GUTENBERG'S FINGERPRINT

GUTEN BERG'S FINGER PRINT

PAPER, PIXELS *and the* LASTING IMPRESSION *of* BOOKS

MERILYN SIMONDS

For Hugh,
and innovators everywhere

HUGH, ME, AND THE BOOK
HUGH, ME, AND THE BOOK
HUGH, ME, AND THE BOOK
HUGH, ME, AND THE BOOK

The project is Hugh's idea. He sends me an email: "I hope you can see all the trouble your writing has caused."

He wants to publish the stories I've been calling *The Paradise Project*. The pieces are slight. Whimsical. I don't know where they come from, and I don't ask.

I'm touched that these stories have got their hooks into Hugh, although I don't quite believe it. I feel like a teenager invited to a party by the most popular boy in class, a boy who can't possibly like me. I suspect a mistake. Or worse, a trick.

Hugh Barclay introduced himself to me more than a dozen years ago, which sounds very civilized, a calling card on a silver salver. Not the correct impression at all. He showed up at my book launch for *The Convict Lover*, which took place in the Penitentiary Museum that occupies the old Warden's House across the road from Kingston Penitentiary, then home to sex offenders and stool pigeons. Canada's Alcatraz, although the architects clearly forgot that Lake Ontario freezes over in winter, a slippery expressway to the United States for anyone who could scale the high stone walls.

On the day of the launch, the museum is packed. The entire village of Portsmouth has turned out, it seems, and half of Kingston, too. During the eight years of writing *The Convict Lover*, I was convinced no one would want to read it. The story was too old-fashioned. Too odd. But here I am, standing at a limestone plinth chiselled by convicts, signing book after book, the room crowded with people bursting with stories of their own: the old man who had a convict as a nanny before he went to school (his father was chief keeper); a woman who, as a girl, passed peaches to the convicts as they marched through the village on their way to the quarry to break stone. The lineup is so long and discombobulating that when my sister hands me her book, I pause over the page, simulating a cough, as I try to remember her name.

I notice Hugh right away. Or rather, I notice his black beret. He's short—something peculiar about the curve of his spine—but his rakish beret keeps bobbing into view until it is right beside me.

"Here!" he says, shoving a green bookmark under my nose. "I'm Hugh Barclay! This is my wife, Verla!" The man doesn't speak, he proclaims.

"We made this!" Hugh taps the length of thick paper.

It is the colour of mashed peas. "We have a printing press. Thee Hellbox Press."

I make noises of gratitude and prepare to add the bookmark to the stack of photos and mementoes others have given me.

"You see. You see," he says, tugging the bookmark back to the centre of the plinth, tapping it more insistently now. "You see? The C and T at the end of 'Convict'? The bit that connects them? That's called a ligature. We chose the type especially. It's like the letters are handcuffed together."

The
Convict
Lover

Merilyn Simonds

MW
& R

Launched April 28, 1996
Kingston Penitentiary Museum

Printed Passage Books Ltd.

Trust me

He is chuckling. So is Verla. They both stare up at me, delighted. Expectant. I look again, more intently, at the bookmark.

Verla's wheelchair has cleared a space like a stage around the three of us. The room and the milling crowd fall away, and it is just the three of us, gazing down at this unexpected chunk of raw, ragged paper, visibly dented with words, letters joined by a curving line defined by a term I've never heard before.

"Amazing," I say. And before I know it, I'm chuckling, too.

Hugh is a fixture about town. His beret, tilted at a dapper angle, can be seen at every literary gathering: book launches, readings, festival performances. He's almost always pushing Verla's chair. And then he isn't.

Hugh is not young, although I can't guess his age. Over sixty. Under eighty. His body is misshapen, as if wracked by some extended, torturing condition, yet there is something child-like about his face. Not innocence: the wisdom in his eyes is hard-earned. Delight, yes. Wonder, perhaps. Optimism, for sure. It's his enthusiasm, I decide, that makes him seem so young. A frank and forthright zeal that cares nothing for propriety or convention, the accepted rules of adult intercourse.

I find myself watching for him at public events, edging over for a chat, craving a shot of his fervour, his wit unstained by irony, unmarred by the faintest glint of condescension or cruelty.

"You know, don't you, that you haven't really made it until you've been published by Thee Hellbox Press," he says to me at a gathering of the Kingston Arts & Letters Club. My husband, Wayne, and I have just presented a talk on the art of collaboration, based on our experience writing a travel memoir together, *Breakfast at the Exit Café*.

"You should send me something," Hugh says.

"I don't have anything." It's a bit of a lie. I'm not a prolific writer, and it's true that I don't have stacks of unpublished manuscripts stuffed in a bottom drawer. But I do have a thin pile of stories, stories I can't yet imagine releasing to the world.

The Convict Lover was my first literary book. Over the next fifteen years, I launched six more: a book of stories, a novel, a travel memoir, a book of essays, two anthologies. When Hugh sent me that email calling me a trouble-maker, I was working on another novel, a long, slow exploration of solitude and refuge. From time to time, as I wrote the novel, bizarre short fictions would flash onto the page. The same thing happened when I wrote *The Convict Lover*, stories that I eventually gathered up and published as *The Lion in the Room Next Door*.

These new stories are different. Shorter. Stranger.

Leftovers, of a sort. Like remnants of a dream that interrupts my consciousness long after I stir awake. For years, I had been writing about my garden. Not just my garden: gardens. My novel *The Holding* began as an exploration of the nature of control and the control of nature. When Alyson and Margaret work their plots, are they trying to make nature do what they want, or are they trying to sidle up closer to it, bring it into their too-concrete lives? *A New Leaf* carried on that conversation within the borders of my own gardens at The Leaf, the patch of woods and cleared land where we lived in Eastern Ontario. It was a gardener, I came to realize, who changed the course of human history, plucking a seed and planting it where she wanted it to grow instead of where it randomly fell. A gardener who made farming possible, and cities, and trips to the moon.

Neither the novel nor the essays contained anything like the lyric fantasies that were erupting now. I had never written anything like them. When I was writer-in-residence at the University of British Columbia, I tacked a few to the end of a reading.

"I don't know what these are," I said by way of introduction.

"They're poems," a friend said afterwards. She is a poet and a teacher; she brought her entire class to the reading. The students vigorously nodded their heads.

"They can't be poems," I protested. "I'm not a poet."

Some were clearly stories—very short stories of a few hundred words or less. Others were lyrical: sixteen words, three lines, a single sentence that trailed down one page and onto a second.

I called them flash fictions and titled each one for an element in a garden—stone, leaf, petal, vine.

"Stone" was the first. It came out whole, each of its 265 words irrevocably attached to the next in ways I could not unlock, could only separate with commas, hitching a clump together here and there, setting a few on a line all their own.

A friend who was an editor at the *Antigonish Review* published "Stone" and a selection of others. More were collected in a special Canadian edition of *Literature and Arts of the Americas*. Both journals were sufficiently distant from me geographically that if critics threw rotten tomatoes, I wasn't likely to know. I needn't have worried: the reviews were kind. Maybe there was something in these stories after all. My youngest son, Erik, is a book designer, and we'd been tossing around the idea of self-publishing some of my out-of-print work as ebooks—and maybe these stories, too. When *Queen's Quarterly*, the magazine of the local university, asked if I had anything they might publish, I emailed a selection of the flash fictions and, in a fit of confidence, copied them to Hugh.

It was a whim. An act of sharing, one literary weirdo to another. I have pressed Send a thousand, a million times. How was I to know that this time it would change my life?

Stone

Every spring, men pried a fresh crop of stone from the field and hauled them on a stone boat to the hedgerow where the boulders heaped, year on year, a hundred years, until the rampart was grown through with willow and alder, dogwood and wild raspberry that tears at the sleeves of the man who pries the stones out, loading them one by one into his wheelbarrow, laying the barrow on its side to take the great slab of limestone or mass of granite, for there are both in this ragged wall, stone from the fire at the centre of the earth and stone from the gentle settling of its first silt, the names springing to his lips, feldspar, domolite, pyroxene, detrital quartz, as he wheels his well-chosen stone away from the field, down the lane towards the house, where he sets it into a low wall around the terrace, admiring the smoothness of the long, subtle curve he has made with all these disparate stones, fitting them together as if he could remake the earth itself, while she takes smaller stones, the ones she comes upon digging in the earth, and lifting them into the light, sets them here and there in the garden, ✻ moving them once or twice, hoping for a pattern, unhappy when none comes to her, but loving each one so, the lines running through it, & the whorls of ancient leaves and nameless living things, that she brings her most precious plants, those with cushioning leaves and a generous, embracing habit, heeling them in, nurselets to the resolute stone.

"This should definitely be in a book," Hugh says when I finally give in to his urging to visit him at his print shop.

Without saying a word to me, he has set the type for "Stone."

"Super stuff," he'd said in response to my email with the poem/story. "It starts movies running in my mind and takes me back to my childhood spent exploring stone hedgerow fences, expecting to find some great treasure hidden in a crevasse."

The test proof he hands me is beautiful. Dark red ink on paper so creamy and thick it might be birchbark or a peeling of sandstone. I run my fingers over it, feel the physical texture of my words pressed into the page. I'm used to the feel of them in my mouth, invisible objects that force my lips into taut circles, a flattened gap, my tongue pressing up against my palate, stroking the inside of my teeth, humping at the back of my throat. But never this.

Hugh has given my words substance.

He takes the page from me and holds it flat, at eye level. Instead of reading the words, I look across the terrain of paper, shaped now into hills and valleys, pools of commas, fjords of *t*'s and *f*'s, rushing rivulets of *s*'s.

"Words make an impression," he says.

Hugh's print shop is attached to his house—almost. The house itself was designed and built specifically for Hugh and Verla, with wheelchair access and a court-yard plan that has every room opening through a large doorway to a central hall. The building that houses the print shop looks like a garage jutting towards the street, connected to the house by a wooden deck.

The shop is a mess. Hugh ushers me in past a counter heaped with paper. The walls are plastered with print projects. One shows a bank of words—*Saffron. Fireflies. Baffle. Truffle*—the lowercase *f*'s in scarlet ink. When I ask what this means, Hugh gets a little irritated.

"Mean? It doesn't mean anything. It's just a gorgeous ligature."

There's a block print of a dancing figure, various quotes, some handwritten, some set in type: *Fragile as I am, I am strong.*

I'm a quick study. I don't ask where the quotes are from.

Once, this shop was hung was prosthetic body parts. Back then, Hugh was into orthotics. He was also writing poetry. In the early 1970s, he met a man named Bill Poole who taught at the Ontario College of Art. He sent Bill his first poem.

"Bill got back to me and said, 'I solved your problem.' I didn't know I had a problem. 'I bought a press so now I can publish your poem,' he said. I told him I'd rather do a book."

A New Respect, Hugh's one and only book of poems

was published by Poole Hall Press in 1972. He helped set the type and run the press.

"That's how I got ink in my veins," he says. He means it metaphorically, but it strikes me as literally true. I imagine the watershed of his body flowing red, yellow, blue. His fingers are perpetually smudged as if ink is leaking out through his skin.

Through the next couple of years, he and Bill produced a magazine called *Symbiosis*.

"People could only pay in kind, and we refused to say what it was worth." Hugh is chuckling again. He seems to be perpetually chuckling, as if life is one big joke. A joke on him. A joke on all of us.

"We had fifty to seventy-five subscribers. We got sent wine, hand-knit mitts and socks. A woman in Newfoundland sent us cod and brewis. One fellow wrote a song about us, 'The Press Gang Blues.'"

As he talks, I lean to look into the other room. The print shop is divided in two: the back room where Hugh does his typesetting and printing and this other room, which is tidier—one long table stacked with various sizes and colours of paper, each in its own neat pile.

Hugh is tapping the test proof of "Stone."

"This should be a book," he says.

I came to Hugh's shop intending to dampen his fire, but I find myself nodding as if what he says makes perfect sense. Yes, these stories should be between covers. *When there are enough*, my saner brain says. *When I hone them to something I understand.*

"I mean now."

"But I only have a dozen." Printed on paper, the book would be so thin it would hardly qualify for the name.

"That's plenty! It will be a handmade book."

I imagine readers paying for the book with macramé hangers, out-of-date pesos, their children's first drawings.

My saner brain tells me I should be appalled. I barely hear it for the chuckling.

STUPID HUGH

Hugh asks to see all the stories, and I send him everything: those that have been published, new pieces, unfinished fragments.

"I've just sat down and read the manuscript and it is amazing. A lot of new pieces, at least to me. Some brought a tear to my eye, but you need to know that my bladder is too close to my eyes."

We agree to meet for dinner to discuss the book.

To my alarm, almost as soon as I sit down, Hugh bursts into tears. We are sitting in the city's finest restaurant, a favourite, we discovered, of us both. The owner, Zal Yanovsky, was lead guitarist in the Lovin' Spoonful, a '60s band I danced to (on tabletops, if I remember correctly). The first time I met Zalman he was on roller skates, scooting around his dinner guests, stopping at my side to ask if I had a cigarette.

"Do I look like a smoker?" I laughed. I was being

taken to dinner by James Lawrence, founder, publisher, and editor of *Harrowsmith* magazine, the back-to-the-land bible of the 1980s, a magazine that was about to get into book publishing. They wanted me to write their first book. None of them smoked anything but weed. I wanted to make a good impression—my Du Mauriers were well hidden—but Zal had sussed me out. I opened my purse and offered him a fag, tossing smiles around the table in penance. Who can resist a man on roller skates?

Now Zalman is dead and Hugh is crying and we are at the worst table in the restaurant, the one in the middle of the room, where every waiter and diner has to pass us by to get in, or out, or serve a dish of Mediterranean stew. We might as well be onstage.

I lean close to Hugh and put my hand on his arm. "You okay?"

He has been telling me about the school children. Immediately after he published his first book of poems, he went out and bought a letterpress. It was a whim, he says.

Hugh, I am about to discover, is a great follower of whims. He set up the press at his daughters' elementary school and worked with students to print their own magazine.

"Those kids! They wrote the stories. They set the type. They did it all!"

He dabs at his eyes with a flowered serviette.

"Don't worry," he says, picking up his fork to attack his stew. "Stupid Hugh cries a lot."

Stupid Hugh has all the bad habits. He forgets the

comma in the first line of type and doesn't notice until the whole page is set. He prints the wrong text over an image. He leaves his fingerprints behind. Until I met Hugh, I didn't realize that I, too, have an incompetent, wastrel twin. Stupid Merilyn was the one handing out cigarettes and dancing on tables. These days, she spends most of her time inserting misplaced modifiers and splitting infinitives in my carefully composed text.

When Hugh points out a mistake in one of the stories, I know exactly what to say.

"Sorry, Hugh. You'll have to forgive her. Stupid Merilyn never learned to spell."

Both Merilyn and Stupid Merilyn have a lot to learn. Hugh will be our teacher. Over the next year, he will rock our world, upend everything we think we know about writing, about paper, words, ink, and presses, and how they come together to make a book.

A PAPER WORLD

My sons and I belong to the last two generations to grow up in an entirely paper world. The first words we read were pressed into paper. By the time I was thirty, I was writing on a computer; by the time my sons were adolescents, most of what they read was onscreen. But our first books, both theirs and mine, were printed much as Johannes Gutenberg printed books six centuries before.

When Hugh proposed publishing *The Paradise Project*, the process he had in mind would have been entirely familiar to Gutenberg: hand-set type impressed on handmade paper with a hand-operated press.

Meanwhile, Erik and I were discussing the production of the same manuscript as an ebook. His daughters were learning to read onscreen. The novels by my bed, as often as not, were ebooks.

We're caught in a paradigm shift. Words are the constant, with paper on one shore, pixels on the other. My sons and I stand in the middle, a foot balanced on either side. My parents would never have believed that a world without paper was possible. My grandchildren will never fully grasp the extent to which paper served us all we wanted and needed to know. I have walled every room in my house with books; my granddaughters can hold more books than that in just one hand.

"So," says Hugh, embracing his print shop with outstretched arms. "Will we do this?"

I feel as if I am being invited to enter Doctor Who's TARDIS. I know what will happen if I refuse: my life will go on pretty much as it has—writing, reading, observing the world from the sidelines, surrounded by what I know.

Stepping inside Hugh's world will change everything.

"Sure," I say, not understanding a thing. "Why not?"

PAPER
PAPER
PAPER
PAPER

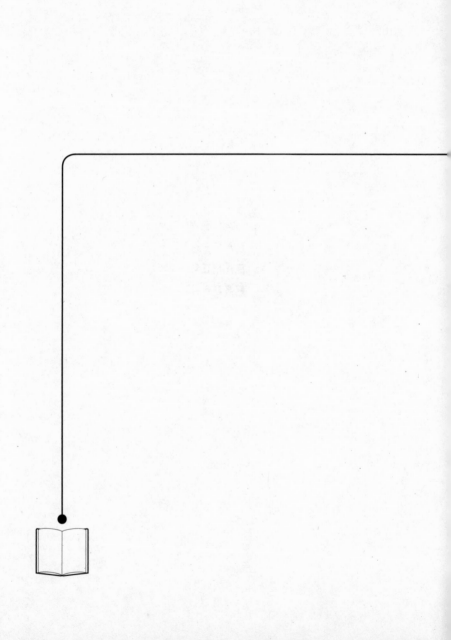

INSTRUCTIONS FROM THE GODDESS

It starts with paper, but it won't end here.

When my firstborn son, Karl, was five, we moved in the middle of the school year. He didn't much like kindergarten in his old school, and he hated it in the new one. I was lonely, stuck with a baby in a big drafty house that had once been a garage on a bleak northern Ontario highway, and so I'd often let my older son stay home from school. The three of us would do things together: make cookies; read stories; sing along with Sharon, Lois & Bram; visit the Acadian woman down the road who made doughnuts by the dozens, heaping them in her roasting pan like a sweet, lumpy turkey.

I don't remember why we decided to make paper.

Karl balled up Kleenex and mounded it in a mixing bowl. I poured boiling water over it; then we took turns pounding the goop with a potato masher and stirring it into a thick pudding with a wooden spoon. He liked that part a lot: the stuff was good and messy.

"We'll have to strain it," I said, trying to sound as though I knew what I was doing. This was in the days before the Internet. We had to figure things out for ourselves.

"And we have to make the sides straight," Karl added wisely. The baby gurgled his approval.

I pushed a dusty print out of an old picture frame, stapled some fine muslin taut across it, set the frame over a brownie pan, and poured on the goop. The muslin was too tightly woven: the goop sat there in a slimy, dripping pool, rivulets of grey water running off the dense sieve onto the counter. I scraped the mushy stuff back into the bowl and hitched the baby onto my hip for a prowl around the rented house, our eyes peeled for something, we weren't sure what.

"How 'bout this?" Karl shouted, pulling me to an old window screen leaning against the furnace.

We propped the screen over the sink and poured on the mush. He stirred it around until it was vaguely the shape of a piece of paper, which is a ridiculous thing to say because, of course, paper can take any shape. But to us, paper meant books, and books were rectangles, so that was the shape of the soggy mess in our kitchen on that drizzly November day. In a moment of inspiration, I grabbed some petals from the roadside flowers I'd hung upside down over the stove to dry and sprinkled them onto the goop: golden brown-eyed Susans, deep purple asters.

I knew next to nothing about making paper. I didn't know that, 1,600 years ago, the goddess Kawakami Gozen—"the spirit who lives above the stream"—came down to the Japanese village of Echizen and said, "This place has such small fields, it must be difficult to make a living cultivating rice. However, this land has beautiful clear water. I will teach you to make paper so that you and the generations following you can survive." Ever since, in the spring, the citizens of Echizen lift a likeness of the goddess into an ornately decorated litter and carry her down from the summit of Mount Omine and through the papermaking districts of the town in a three-day festival of paper that celebrates the goddess who was a "harbinger of good fortune and the bearer of an enduring gift."

A hundred years ago, there were 70,000 papermaking workshops in Japan. Now, there are fewer than 300, a number that shrinks every year. The goddess would not be pleased.

She must have learned her craft from the Chinese, because that's where the world's oldest fragments of paper have been found. I think I knew that much: the Chinese are famous for their invention of paper, gunpowder, and that brilliant interface of gunpowder and paper, firecrackers.

Paper made its debut in written history in 105 CE, when Cai Lun, an official at the Imperial Chinese

Court, announced its invention in a report that laid out precise instructions for manufacturing paper from tree pulp, hemp, old rags, and frayed fishing nets. Bits of paper at least 250 years older than that have been found in Chinese tombs but, even so, Cai Lun has held his place as the inventor of paper, his name known to every Chinese school child in much the same way that North American children hail Thomas Edison as the inventor of electricity, glossing over centuries of experimentation by scientists before him.

My son and I had unwittingly followed Cai Lun's instructions for making paper: mix fibrous material with water and beat it to a pulp—papermakers call it "stuff," and in our wise ignorance, we did, too—then ladle it evenly over a screen mould.

Our paper came out lumpy and grey. After days of drying and pressing under a stack of encyclopedias, it still resembled a grey mass of used Kleenex. When we tried to draw on it with a pen, the ink spread like freshly hatched spiders. Crayons humped off the paper landscape, leaving gaps in the coloured contrail. My delicate petals looked like specks of splattered mud.

What I was hoping for was something more like the paper of Xue Tao, a poet of the Tang Dynasty and China's first female papermaker. Xue Tao added red hibiscus flowers to her pulp, producing paper that was a delicate, distinctive pink.

We didn't have hibiscus blossoms. Our water wasn't pure. We didn't know enough to size the paper to close the fibres so that ink would stand boldly on the surface instead of tunnelling every which way. Worst of all, we did not enter our papermaking project in the correct frame of mind. By the time we found the basement screen and got it centred over the sink and the stuff smoothed over the surface, the baby was fussing and my son's interest was waning at approximately the same velocity as my patience. I just wanted the thing over and done with so I could drive to the store and buy a nice thick pad of newsprint for the kids to scribble on.

"There can be no anger, and no irritation," says Ichibei Iwano IX, Japan's most famous contemporary papermaker, named a Living National Treasure for his papermaking skill, which he learned from his father, also a Living National Treasure. (Picasso drew on paper made by Ichibei Iwano VIII.)

"My paper is closest to the paper taught by the goddess," Iwano IX told Nicholas Basbanes, author of the brilliant history *On Paper*. "This paper will last for a thousand years."

Recently, the last independent papermaker in China, a man whose family has made paper on the same site for six centuries, went out of business. In Japan, as in China, papermaking runs in families, and those families are dying out. In the Iwano family, the name Ichibei is reserved for the heir who declares a desire to continue in the family papermaking business. Ichibei Iwano IX is the ninth in his family line; his son has recently agreed to become Ichibei X.

I watch Ichibei Iwano IX making paper on YouTube. If I close my eyes, I can almost feel him in the room with me, the rhythmic slosh, slosh, slosh of his screen dipping through the pulp—lifting, dipping, sloshing, the soft percussion of papermaking.

My son and I were crude, clumsy beasts by comparison, our paper stuff thick as gruel, no sloshing, only scooping, the paper heavy as oatmeal—not at all what Hugh hands me one day as I enter his print shop. Gorgeous green and gold and russet fibres thread elegantly through the sheet. If the movement was more regular, you'd think it was woven by a hundred-handed goddess from exotic plants she gathered on a forest floor.

"It's from Japan," he says, handing me another page, this one like shells overlapping on sand, tiny translucent rounds pink as a baby's fingernails. "What do you think?"

Who made this? is my first thought, a thought that has never before whizzed through my brain, not in the thirty years I've been a writer, not even on those days I sat in publishers' offices discussing the production of a new book. "Who made this lovely paper?"

Hugh beams. He knows he's got me now. "The first one is called 'Storm.' This lighter one is 'Hyacinth.' I'm thinking of them for the cover of the book."

"Really?" They seem too beautiful to be put to such a utilitarian purpose. I want to frame them and hang them on the wall.

"Really," Hugh says, pulling me deep into the print shop and closing the door behind us. "And this is just the beginning!"

The papermaking process was mechanized, like most everything else, during the Industrial Revolution. Even at the height of that love affair with the machine, however, handmade paper never entirely disappeared. During the second half of the nineteenth century, "luxury papers" were all the rage, used to make everything from toy theatres to brightly coloured, glossy miniatures of carriages, drawing rooms, soldiers, and Persian princesses.

The Arts and Craft Movement, which began in Britain around the 1880s and moved into Europe and North America in the early part of the twentieth century, elevated traditional crafts such as hand papermaking to an art. Pablo Picasso and Georges Braque used newspaper clippings and wallpaper scraps for their collages, and from this developed *décollage*, tearing away at the layers to create an image thrown into relief by the surface structure of the paper.

In the 1950s, in America, the damp fibrous stuff became an art material in itself, shaped and worked into something hardly resembling paper at all. In the '60s and '70s, handmade paper was part of the back-to-the-land, do-it-yourself renaissance—the one my sons and I were part of—and now, at the beginning of the twenty-first century, papermaking, like cheesemaking and winemaking, is undergoing a more refined, artisanal rebirth.

Hand papermaking has endured, I think, because the process is relatively simple. And for the person willing to hone the skill, it offers lavish aesthetic rewards. Handmade paper is now produced, sheet by sheet, in studios around the world, though most of it does not end up in books. This is not paper in the service of story. It is art paper. Paper for paper's sake.

Emily Cook makes art paper. We first meet in our favourite Kingston restaurant, at a table tucked in a corner under the stairs. Hugh has made the arrangements. He hovers like a matchmaker as we shake hands and settle in.

I am immediately charmed. Emily is beautiful, her skin the most luminous alabaster I've ever seen, smooth in a way that only an older woman can truly admire. She has the broad cheekbones and wide eyes of a Slovak princess, but her hair is platinum, as white as mine, although she can't be more than thirty. A barely controlled wave dips playfully across her forehead.

Within minutes we are comparing hairdressers and life with curls. I tell her my hair went white in my thirties. She tells me hers has been this colour always.

While we wait for our food, Emily reaches into the black portfolio case leaning against the wall. My baby son has grown into a visual artist, but I've never seen a case like this, big as a card table. She dives into it, rifling through until she pulls out two sheets of paper, one for Hugh and one for me.

The sheet seems more like a weaving, fashioned from the filaments of exotic plants or gigantic silkworms or the nests of fantastical birds. I've always thought of paper as flimsy, fragile, easily torn and bent. Even the

Japanese papers Hugh handed me seemed vulnerable, needing protection. But Emily's sheets are something different altogether: robust, stroppy, bursting with character. More like worsted woolens than tissue.

I am stunned. Emily has accomplished in paper what I have tried to do in *The Paradise Project*: forget what stories are supposed to be and let them come out rough and ragged, not necessarily lovely, but true. True to themselves, at least.

"It seems wrong to call this paper," I say. "The word is too mundane."

"Let's see some more," booms Hugh. "Show us everything you have in there."

I realize, suddenly, that this is an audition. I am only an observer; Emily is performing for Hugh. She pulls out sample after sample until the exquisite mats of fibre take over the table, the extra chairs, our laps.

Hugh waves the waiter away: there is no room here for salads.

Hugh commissions Emily to make the endpapers for *The Paradise Project*.

Publishers don't make much of a fuss about endpapers anymore: the sheets that join the cover to the bound pages are most often simply plain white or coloured stock chosen to match the cover of the book. It wasn't always like that. I remember the books in Mrs. Ronald's stone farmhouse, which I visited each spring and fall throughout my teens to help with her semi-annual housecleaning. In the evenings, I'd plunder her bookshelf, lifting the glass front to pick out *Helen of the Old House* or *The Wayside Cross*, *The Book of Ultima Thule*. The endpapers of books of that era were often lavishly marbled, but these volumes opened with woodcut landscapes or interlocking patterns of wild birds, designed by Thoreau MacDonald, Frank Johnston, or some other artist of the Group of Seven. The Everyman books were my favourites, with their maroon leather covers and gilt-edged pages, the endpapers drawn by the great nineteenth-century British Arts-and-Crafts designer William Morris: wildly swooping stems and leaves embracing a pilgrim on the right and, on the left, the words *Everyman I will go with thee and be thy guide, in thy most need, to go by thy side.* No wonder I thought of books as my friends.

Late in the summer, Hugh meets Emily at the Kingston train station and drives her out to The Leaf, our property in eastern Ontario where we've spent fifteen years converting grass to gardens on the verge of a maple wood. We moved here from a small city lot that backed onto an old stone quarry, a grotto that I filled with gregarious shade-loving plants. At The Leaf, I plant in great, sunny swaths: one garden alone is 160 feet long and 40 feet wide. The beds were populated first with fast-growing, spreading species such as creeping Jenny, brown-eyed

Susans, and grasses, the plants every gardener hauls out by the wheelbarrowful each spring. Over the years, I've replaced those aggressive spreaders with more delicate blooms, flowers I babied into existence, coddling them through the winter, shielding them from the summer sun.

I offer Hugh and Emily peach cream pie and coffee on the screened terrace, then invite them into the gardens.

"How many varieties do you have?" Emily asks.

"Of plants? Goodness, I have no idea." I have never thought to count. Mentally, I tote them up: a few dozen kinds of hosta, at least as many daylily species, scores of sedums planted in a mosaic, grasses, hibiscus, echinaceae, peonies, roses, campanula, hydrangea, spirea, lilac, magnolia, violets, polygonums, ferns, mosses; really, it's too much to contemplate. "Thousands, I imagine."

During our years at The Leaf, I dreamed of picking a stem and flower from every variety of every species that grew there. I'd tape them neatly in a book, the dried plant on one side and a pencil drawing on the other to show the reproductive parts, the flower in full bloom, delicate renderings like the ones Agnes FitzGibbon painted for Catharine Parr Traill's book *Canadian Wild Flowers.* Under the specimen and the drawings, a description of the plant's preference in soil, light, temperature, mating, the traits I like best and what I find irritating, disappointing, hard to control. A botanical diary. A dry garden—*Hortus siccus*—that's what these albums of desiccated, labelled specimens were called. Years ago, in a used book store somewhere along the

Atlantic seaboard, I discovered a photography book based on just such a diary that had been created by an anonymous young woman in the late nineteenth century. The photographer, entranced by the way each plant specimen left its imprint, its shadow self, on the opposing page of text, had captured perfectly the overlay of nature on human words.

I'd like to gather such a plant collection, and I'd like someone to find it, to write a book about it, and someone else to find that book and write another book inspired by it. I love these creative daisy chains. But I am not a collector at heart. There is no order to my gathering. I am a magpie. I'm the one who finds the odd books and carries them home to rest higgledy-piggledy on my shelves. The writer who tucks a found story into another story, the way I embedded that botanical journal into my novel *Refuge*.

I find it hard to admit: I will never draw every species in my garden.

Emily is fondling leaves as we walk among the plants. Not fondling—that implies a kind of seduction. Her touch has more practical purpose to it. She holds a leaf the way a tailor might finger a length of cloth, assessing its texture, its weight, its willingness to be cut, to drape the human form.

"This might work," she says, sliding her hand along a length of daylily leaf.

I grow great swaths of daylilies, which aren't really lilies, although they are members of the genus *Lilium*. True lilies grow from bulbs, daylilies from crowns with roots that thicken to look like tubers. The daylily she is holding is a *Hemerocallis*, a genus of plant that roots and reproduces as profligately as teenagers. Unlike true lilies, they are immune to the appetites of the scarlet beetle that has recently made its way north. Tolerant of poor soil, summer heat, and deep shade, daylilies serve as excellent fillers for out-of-the-way places: a forty-foot swath by the old stone turkey shed on the eastern edge of the property, a waterfall of colour that flows down from the woods onto the lawn behind the house, a railing of pale pink Mrs. Bradshaws to flank the curving steps that lead down to the stone terrace.

I'm not sure whose idea it was to make the end-papers from plants from my garden. Not mine: I didn't know such a thing was possible. And probably not Emily's: she had no way of knowing my gardens were of a size to accommodate such a scheme.

The idea has Hugh's fingerprints all over it. He is never content to do things the easy way, the practical way, the way everyone else has done it. "Tried and true" is a not an adage that will ever hang on his wall. He has an almost miraculous capacity for seeing with fresh eyes and a stubbornly iconoclastic desire to try the untried. He isn't interested in new for its own sake: rather, he wants each phase of his project to be perfect unto itself, the pages as unique as the stories.

"The fibres seem long enough," Emily says pensively, her hands moving from one lily leaf to another. I'm not sure she even sees the searing red and yellow trumpets of the blooms.

"And that's good?" I ask.

"We're looking for a fibre that will feather apart, something that will dissolve in water and suspend, but also bond with other fibres, not hang out on top on its own. So yes, that's good." And for the first time that day, Emily flashes me a smile.

For 2,000 years or so, the lion's share of European writing was done on parchment, the scraped, stretched, dried skin of a goat, sheep, or cow. By the fourteenth century, papermaking had made its way onto the continent, although it was expensive and slow to catch on. In the early 1700s, the invention of the spinning wheel created an explosion in linen goods—shirts, bed linens, towels. Not surprisingly, within a few years, there was a complementary explosion in rags. Rags were so plentiful that the price of rag paper plummeted to about a sixth of that of parchment. Paper was suddenly popular. Soon the demand for paper was so great that the rag trade couldn't keep up. Rags were imported from Asia and Africa, but even that wasn't enough. Newspaper owners ran advertisements apologizing for printing only half the news because rags were so scarce.

There's something prophetic in those 200-year-old ads. The shift from parchment to paper was a direct result of an oversupply of rags. Pulp from the vast and seemingly endless forests replaced rags, and now alarm over disappearing woodlands is fuelling the enthusiasm for digital books.

Buy a paper book, save a herd of goats.

Buy an ereader stocked with sixty-two books and save a tree.

By the middle of the eighteenth century, paper-makers were desperate for a more readily available source of cellulose, the essential ingredient in paper. Rags were one option; trees were another. But what about grass? Leaves? Stems? One of the people looking around for a cheap, plentiful alternative was Jacob Christian Schäffer, a German botanist and ornithologist, author, and collector famous for his cabinet of curiosities. He also conducted experiments in electricity, colour, and optics, inventing, among other things, a washing machine, a saw, and a furnace. Between 1765 and 1771, he turned his febrile mind to paper. He spent hours plucking plants and stems from his garden just as Emily and I are doing in mine. He chopped up everything he came across—wasps' nests, mosses, hops—macerating them to a pulp in "stampers" and making small squares of sample paper. A few years later, an entrepreneurial British papermaker, Matthias Koops, decided straw was the next big thing. (Koops was also the first to produce paper from discarded paper.) He opened a factory near London, England, where he produced reams of straw paper. Basbanes, in his book *On Paper*, recounts handling a book printed on straw. After 200 years, he writes, the paper still held "the agreeable aroma of fresh-cut grass."

Hugh trails behind Emily and me as we pause at one plant then another, bagging leaves like forensic samples: hosta, hibiscus, queen of the meadow, hyacinth. Into larger bags, she stuffs stooks of bright green daylily leaves, burgundy canna lily leaves, grey-blue spikes of iris.

Hugh is not as interested in this stage of the paper-making process as I expect him to be. When I ask if he has ever made paper, he tells us that, twenty years ago, he visited Walpole Island First Nation with his two adopted daughters, who are of Cree heritage. Together, they went on a hunt for sweetgrass, used in smudging ceremonies and prized for its sweet vanilla fragrance, even when dried.

"I picked a bundle with the intention of making paper from it. I hoped the paper would pick up the scent." He soaked the sweetgrass and used the kitchen blender to beat it to a pulp. "Smoke rose from the motor. Verla suggested in no uncertain terms that I should leave that project for a more favourable time." Hugh sighs. "The paper never got made."

Emily and I are finished culling leaves. Now we're filling small plastic bags with flowers, looking around for tough, brightly hued blooms, petals that keep their colour when dried. I suggest sedums. Maybe silene. Astrantia. Bee balm. Spirea.

The flowers are for Hugh. At our first lunch, he brought a sample of what he had in mind for the end-papers: a pale Japanese sheet with a faint pink cast to it, the pink I imagine the poet Xue Tao achieved with hibiscus tea. The surface was strewn with small bits of leaf and petal, exactly the effect I was hoping for when I sprinkled roadside flowers over that first sheet of paper I made with my sons.

In the restaurant, Emily had squinted at the paper Hugh handed her. She held the sheet inches from her face as if, in that moment, nothing else in the world mattered. "It's not easy," Emily said then, and she says the same thing now. "It's not easy, adding bits of flowers to the process."

She's squinting again, despite the dark sunglasses. Like many people with albinism, her eyesight is compromised. Sunlight is painful, even under the shade of her thick white lashes. We move deeper into the shadows.

"The flower bits will look like flecks of mud. Or they'll fade away altogether. There are things you can do, chemicals you can add to keep them looking fresh, but that's not the way I make paper." She has an artist's stubborn confidence in her own vision.

"Not a problem," Hugh says, repeating the phrase, as he does when he gets excited. "Not a problem. No. No. It's your paper! Go for it!"

Emily is travelling by train, so we limit ourselves to two rather large soft-sided pieces of hand luggage, stuffed with plant material. Through the summer, she will beat them, species by species, into stuff, making sheet after sheet of test paper. I try to imagine the process, falling back inevitably to the scene at my kitchen counter, the old window screen, the thick oatmeal slurry, my whining boys.

Early in the fall, Emily, Hugh, and I convene again at the Kingston restaurant to see what she's made.

I gasp as she pulls out what looks like a swirling cloud of green roiling down across a pale landscape.

"I love this!" I say, and she smiles. "Which plant is it?"

"Daylily fibre." She looks at it critically. "The greener it is, the more fugitive it is," she says. "Chlorophyll's not a great dye. With the green stuff, I'm worried that it won't be stable, that it will fade out over time."

"I don't know. I don't know." Hugh is the one squinting now. "You know. You know. It looks muddy to me. Did you try the flowers?"

She pulls out half a dozen sheets labelled *Creeping Jenny*, *Sedum*, *Violet*. Even Hugh has to admit that the strewn leaves and petals look like specks of dirt. Not at all what he was hoping for.

"Commercial printers can do that sort of thing, put flowers in. A paper artist can't. If that's the look you want, you should buy ready-made paper."

I wince. Hugh looks wounded. But she's right, and he knows it.

Emily offers a compromise. "I'll use a white base, with the plant material added later. It will look more like a garden flowing through a landscape."

"You're the artist," Hugh says, raising his hand in the air as if he's calling off a match. "You do what you do. It will be just right."

Emily scoops something that looks like cooked spinach out of a small plastic bucket and trails it over the water in the wooden box.

Except that it's not spinach, it's not water, and it's not just any old box.

Earlier that spring, I took my Japanese knife to my gardens and hacked down great swaths of daylily leaves: twelfth-of-July lilies, forty feet of them or more; smaller clumps of citrinas, Catherine Woodburys, Crimson Pirates, Gentle Shepherds, Stella d'Oros, and Happy Returns. I drove them to Toronto and left them on the doorstep of Emily's studio on my way through the city. She was sick and didn't get to work for several days, by which time the leaves had cooked inside the black plastic to a stinky, slimy mess. So I picked more and stuffed them into garbage bags that I shipped by bus to the city. Emily hydrated the pulp and put it through her Valley Hollander beater, which doesn't cut the fibre, she assures me now, so much as fluff it up, separating it into shorter strands. She keeps the green "stuff" in yogurt containers in the fridge, mushing it into water when she's ready to make paper.

We are standing in her studio at the Ontario College of Art and Design (OCAD) in Toronto. Other than the paper I made with my sons when they were children, I am a papermaking virgin. Even Hugh has more experience than I. Years ago, when he was teaching a seminar at OCA he called Designing Outside the Box—a skill he has in spades—he met the papermaker Wendy Cain. When she told him she was teaching a workshop near Kingston, he decided to give papermaking a second chance.

"You need to know that when I attend a workshop, I have to be able to produce a masterpiece in the first few days," says Hugh. "Well, that didn't happen. I did manage to make a bit of paper, but it was really only suitable for taking home to show Mommy what I had done."

Emily hands me an apron. "Basically, you can make paper two ways: by dipping the screen in the pulp, which ends up with a very homogenized paper. Or you can make it the Japanese way, by draining pulp through a screen in a box. This process is harder to control, but I seem to need to do things the hard way."

She says the last bit with a shy smile. She and Hugh make a very good pair.

The papermaking box is properly called a deckle box. This one has been designed and built specifically for *The Paradise Project*. It is a lovely wooden oblong, with a wall down the middle creating two spaces exactly the size of each endpaper in the book. The endpapers are made in sets of two, so that the design trails from front to back, enclosing the text.

The bottom of the box is screened to let the water flow through, leaving behind a film of fibre. Emily lines both compartments with plastic, then fills them with abacá fibre hydrated to a pale, glutinous liquid. Abacá is a kind of banana tree that grows in South America and the Philippines. Its scientific name is *Musa textilis*.

I like the literary lilt of the name, as if the plant is muse to the paper.

Musa textilis grows quickly to about twelve feet, with the base of the leaves forming a sheath around the trunk to create a kind of false trunk. These sheaths, about twenty-five of them per tree, contain the fine, soft, silky fibres that are often as long as the tree is tall. The fibres, rich in cellulose, lignin, and pectin, were originally used for making rope. Today, most of it is pulped for specialty paper products such as diapers, coffee filters, and money. Abacá fibre is also a favourite of papermakers. Emily doesn't have to grow it herself or find a willing Peruvian farmer to ship her bagfuls, and she doesn't have to cook the raw strands to break them down. She orders sheets of prepared, unbleached fibre: add water, stir, and, presto, she has pulp.

Both sides of the deckle box are filled with the milky abacá. She works quickly now, drizzling the green lily-fibre into the abacá "stuff," drawing green swirls into the abacá with her fingers.

"Now for the fun part," she says. She grasps the side of each plastic liner and, like a magician with a table-cloth, whips them out from under the liquid. "Ta-da!"

Suddenly, liquid is gushing out the screen at the bottom of the box, which isn't sitting quite level. One side is draining faster than the other. Emily rushes to prop it up.

"I met a boy," she says, her eye fixed on the gushing fluid, which is now draining evenly. "My brain's a bit of a mess."

And her heart is on the wrong side of her body. She told me that the day we met.

As the runoff drains, she swishes the box gently, urging the fibre to interlock. When the last of the liquid has drained away, she unhinges the bottom of the box. A thick, familiar-looking wad lies limp on the screen. Soaked Kleenex.

"Everything that happens from this point on is recorded in the paper," she says. I look past her to the handwritten sign on the wall. *No Glitter!* She follows my gaze. "Glitter is the STD of the craft world," she says.

She lifts the screen to the other end of the table, where squares cut from old blankets are stacked. Earlier this morning she soaked them and squeezed out the water. Now she upends the screen, and, in one deft flick, the gooey sheet of paper is released onto the wool.

"It's called couching," she says, pronouncing it "kooching," as in smooching. It comes from the French *couche*, which means a lot of things, from diaper to social strata. In this studio, it means to lay the paper down.

"After my last relationship broke up, I couldn't make paper," she says. "It just wouldn't couche."

I'm delighted by the language. "Tell me more."

"Well, the other way of making paper is to have a vat of hydrated fibre and dip your screen into it. When you pull the screen up, you smack it against the water to release the sheet. That's called kissing off.

"He plays the ukulele," she says wistfully. "How good is that? Last night he played 'When We're Dancing.'"

She hums the tune as she sets up the paper press,

which will exert 60,000 pounds of pressure on every square inch of the newly made page. Because the pages are relatively small, they will be unforgiving, prone to distortion. She stacks wooden pallets inside the press, lays on the blanket, the sheet of paper, another blanket, and more palettes, taking time to make sure the registration is perfect. Then she flips the switch, and the paper press grinds down.

Traditionally, the wool blankets sandwiching the fresh paper are called felts. The texture of the felts has a lot to do with the appearance of the paper. In the early days of papermaking, the felts were often non-woven; the interlocked hairs gave the paper a distinctive "chicken skin" texture. You can still see the impression of woven felts in the surface texture of contemporary hand-made paper, although the pressing diminishes the effect.

Our freshly made paper gets two pressings, the first one five minutes and another, fifteen minutes. The sheet she lifts from between the blankets looks like paper now, limp paper on a very humid summer's day, but recognizable nonetheless. She bends close to scrutinize what she has made.

"See that?" She points to an almost imperceptible indentation, a thin area surrounded by an infinitesimally thicker ridge. "That's called a papermaker's tear."

I imagine her crying onto the sheets, her heart broken by her new beau.

It is hard to think of this as an imperfection. There are dips and clumps, knots and swirling fibres, as if the paper itself is supple, complex, alive.

She places the two freshly made sheets gently between blotter paper and triple-walled cardboard with a weight on top so the pages won't shrink, then arranges a fan to blow over them for twenty-four hours until they are dry.

It has taken an hour to make one pair of matching endpapers for the front and back of one copy of my book. Hugh will print 300 copies of *The Paradise Project*. The prospect of another 299 hours of work doesn't seem to daunt Emily.

"After I make a hundred or so of these, I'll figure out some tricks. And my boyfriend says he'll help. Isn't that sweet?"

THE FLIGHT OF BIRDS THROUGHOUT THE AIR

Paper is not forever: it can be burned, cut, torn, crumpled, lost; it can rot, discolour, disintegrate; be eaten away by mice and mould. Even so, it is more enduring than what we think or what we say. It has the strength to carry words across vast landscapes, from one time to another, from one person to hundreds, thousands, even millions.

In 1815, John Adams, the second president of the United States, wrote to his grandsons as they were preparing to cross the Atlantic to join their parents: "Without a minute Diary, your Travels will be no better than the flight of Birds throughout the Air. What you write, preserve. I have burned Bushells of my Silly notes, in fits of Impatience and humiliation, which I would now give anything to recover."

I received my first diary as a going-away gift when I was seven, on my way to Brazil with my family. I wrote in it daily until I was a young woman, and I've kept one ever since, although never consistently enough. When I visited Frida Kahlo's Casa Azul in Coyoacán, I was filled with guilt and longing at the sight of her rows of boxed diaries bulging with clippings and sketches and her impressions of what seemed like every moment of her life.

Leonardo da Vinci, one of the world's great diarists, left 13,000 pages of notes containing his observations, speculations, plans, and fantasies. Paper had just arrived in Italy 200 years before he was born in 1452. What if there had been no paper? Would he have scratched his ideas in the sand, to be washed away in a storm? Painted them on a wall? He could have used parchment, but that medium was expensive and relatively scarce, the purview of monks. The supply of paper must have been limited, too, yet Leonardo didn't stint. Of his finished works, only some fifteen paintings and a few sculptures survive: his reputation rests not on these so much as on the enormous body of sketches and notes for his precocious inventions, all recorded for the future on paper.

Beethoven's compositions were captured and preserved on paper, too, written in his distinctive, erratic hand. It is estimated that if all of Beethoven's works were written out in musical notation, they would fill 8,000 pages. Thomas Edison's notes, including his sketch for the first phonograph, run to over five million pages. Canadian novelist Robertson Davies kept a diary all his life; it took his daughter fifteen years to transcribe the over three million words into digital files. Literature and science, music and visual art, even dance choreographies are all notated on paper, giving us the closest thing we have to a glimpse inside the creative mind.

And then there is Joe Blades, the poet in Atlantic Canada who builds amazing books that might be called diaries—splayed *objets d'art* whose every page is pasted with ephemera. These are books that never close, gaping bindings of pages that, taken together, offer a snapshot of a culture at this moment, and this, and this.

We say we keep a diary. More to the point, a diary keeps us on its crumbling, rotting paper pages. Such a fragile substance to carry so heavy a burden: the preservation of a culture.

WHAT LIES BENEATH

I've always thought of paper as a kind of silent butler that delivers words and images to a reader. But the paper itself is telling a story quite apart from the one that is told in ink.

Paper's own history runs underneath, around, and through the story that is printed on it, a *sotto voce* narrative of conquest and invention. The art of papermaking travelled eastward from China to Korea and Japan, then westward along the Silk Road into modern-day Burma, to the central Asian city of Samarkand. Chinese prisoners captured in Samarkand brought papermaking to the Arabs, who took the process to the Middle East, Egypt, and North Africa, where Muslims recorded the insights of the Islamic Golden Age for posterity. By the Battle of Hastings in 1066, paper itself was in Spain, although papermaking didn't make its debut there and in France until around a hundred years later. The famed Fabriano paper mills of Italy started up in the late 1200s; Austria, Germany, and Switzerland were making paper by 1411; Flanders, Poland, and England around the time that Columbus sailed. A hundred years later, Bohemia, Russia, and Holland adopted the invention. Scotland, by 1591. The Spaniards were operating a paper mill at Culhuacán, Mexico, as early as 1575. The first American mill was established in Germantown, Pennsylvania, in 1690. And the first paper mill in Canada started production in Argenteuil, Quebec, in 1805.

Our world is now so heavily papered that it is hard to imagine that paper was first met with suspicion and fear. But to Europeans seeing it for the first time in the hands of Muslims, paper was heathen. It was weak: look how easily a sheet could be crushed and torn! Paper was ephemeral: it wouldn't last a year. A substitute for parchment? Ludicrous! Parchment, and its rich cousin, vellum, could preserve thoughts as words for centuries.

But parchment was laborious and expensive to make. An average-sized manuscript required the skins of twenty sheep or goats for parchment, even more lambs, calves, or kids if it was vellum. And by the beginning of the thirteenth century, the copying of manuscripts was a growth industry: the production of scrolls was moving out of monasteries and into the city, where scriptoriums housed writers, illuminators, and book binders working together to fill the libraries of nobles, wealthy merchants, and municipalities. Making paper from plants and rags was far faster, easier, and cheaper than scraping and curing the skins of beasts.

The first paper to make its way to Europe was thin, soft, and pliable—a bit like our toilet paper. It was ideal for Chinese calligraphy and block printing, but much too soft for the sharpened quills of the Europeans. It was the Italians who hardened paper by adding animal gelatin to the "stuff," producing a stiff, impervious surface that could take the scratch of a pen on both sides without the ink showing through.

When Johannes Gutenberg began his experiments with mechanical movable type in 1440, paper was one of the first of the problems he had to overcome. Ironically, the stiff paper developed for quills and scribner's ink resisted the imprint of type. Gutenberg tried dampening a sheet before putting it through the press, and suddenly, the metal letters were able to make their mark. Dampening was tricky, though. Too much moisture and, the paper turned to mush; too little and the type bounced off the surface. Eventually, Gutenberg discovered the trick of dampening every other sheet and pressing them together for a few hours, just long enough that the moisture would equalize—the same way my mother taught me to dampen one side of a cotton sheet, then fold it over and in on itself, leaving it until the fabric was uniformly damp enough to iron smooth.

Dampening the paper solved the problem of creating an impression to hold the ink, but it caused another: not only did the ink have to dry, now the paper had to dry, too. This is the creation chant of paper: each solution provoked a new problem to overcome. After Gutenberg came the coaters and the millers, all the thousands of entrepreneurs and inventors who make possible the thick, slick papers in art books today; the lightly toothed pages of poetry chapbooks; the rough, brown pages of pulp novels.

Every sheet of paper is infused with the saga of its own evolution, but it can carry a personal story, too. In 1987, when I moved to Kingston, I found a cache of letters in the attic of my house. Hundreds of pieces of paper were strewn across the rough plank floor, spilling out of boxes, bags, and rusting cookie tins. Among the tracts and letters and diaries was a distinct and startling correspondence: seventy-nine letters from an inmate in Kingston Penitentiary to a girl of seventeen who lived in Portsmouth, a country village that has since been swallowed by the city. The inmate's letters—kites, as they are still called on the inside—were written on whatever he could beg, borrow, or steal. The back of a calendar. Toilet paper. Stationery lifted from the warden's office. No other correspondence like it exists in the English-speaking world: dozens of letters written from inside a prison and smuggled over the wall, uncensored.

For eight years, as I wrote *The Convict Lover*, I kept the rolls and squares of pilfered paper close. I transcribed the words on the pages into computer files that I printed out so that I wouldn't have to touch the crumbling paper any more than necessary, but the actual letters never left my desk. Those papers held the convict's touch. His fingers, stiff with cold in his unheated cell, had made the clumsy folds, tied the butcher's cord and, once, a pale blue ribbon, around the thin rolls. His calloused palm hid the note until he could slide it under the guards' shack in the centre of the stone quarry, where Phyllis Halliday found it, grasping it in her hand, holding it tight in her apron, hiding it in an Ovaltine tin shoved under her bed, moving the letters house to house for seventy years, until I lifted them from her attic into the light.

When I finished writing the book, I donated the convict's letters to the Queen's University archives. Months later, I was invited to view the collection. I felt as if I were coming to visit a long-time friend, one who was a little worn out by his travels, but who was safe now from the deterioration of age and circumstance.

I was shocked to see the rolls and squares of paper pressed flat, trapped rigid between plastic sheets, the life drained out of them. The words were still there but, for me, the words had been such a small part of the story. Gone was the convict's touch, the possibility that my thumbprint might land exactly where his had pressed almost a century before. It hardly seemed to me like paper. More like concrete. A monument. Moribund.

I have another letter that I doubt will ever end up in an archive. I found it stuffed into a purple velvet Crown Royal bag that was balled up inside a pillow case that huddled in the corner of an old box I found at the bottom of the cedar chest my aunt kept at the foot of her bed for as long as I knew her. My aunt and uncle had no children: when they died, it was left to my sisters and me to clear out their apartment.

The letter was torn into tiny bits. Throw it out, my sisters said; it's private. But I couldn't. We tear up letters to get rid of them; we put them in a cedar chest to keep them. This was a letter my aunt wasn't willing to part with.

I spent the better part of a week putting the letter back together. The pieces were tiny and thoroughly mixed up, as if my aunt had ripped the letter in a frenzy and pitched the pieces into the air, then patiently gathered them up and looked around for something to hide them in: the velvet bag that had held her husband's quart of whisky.

She hadn't found all of them. Even after I placed every fragment, sentence to sentence, there were still gaps in the jigsaw puzzle of the letter. The single page had been closely written on both sides, with sentences trailing up the narrow margins. It was from a woman, addressed to my uncle. The date was missing. But the paper was one of those thin blue airmail sheets with glued edges on two sides, a letter and envelope all in one; it had been sent from England, where my uncle, a pilot, was stationed during the Second World War. The return address was Sussex. The woman was pleading. Some of the ink had run; across the centre, the paper was buckled, as if soaked by tears, or maybe spilled tea. Each scrap of paper was smaller than my thumbnail, yet they were all deeply creased, as if the letter had been crumpled in my aunt's fist before she ripped it to shreds.

I taped the pieces to a clear sheet and put the letter fragment in a plastic sleeve, not unlike the ones that hold *The Convict Lover* kites. When I die, one of my children, or a child of their children, will find it. They'll ponder the torn paper, trying to decipher the story it tells, or they'll toss it into a dumpster already overflowing with the paper detritus of my life.

PAPER, SCISSORS, ROCK

I am a messy gardener and a messy cook. My old cookbooks are splattered maps, like those of my mother and my friend Ida, who writes *NOT GOOD!!!!* or *Tasty!* beside the titles of recipes.

I hardly use cookbooks anymore. I look up recipes online. I trace my finger down the screen, a greasy stripe that I wash away with a cloth dampened with vinegar. My children and my children's children won't know which recipes I liked best or why.

I have abandoned legacy for the sake of convenience. I am not the only one. In the 1990s, the New York Public Library—and ultimately every library in the country—gave up its card catalogues in favour of a searchable database. I used to spend hours with the card catalogues in my local libraries, idly thumbing the cards, waiting for the inspiration of coincidence: looking up monarch and finding Malcolm Lowry loitering nearby, which led to *Lunar Caustic* and the lovely, pale green luna moth. I loved the jittery type across the top of each card, the *o* and *e* filled in by the ink-caked keys of some ancient typewriter and, below the essential details of title and author and number of pages, notations in black ink or blue, handwritten by one librarian after another. On the backs of the cards, spelling corrections and comments, mini reviews and recommendations, directions to other books by the same author, catalogued under her secret *nom de plume.* The cards were coded conspiracies among readers, like the pin-pricked notes that inmates would leave in prison library books, a silent telegraph from one book-lover to the next.

When my local library threw out its card catalogue, stacks of cards lay on the checkout counter, free to readers needing bookmarks. I took as many as I dared, worried that some catastrophe would shut down the electrical system and the new digital database with it. I didn't worry about an obliterating fate like the fiery one that destroyed the library at Alexandria (not then, I didn't) but a lesser catastrophe: books still on the shelves but no way to find them.

I suffer the anxiety of a culture in flux. I imagine a shepherd a thousand years ago hoarding the hides of his flock in the event the flirtation with paper turned out to be nothing but a passing whim.

A PUZZLING OF PIXELS

Paper, in contemporary jargon, is a display technology. So, too, is the screen of a computer or an ereader. As we prepared the ebook of *The Paradise Project*, my son Erik and I blithely skipped past all the paper decisions: heft, texture, colour, source. The history of paper seemed immaterial as we considered the digital version of the manuscript. Surely a plastic screen was as great a deviation from tree pulp as the scraped skins of donkeys were from stone tablets. Yet paper continued to be strangely present, I discovered, in the evolution of digital displays.

The first electronic paper—epaper—came out of the Palo Alto Research Center in California, where, in the 1970s, Xerox gathered a world-class team of scientists to become what they claimed would be the "architects of information." Nick Sheridon, the inventor of the first epaper, called his brainchild Gyricon, a name that has nothing to do with paper and everything to do with how its plastic surrogate is made. Microscopic polyethylene spheres (75–106 micrometres across) are embedded in a transparent silicone sheet, each tiny ball suspended in its own bubble of oil so it can rotate freely. The spheres are Janus particles: their surface boasts two or more distinct physical properties, so that two different types of chemistry can occur on the same particle. In the case of the Gyricon, the Janus particle is composed of negatively charged black plastic on one side and positively charged white plastic on the other. Depending on the polarity of the voltage applied, the white or the black side is face-up, giving the pixel a white or black appearance.

That's a wildly simplified explanation, but you get the drift. Epaper made ereaders possible, and in 2004, digital readers using the paper substitute started hitting the market. It wasn't a complete success. Although the new epaper was reflective (about as reflective as a newspaper, but not as reflective as good white bond), it was slow to refresh, which meant it held onto one image for a second or two after the next image appeared. This "ghosting" is not the same as what happens when a computer screen is left on too long. With epaper, the ghost would disappear if the device was turned on and off repeatedly until the pixels normalized. Some devices would flash the entire screen white then black when loading a new image.

Over the past dozen years, the architects of information, these modern-day Cai Luns, have been refining their invention, getting rid of the ghosts, striving to produce a plastic that acts as much like paper as is humanly, mechanically, and digitally possible. They are motivated by studies that show, despite every technological advance, many readers still prefer paper.

The earliest studies—done before 1992 (and before epaper) when only a few of us were reading on our computers—found that comprehension, speed, and accuracy were much lower onscreen. Recent studies, however, find little significant difference between the two. Despite this, many research subjects continue to state a preference for paper. They like the way paper feels. They like being able to shuffle quickly between pages that are chapters apart. They say they don't feel as tired after reading a paper book.

Are these just the nostalgic musings of a transitional reading generation?

I don't think so. Comprehension matters, but so does comfort.

Epaper has come a long way since the cathode ray tubes of early computers, but even so digital displays with their glare, pixilation, and flickers can be hard on the eyes. Eye strain, headaches, and blurred vision are so common—affecting around seventy percent of people who work long hours in front of computers—that the American Optometric Association has officially recognized computer vision syndrome (CVS). At least one study claims CVS is epidemic among North Americans.

Reading from paper is less work, on a whole lot of levels. Working memory is a finite resource: the harder it is to read, the less brainpower is available to shift what we read into memory. Because we weren't born with specific brain systems for reading, our bodies have had to invent them. Some researchers believe that, as well as reading the actual words, the brain perceives a text as a kind of physical landscape, building maps not unlike the maps we make of hills and valleys and halls and rooms. A paper book presents a more complex topography with more variations on which to hang our memories. The paper itself has texture. It drapes to the left or right when a book is opened. Touching the thickness of the paper and turning it leaves a kind of fingerprint in the mind, a marker of what has been read. It is easier, researchers believe, to make a coherent mental map of a long paper text because of these markers. By comparison, onscreen text is an endless scroll with little physical texture or variation to help fix the words and their meaning in the memory. No wonder we get tired.

Subconsciously, we understand this. In study after

study, students consistently prefer paper over screens if they really need to understand what they are reading. Typically, they'll cruise a screen to find what they want, but turn to paper to read it intensively.

The most recent research suggests that reading onscreen is as *effective* as reading a printed page—exactly what digital devotees want to hear—but there is a difference between effectiveness and pleasure. As Alberto Manguel points out in *A History of Reading*, our species has had to learn to read: we aren't hard-wired for it, the way we are for speaking. And we have only been reading silently inside our heads for a thousand years, a drop in the bucket in evolutionary terms. Once we stopped reading out loud, Manguel writes, "the reader was at last able to establish an unrestricted relationship with the book and the words." That relationship is not insignificant, and like all relationships, it is both sensual and intellectual. And reading on paper is still, at this point, a much more sensual experience than reading onscreen.

Interestingly, a 2011 study by the cognitive scientists Rakefet Ackerman and Morris Goldsmith found that the expectations of readers—that print or digital would be more efficient and effective—were in fact self-fulfilling. Those who believed print was better scored higher in recall and comprehension when reading from a printed text. And those who believed digital was better had a psychological bias towards etext that made them score better in onscreen reading.

I wonder if the intangibility of onscreen text plays a role, too, in the paper/pixel preference game. I've suffered enough computer crises to know that digital storage is not to be trusted. I now keep backups of my backups. Paper may be fragile, subject to tearing and rot and spilled coffee, but printing words on paper is like carving them in stone compared to the ephemeral world of pixels, where words can disappear from epaper as if written in invisible ink.

For whatever reason, after almost fifty years of digital innovation, physical paper remains the gold standard. Engineers, designers, and user-interface experts are engaged not in invention but in technological mimicry, working hard to make reading on an ereader or tablet as close to reading on paper as possible. The Kindle screen looks like a page in a paperback. iBooks includes fairly realistic page-turning. Both of these will seem like square wheels if South Korea's KAIST Institute of Information Technology Convergence perfects its interface that will allow a reader to see already-read pages on the left and unread pages on the right, exactly like a paper book.

But the question remains: why are scientists working so hard to make plastic screens exactly like paper? Can't we have both—eat our cake and pie, too? Paper is lovely to touch; screens are workhorses at scrolling and searching and ferrying volumes across oceans and continents.

I want both.

I have walls of books and stacks of diaries and reams of scribbled-over pages. I also love Atavist publishing and storytelling platform, which brings me long news stories with embedded interactive graphics, maps, timelines, animations, and soundtracks. And I am excited by each new installment of interactive fiction from Kate Pullinger and her digital-wizard collaborators, a literary experience that could not possibly happen on paper. The personal, contemplative space created by reading silently can open up around an iPad just as easily as around a paper book. Paper and pixels both are tools, substrates, display technologies: how well they work for us depends on how we use them.

Why is it that we assume each new thing condemns what went before as obsolete? We know that's not true. We can read a book, stream a Netflix movie, then listen to the radio as we drive to the opera, read a précis of the narrative on our iPad as we wait for the performance to begin.

We *can* have it all.

KEEPER OF THE WORDS

"Salad paper," Hugh says by way of greeting as I enter his print shop one bright August morning. He shoves a sheet of pale paper at me.

I can always tell when Hugh has something up his sleeve. He bounces around me like a leprechaun. "Salad paper. Perfect for our paradise project, don't you think?" He winks.

I run my hand over the sheet. It feels as thick as a communion wafer, but more appealing. A fine cream biscuit.

"Is it handmade?" I ask.

"Well, well, well now. Let me tell you. It is, in a way. It's from Saint-Armand."

Saint-Armand is a Montreal papermaker known for its fine handmade and Fourdrinier papers. Handmade sheets are produced one at a time, much the same as the process I saw at Emily's, although on a larger scale. Screens are dipped in a vat of stuff, the water is drained off, and the paper is pressed and dried in sheets that have four deckle edges and no grain, the fibres knitting together randomly. With Fourdrinier papers, the process is mechanized: a continuous sheet of paper is formed on an endless woven wire cloth that holds the paper fibres on top while the water drains out below. The paper is pressed and dries as it moves over forty feet of heated rollers, then it is wound onto spools and cut into thirty-inch lengths. The process by its nature aligns the fibres, so that the paper has grain in the long direction, which means it can be torn neatly. Sheets cut from a spool of Fourdrinier paper have two deckle edges and two straight edges from the cuts.

David Carruthers founded the Saint-Armand paper mill in 1979. That same year, Hugh met David at one of the first Grimsby Wayzgoose book fairs.

"What's a wayzgoose?" I ask. My ignorance is legion.

"When an apprentice printer became a journeyman about to start out on his own," Hugh explains, "the proprietor of the print shop would throw a going-away goose dinner. After a while, this evolved into an annual picnic for all the staff around the end of August. Saint

Bartholomew's Day, I think it was. That day marked the end of summer and the start of working by candlelight. Can you imagine that? Printing by candlelight! And we think we have it hard. They coined the word 'wayzgoose' to describe the dinner, shortened from 'going-away goose,' I suppose. Apparently they thought it sounded better with a z stuck in the middle. After a while, any party for the printers at a print shop or a newspaper was called a wayzgoose."

(According to my etymological dictionary, the derivation of the term is in doubt. It could also be a misspelling of wasegoose, from *wase*, which is sheaf in Middle English, indicating a harvest goose, like the stubble-goose Chaucer mentions in "The Cook's Prologue." More likely, my dictionary says, the word comes from the early modern Dutch *weghuis* or way house, which refers to an inn and also a banquet. Apparently, English printers often apprenticed in the Low Countries and brought printing terminology back with them.)

Some individual presses still throw an annual wayzgoose to celebrate their work and workers: Coach House Books in Toronto has been doing so since 1965. In 1979, a small gathering of friends in the bookmaking arts—letterpress printers, printmakers, papermakers, and hand bookbinders—decided to get together to talk books and paper and printing, and to exhibit their wares. They called it Wayzgoose, after that long printing tradition, and the annual gathering has been growing steadily ever since. Held each year on the last Saturday in April in Grimsby, Ontario, it now attracts over fifty artisans and more than 2,000 visitors.

"We were essentially in it for the kicks," Hugh laughs. "We had to be. We didn't sell enough to pay for the beer we drank afterwards."

This year, I make the trek to Wayzgoose. Hugh's heart is acting up—that's the way he puts it—and he's on the list for a new valve, borrowed from a pig. His booth is womanned by a young book artist who has fallen under the sway of Hugh, another acolyte who feels ink stirring in her veins. Dozens of book artists are set up in the hallway of the Grimsby Public Library, their books arranged on tables in front of them. Not stiff towers of the sort of books found in a bookstore: these are softly covered, thick-paged, gorgeous books filled with pages with ragged edges that reverent readers delicately lift and turn in their hands as if the book were a rare work of art, which each one clearly is.

"David and I always see each other at Wayzgoose. We both have a sense of humour. You need one of those to cope with such desperate enterprises as making paper and publishing books."

Just as ink is in Hugh's blood, paper—or maybe pulp—is in David's. His grandfather, George Carruthers, owned a large paper mill and wrote a book, *Papermaking*, that traced the history of papermaking in Canada up to 1905. David's father was a paper salesman with the family firm. David himself started out working at the Pulp & Paper Association of Canada, but his knowledge of the paper trade convinced him to set up a handmade paper mill "with a dash of technology," as he puts it.

The early years were tough. His nascent mill was plagued with floods, machinery failures, and unhappy neighbours. But he persevered, selling his handmade paper to art suppliers in Canada, the United States, and abroad.

In 1992, David had the chance to buy a thousand-pound Hollander beater from Massachusetts. His paper was and still is made primarily from rags, mostly cotton off-cuts from local clothing manufacturers, but it can also be made from linen, flax straw, jute, sisal—any kind of organic fabric. His shop floor in an old industrial and rapidly gentrifying suburb of Montreal is littered with huge bags of cuttings from what David calls "the bed-sheet ladies" and "the long-underwear guys." A machine chops the fabric to uniform shreds that are pulped in the giant beater: 500 pounds of chopped rag to 20,000 litres of water. Nothing else is added: no chemicals, no bleach. White paper is made from white underwear off-cuts, blue from blue denim.

At the same time as he acquired the 1903 Hollander, David bought a Fourdrinier papermaking machine. The Fourdrinier was invented in 1799 in France, at the height of the French Revolution. It was financed (not invented) by the Fourdrinier brothers, who lost their shirts in the venture but had their name attached for-ever to the first break-through in papermaking since Cai Lun set out his instructions in 105 CE.

The Fourdrinier revolutionized papermaking and put it at the very cutting edge of the Industrial Revolution, so much so that the proper name has now become an adjective. When David set up his rescued Hollander and his 1947 Fourdrinier, no one in Canada was making handmade paper on a large scale. His Fourdrinier was probably the only such machine set up since the 1920s. He was bucking a trend.

"Paper is life's hard copy," David says. His rumbling, sloshy basement in Quebec produces the only fine art rag paper in Canada, one of a handful of such paper-makers left in the world. "Paper has to survive."

Saint-Armand refers to its Fourdrinier papers as Canal paper (named after the Lachine Canal, near where David finally settled his factory). The company

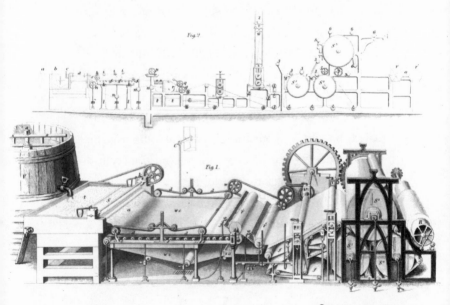

sells twenty different grades of Canal papers, made from cotton, sisal, linen, or flax straw. If the order is big enough, David can mix a customized pulp. He has made patterned papers with spots and stripes, papers scattered with coffee beans, vine leaves, apple leaves, die-cut letters, and photocopied images. He's made paper that imitates marble, bark, animal skin, and even an old wooden door.

Hugh wants Canal paper for *The Paradise Project*. He has designed the book to be fifty-seven pages long, each page measuring about five by eleven inches. Each sheet of Canal paper is roughly twenty-two by thirty, which means that Hugh can get twelve *Paradise Project* pages out of a sheet. For 300 books, he'll need roughly 1,500 sheets. Not a big order by commercial paper-making standards.

"Of course, depending on the fibres, the sheets are going to shrink a bit. You might end up with a sheet that is twenty-one inches after it dries. The sheets will vary in thickness, too, depending on where in the roll they are cut from," Hugh explains. He winks. "Nothing is ever as straightforward as it seems."

That thought tires me, but it fires Hugh up. "The first sheets off the batch will be slightly thicker because there will be more fibre in the same volume of water, and this can affect the printing impression. A man on a galloping horse wouldn't notice, but it can be a problem to an anal person like me."

If Hugh sometimes comes across as a fanatic, he isn't a patch on Dard Hunter.

From 1922 to 1950, Hunter produced eight limited-edition books, handmade in a way that Hugh only dreams of. Not only did Hunter make his own paper, he bought a property with a running stream so he could produce the power to run the pulping stampers. His goal was to produce a printed book that was, down to the very last detail, made entirely by himself. He accomplished that eight exquisite times. One of those books, which he both wrote and printed—*Papermaking: The History and Technique of an Ancient Craft*—was in part responsible for the post–Second World War revival of hand paper-making and handprinting in the United States.

Hugh is prodding me with the Salad paper.

"It's made from cotton fibre and it is acid-free," he says. "It will last forever—or 500 years, whichever comes first—or we will give you your money back."

Hugh is watching me like a five-year-old with a secret.

"Don't you want to know why it's called Salad paper?" he says finally, taking the sheet out of my hands.

I play along. "Sure. Why is it called Salad paper?"

"Well. David had a call from a printmaker in New York. The man was very insistent. He wanted to know if the paper David was selling him was good for 'salad' prints."

Hugh is chuckling wildly to himself. I can't imagine where this is going.

"The man was from Brooklyn. It took a while, but eventually David realized that the printmaker was saying 'solid' prints." Hugh does a very bad imitation of a nasally, wide-mouthed New York City accent: "Solid. Salad. Get it?"

I laugh. Hugh is irresistible. He always makes me laugh.

"So David named it Salad paper. He figured it would be a big seller among the greengrocers."

THE SOUND OF SILENCE

Paper rustles. It snaps. It swishes. It riffles, slides, and flumps. If someone asked, I would say this is the sound of books, but I'd be wrong. It's the sound that paper makes.

Imagine a library completely stripped of paper books. We're almost there: my local library is alive now with the chirp of keys, the click of mice, the whoosh of emailed words sucked up into cyberspace. Mechanical sounds. But go to the shelves (yes, there are still public shelves for browsing) and leaf through a book. Close your eyes. Listen.

The manufacturers of digital readers must be aware of how much we love the sound of paper because most of them have taken pains to add sound cues that simulate the turning of a page. They've tried to mimic the physical turning, too, even though with an ereader there is no page to turn, just a soundless scrolling of text and image.

The whoosh of a turning page on an ereader is a sop. It's like the gear shift in my Toyota Prius, which serves no purpose other than to reassure me that what I am driving is a car in the way I still understand the word "car," as a machine with an internal combustion engine. I press a button to start the car and I could just as easily press buttons to shift from Park to Reverse, but Toyota gives me a gear-shift knob instead, to create the illusion that I am personally putting the car through its paces.

I suspect that the future in which we give up this pretense is not too far away. The images on our ereaders will scroll silently one to the next. No faux page lifting at the bottom right-hand corner. No surrogate sound of rustling paper. No attempt whatsoever to reproduce the visceral sensations of reading on paper.

In 2006, I was Writer in Residence at Green College, University of British Columbia. Green is a multidisciplinary graduate student college modelled on Green College, Oxford, and endowed by the Texas Instrument philanthropist Cecil Green. My only job, apart from writing a novel, was to engage in dinner conversation with the residents, one of whom was doing post-doc research on ereader screens, although the devices weren't called that at the time. They hadn't been around long enough to warrant a generic name.

"We have to make the reading experience onscreen as much like reading on paper as possible," he said, and even then I wondered why. Did papermakers in the fourteenth century think that way, too? Did they try to make sheets of paper look as much like parchment as possible?

The curse of the innovator: to make the strange familiar.

Will historians of the future look back with awe at

the first ereader screens, touch them as reverently as paper historians touch the ancient fibrous relics found in Chinese caves? Will they wonder where the screen was made and by whom? Or will they shake it vigorously, bash it against a tree, puzzled by what this inert rectangle of plastic was meant to do.

Before I met Hugh, I might have said I had no opinions about paper, but it seems that I do. I buy my notebooks in Mexico because I like the tissue-thinness of the paper in the 10-peso scribblers, the slightly waxy coating that speeds my pen along. I don't care for paper with "tooth." And I don't like paper that thinks it's a blotter, spreading my ink like a bruise.

"Paper" didn't appear as a word in the English language until around 1350, during the last days of the Dark Ages, at the height of the bubonic plague. The word derives from *papyrus* and comes ultimately from the Egyptians who made paper from that genus of plant. "Page" comes from the Latin *pagina*, a strip of papyrus fastened to another strip to create a scroll. "Page," meaning a sheet of paper, came into English some 200 years after the word "paper." In 1993, "home page" was coined, and now page refers not only to a physical sheet of paper but to a block of information that fills the screen at a single Internet URL.

Language is in transition, and so are we.

I write on paper. I write onscreen. I like writing

on paper better, or I used to. I have to recalibrate that phrase daily as my habits change. The drag of paper irks me when words are clamouring to stream out. Words onscreen come with a ready-made gloss, the margins automatically justified so that the page looks like it's part of a book long before the words have any right to call themselves anything but a raw heap of alphabet.

In the first years of settlement on this continent, paper was such a precious commodity that people wrote over the sheet twice, once in one direction, once in another, a crosshatch of stories. I've read diaries by pioneers and letters from settlers that were almost illegible, the words were so entangled. In my novel *The Holding*, Alyson, a back-to-the-land gardener, finds an old cookbook in a collapsed log cabin, the last pages written in exactly that way:

> at the end, a few sheets closely written
> in cursive script, the paper written
> over twice, side to side, then top to
> bottom, so that the sentences seemed
> woven together, and she knelt there
> by the logs, the wind worrying at the
> pages as she tried to tease the phrases
> apart, until she found an opening and
> tracing her finger along the lines, she
> came at last to the beginning—

Not only did early settlers write crosswise, sometimes circling the margins, too, but the penmanship itself was cramped, letters jammed up against each other, the ascenders and descenders held under tight rein. I can imagine the writer, hunched into herself, the pen held rigid, as frugal with her words as with her paper.

There is no such parsimony now. Digital screens make us garrulous, no paper to consider, just endless letters jostled into words and strung together in sentences (or not), our posture loose, our mouths flapping, fingers flying, an endless spew.

Pixel or paper: is one better than the other, more lasting, more real? Or in the end, are both as desperately inadequate as Franz Kafka bemoans in his letter to his beloved Felice:

"May I kiss you then? On this miserable paper? I might as well open the window and kiss the night air."

A LASTING IMPRESSION

The page that Hugh hands me is a material object. It does not yet hold any information except the story of its own history and making. It rustles slightly in my hand. I look at it head-on, as I might look at a painting. Then I hold it up to the light, as Emily taught me to do, to look for variations in opacity and how the paper fibres are dispersed. This is the look-through. Then I hold it at a raking angle to the light—the look-down—to check the texture on the surface caused by the felts, the moulds, the fibres. I look for the papermaker's tears.

Hugh plucks it out of my hand and offers it to me again.

"Like this," he says. He holds it perfectly flat, at eye level.

I look across the terrain of the paper, its landscape of hills and hollows. I could get lost in there.

"Feel how soft it is," Hugh says. "On paper like this, words make an impression."

TYPE
TYPE
TYPE
TYPE

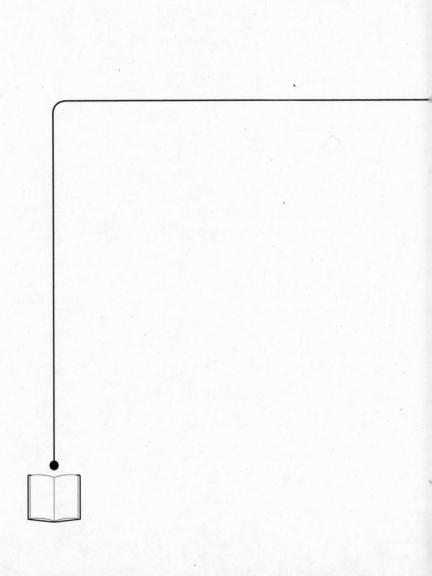

THE PRINTER'S DEVIL

Hugh is in love with words, but his love is different from mine. I adore the shape of words in my mouth, the music of them in the air, the way a word can be a Proustian *madeleine*, springing the door on a full-blown movie of memory. Hugh, on the other hand, craves the feel of words under his fingers, the press of them against a sheet of paper. Not storytelling, typography.

It doesn't surprise me that Hugh's first idea for the endpapers of *The Paradise Project* is typographical.

"What I have in mind is to print with wooden type, in two shades of yellow, words and phrases taken from your work," he writes by email. "These words will range from one inch to three inches in height and will run horizontally across the endpapers. I must use *TRUST ME* from *The Convict Lover*. If I don't like the effect, it will end up in the garbage. Don't worry. I need to feed my addiction to the press, and this will be my fix for today. So just sit back and relax until I get something to show you."

In his book *The Gutenberg Revolution*, John Man theorizes that there have been four crucial turning points in "the line zooming from grunt to email." The first was the invention of writing. The second was the invention of the alphabet, which simplified writing and made it accessible to everyone. The fourth is the turning point that is spinning us dizzy right now: the invention of the Internet.

The third turning point in human communication was the invention of printing with mechanical movable type.

Before Gutenberg, books were produced by scribes toiling away in scriptoriums, each manuscript copied by hand. A book would take a month or two, at the very least, to produce, working by sunlight then candlelight on sloped desks that torqued the body. The margins of medieval texts are littered with scribe complaints:

> *This parchment is hairy. The ink is thin.*
> *A curse on thee, O pen!*
> *Writing is excessive drudgery.*
> *Thank God it will soon be dark.*
> *Oh, my hand!*

In 1438, just before Gutenberg unveiled his invention, a 1,272-page commentary on the Bible was finally finished: two scribes had worked five years on the project. Only a few years later, with mechanical movable type, 500 copies of such a book could be produced in a week. The implications were staggering: information was no longer a guarded secret available only to the rich and powerful. Through a printed book, anyone could travel the world.

The paradigm shift currently rocking our world is of equal magnitude. A writer no longer has to wait for someone to select their manuscript, edit it, typeset and print it, move it to a warehouse, then ship it out to bookstores by truck and train. Writers don't have to wait for a publisher, and readers don't have peruse the shelves of a store or library in search of a title. Book warehouses are all but obsolete. The gatekeepers are leaving the building. Now, within minutes of being written, a book can be simultaneously in the hands of readers in China, Chile, and Chattanooga.

Surely turning point is too mild a term. These four inventions have acted as detonators for worldwide explosions in literary outpourings. At the time Gutenberg printed his first book, all the books printed in Europe could be hauled in a single wagon. A mere half century later, tens of thousands of titles were in print. Today, some 10,000 million books are produced every year worldwide. John Man offers a compelling image. "One year's production would make a pile four times the height of the Great Pyramid." Multiply one giant pyramid by five centuries of printing and we humans have produced a Rocky Mountain range of printed matter.

Like Gutenberg, Hugh is an inventor, although he prefers the term innovator. Before he became a letter-press printer, he was a certified orthotist, working as a consultant. In the early 1980s, he was spending two days a week at Ongwanada, a Kingston facility that provides community support, including rehab, research, and radiology, for the developmentally challenged. Hugh's job was to shape seats that would fit within a wheelchair frame to improve the comfort and health of children suffering from postural deformities such as scoliosis.

One day he observed to his horror that the spinal curvature in his young patients wasn't getting better, it was getting worse. X-rays confirmed his suspicions.

"I can remember driving home and thinking, *What are you doing, Hugh? You're saying to these kids, 'Oh I'm sorry I've made your back worse, now I'm going home to have some red wine.'* It wasn't enough to say sorry."

Instead of taking that glass of wine, Hugh went into his workshop. In those days, the back and seat of a wheelchair were fixed at a 90-degree angle. When a physically challenged person sat in a wheelchair, the spine necessarily slumped; the part of their body that supported the weight inevitably developed pressure sores. Hugh knew that lying flat produced the least pressure on the spine and that sitting up straight pro-duced the most. What if he could design a chair with an adjustable seat, one that could be tilted so the person was optimally both upright *and* relaxed?

He built a tilting chair and chose six children whose backs had worsened and arranged to have them x-rayed lying flat, sitting up, and reclining.

"The effect was almost immediate: five of the six improved. But I couldn't stop thinking about the one that didn't get better. Then the light bulb flashed on: it wasn't only the weight on the spine, it was the fact that this child was spastic. So we tilted the chair a little more, enough that the muscles relaxed, and, bingo, that child improved, too."

His wife, Verla, had been confined to a wheelchair since 1948. For thirty-two years she'd battled pressure sores. Hugh made her a tilt chair, and within three months the sores were healed.

Hugh tried to sell the medical community on his new adjustable tilting wheelchair. "I went to a conference and I gave a paper on the tilt chair, but I might as well have stood on the street and talked to the squirrels." When he failed to interest a manufacturer, Hugh started a company, Advanced Mobility Systems, to produce the dynamic-tilt wheelchair. He was too busy filling orders to file for a patent, and soon others were manufacturing their own versions, advertising them as lighter, cheaper, stronger.

"I couldn't compete, but that doesn't matter. What matters is that things got a whole lot better for people in wheelchairs."

Brilliant new concepts rarely appear out of the blue. More often, the key elements have been bumping up against each other for a while, waiting for someone with the insight, the foresight, and the audacity to try something new.

"More *Aha!* than *Abacadabra!*," I say to Hugh.

"Good girl. You've got it!" he says, and I beam ridiculously.

༅

What were the elements, I wonder, that came together for the invention of mechanical movable type?

Johannes Gutenberg was born in Mainz, Germany, around the turn of the fifteenth century. His father was a Companion of the Mint. Young Johannes would have seen coins struck, a process by which gold or silver was poured into a mould made of two dies, one for each side of the coin. The dies were made with a punch—a shank of steel engraved with an image. When the punch was struck with a hammer, the image transferred to the softer metal of the die.

Punchmaking was an art that required not only metallurgical skill but also proficiency in the engraver's art. We are smug about the ever-increasing resolution of digital technology, but the men that young Johannes would have seen cutting letters into steel punches were achieving resolutions of at least six and in some cases sixty times the resolution of a modern laser printer.

Was Gutenberg himself a punchcutter? He is described as a goldsmith and a member of the bourgeoisie, but, really, the historical record is slight. What *is* known for sure is that in his early thirties, this well-educated bachelor received a windfall—the equivalent of five years' salary in one lump sum. With it, he bought a house outside Strasbourg, a city that straddles the Rhine and is now part of France but at the time was an independent republic boasting the tallest building in the world, the Strasbourg Cathedral.

Gutenberg was young and ambitious, an entrepreneur: he decided he could make a fortune selling 32,000 mirrors to pilgrims flocking to Strasbourg to see the relics of Emperor Charlemagne. (Mirrors were thought to concentrate the healing power of the relics.) The venture collapsed when the pilgrimage was cancelled due to a recurrence of the bubonic plague, but here's where it gets interesting, as Hugh would say. In the court records of his business failure, Gutenberg offers to appease his disgruntled investors by sharing the secret of something else he's working on, something so surefire that they immediately drop their lawsuit against him.

The court records mention a "secret art" that Gutenberg developed sometime in 1438. He calls it *kunst und aventur*. Art and enterprise. At one point he orders the melting down of all the "formes" that have been created, formes that are described as "four pieces" held together by "two screws."

Were these formes designed to hold type for a press? Screw-based presses were commonly used in fifteenth-century Europe for pressing olives and grapes and for squeezing paper dry. Press, paper, ink, punch-cutters to create moulds for letters: all of these technologies were at hand. So what was the catalyst that sparked the invention of mechanical movable type, the missing element that would make the printing press possible?

For the answer, it may help to step back from Gutenberg to look at the time in which he lived. Gutenberg was born exactly halfway through the century of the Black Death, the plague that buried somewhere between thirty and sixty percent of the population of Europe. Those who survived were reeling from grief, yearning for an explanation, and desperate to prevent the disease from wiping humankind off the map. It was a turmoil tailor-made for religious fervour, and, sure enough, a vision arose of a single Christian church, with the devout all saying the same prayers, singing from the same songbook, reading the same psalms. A standardized missal. One true Bible for everyone.

I am an inveterate watcher of clouds, my eye trained for the bright flash of lightning among the thunderheads. So I think, *Yes, that could be it: the Black Death itself prompted the "what if" that sparked the invention that cracked open our lives.*

A SHORT HISTORY OF ARTIFICIAL WRITING

Even in Gutenberg's day, there was nothing new about making multiple, identical copies of a single, approved original. Whether the human animal is intrinsically lazy or hard-wired for efficiency, the fact is that almost as soon as writing was invented—in Mesopotamia in

3200 BCE and independently in China in 1200 BCE and in Mesoamerica around 500 BCE—people were trying to figure out how to reduce the work of drawing each glyph or character by hand.

The solution was some sort of stamp. In 1700 BCE, an enterprising Minoan produced the Phaistos Disc, a clay circle the size of a bread-and-butter plate with 241 images pressed into the clay with metal stamps. Ancient Egyptians stamped hieroglyphs on tiles with carved wooden blocks. Paper was a more fragile medium, but even so the Chinese perfected stamping on paper in the fifth century; by the 700s, printers in China, Japan, and Korea were all producing books made up of pages stamped with a single carved block of wood or stone. In the tenth century, the Chinese used that method to print the entire Buddhist canon of 130,000 pages.

There was even movable type, of a sort. An eleventh-century Chinese printer named Pi Sheng incised separate characters in reverse in wet clay, then baked them in a kiln. To print, he chose the characters he wanted, mounted them in a frame, inked them, laid on a sheet of paper, and rubbed to get an impression. Clay characters gave way to wooden blocks and, eventually, characters cast in bronze, copper, tin, iron, and lead. Even so, the selecting and arranging of the elements of a text and the rubbing continued to be done by hand. The practice wasn't widespread partly because there was little demand for printed matter beyond the emperor's palace. There was no real need for a press because the paper in that part of the word was delicate and didn't require the forceful stamp of a screw press. Hand-rubbing worked just fine.

Even if someone had thought up a press, no machine at the time was up to handling the multitude of characters that make up an Asian language. The Koreans took movable type to its highest sophistication, but they still had to hand-select from among 40,000 characters and take a rubbing, a labour-intensive process. In the end, these calligraphic writing systems were simply too complex to spawn a printing revolution.

An alphabet, however, condenses the vast array of human linguistic sounds into a few symbols; twenty-six, in the case of the English alphabet. Alphabets are imprecise, which makes for less nuanced written communication, but the pared-down simplicity is a huge advantage when it comes to mechanizing a writing system.

"When Gutenberg came along, the word 'modular' hadn't even been invented!" Hugh exclaims, and he's right. I checked. The first recorded use of modular to mean "composed of interchangeable units" was in 1936. "And there he was, five hundred years before the rest of us Neanderthals caught up, developing a modular system for making words with metal type. He mechanized it, and the rest is history!"

Gutenberg's modular innovation took two forms. He developed a hand-held mould that allowed printers to cast a letter accurately again and again from one original punch. In the course of printing, type wears out, gets chipped and bent and generally banged up. Re-cutting a punch every time that happened would be expensive and time-consuming. Gutenberg's handheld mould allowed a printer to cast endless units, either from new metal or from the old letters, melted down.

Gutenberg's second modular element was a technique for bringing together the letters of the alphabet into an endless variation of words and sentences and fixing them so that page after identical page could be printed, then the letters released to be reused to create other pages.

Gutenberg wasn't the only one keen on figuring out how to mechanize type. That's usually the case with inventions: Tesla and dozens of others were tinkering with the light bulb when Edison brought his version to market; my father spent years in the 1940s trying to invent instant coffee, unaware that a process had been patented in 1890. Coincidentally or not, just as Gutenberg was launching the first movable type, a goldsmith named Procopius Waldvogel turned up in southern France carrying two steel alphabets and various metal formes, offering to teach "the art of artificial writing." (Scribes of the day referred to their calligraphy as "artifice," so "artificial writing" may indeed refer to printing.) Gutenberg probably didn't know of Waldvogel's existence and the "forest bird" disappears after this one puzzling mention, but the speed with which Gutenberg's invention was taken up proves that the time was ripe. If he hadn't done it, chances are someone else would have.

"I'm not sure if I'm going to lie to you or not," says Hugh, "but in those years 1980, '81, '82, I gave something like twenty papers at national and international conferences on my innovations in orthotics." Hugh isn't boasting. After the dynamic-tilt wheelchair, he produced dozens of innovative orthotics, including an invisible body brace and a wrist-driven flexor hinge splint. "Because of all that, I was invited to teach a design course at the Ontario College of Art in problem-solving. Designing Outside the Box, I called it. And I'll tell you something. Inventing or doing artwork, they both take the same sort of thought. You don't get where you need to go by looking for what is bad. You have to look for the good, and build on that. That's Barclay's Law #27, by the way. Look for the good."

THE MOST HATED FACE IN THE WORLD

I started writing on a portable Smith-Corona type-writer. Type Writer. When I pressed a key, a metal letter at the end of a long arm was propelled toward the page, where it whacked a ribbon inked with two bands, black and red. The typeface was probably `Courier`. I don't remember. It never occurred to me that there could be more than one.

Half a century later, when I begin a new book, I choose a fresh face for the project. I spend hours peering at the 120-plus typefaces that are standard equipment on my MacBook Pro. A name will attract me first, but it's the shape of the letters I'm interested in. Baskerville, for instance, sounds strong and noble, but its squat letters give me a headache. **Myanmar MN** seemed perfect for my novel set partly in Burma, but this alphabet goose-stepped too aggressively across the page.

I have only two rules when choosing a typeface for a writing project: it has to be a face I will be happy to look at every day for several years, and it has to reverberate in some way with the nature of the book. In the past, I've written books in Times New Roman, Palatino, Avenir, American Typewriter, and Arial—traditional, romantic, literary, journalistic, practical. With *Gutenberg's Fingerprint*, I was tempted to give each chapter in its own face—Papyrus for "Paper," Franklin for "Press," COPPERPLATE for "Type." Editors don't like writers getting fancy with typography: it's harder to catch errors and to calculate pages. But with a computer, I can revert to standard Times with a click of a key, so I am free to indulge myself.

In a fit of whimsy, I consider Comic Sans, a typeface developed twenty years ago by Microsoft typeface engineer Victor Connare. When Comic Sans was released in 1995, type-lovers were so outraged that they set up BanComicSans.com, where they sold anti–Comic Sans mugs and T-shirts to help finance a documentary called *Comic Sans; Or, the Most Hated Font in the World.*

Comic Sans Must Die went further. It deconstructed the face, glyph by glyph, until the typeface was finally declared officially dead on December 5, 2012. You can witness its demise at ComicSansMustDie.tumblr.com. But check the pull-down font menu on your computer: chances are that Comic Sans is still there, with its goofy, round, erratic letters that look like a child's handprinted sign for selling lemonade at the curb. Brownies use it for bake sales. Families use it for birthday invitations. On *Orange Is the New Black*, Piper uses it for her prison newsletter. Even Pope Benedict XVI used it for the tag lines in the online photo album that commemorated his papacy. His resignation letter is there, too, printed in the same innocently charming **Comic Sans**.

Comic Sans isn't the only typeface to rouse strong public opinion. When the movie *Avatar* was released, fans were appalled at the Papyrus typeface James Cameron chose for the subtitles that ran through the film. When posters were unveiled for *Star Wars: The Force Awakens* (Episode VII, released in 2015) there was a happy outcry: the title was set in ITC Serif Gothic, the same typeface used in the promotion of the first *Star Wars* movie—a curvy, iconic '70s face that has since been used on everything from *Eraserhead* posters to the cover of Colleen McCullough's blockbuster novel *The Thorn Birds*. The C's and E's are throwbacks to F. Scott Fitzgerald's Roaring twenties; the AV, TY, and TH ligatures are brilliantly nestled together, the Z a lazy, elegant coda to this pop-culture alphabet.

Most of us can't imagine getting that exercised over a typeface. Thirty-five years ago, when my publisher suggested Bembo for my first book, I shrugged. Fine by me, I said. I was hardly aware of the existence of typefaces. I do remember firing up my first computer and being vaguely disappointed at the utilitarian Helvetica, but I wouldn't have gone so far as typeface maven Bruno Maag, who calls Helvetica a "cultural blight. If you think of ice cream, [Helvetica] is a cheap, nasty, supermarket brand made of water, substitutes, and vegetable fats." Mike Battista, a blogger at Phronk.com who claims he is tired of the typeface wars and what he calls "the font police," nevertheless champions Univers, also a Swiss design. "There's no fuss and schmuss about it, it's a clean, tight design. If Helvetica is Julia Roberts—pretty enough— then Univers is Uma Thurman—really cool."

One of the consequences of the digital revolution is that even a six-year-old is likely to be conversant in typefaces. Coca-Cola and Pepsi have always known that typeface matters, but now Two Men and a Truck and the Limestone Cupcakery are aware of it, too, and so is the student formatting her résumé for her first job application and the little boy hammering out invitations to his Hallowe'en party.

In the end, I chose Book Antiqua as my typeface for writing *Gutenberg's Fingerprint*. Readers will never know that unless I tell them: they see only the typeface that the designer chooses to present my words. As I write this, I have no idea what that might be, although I hope I am consulted. I promise I won't shrug. Like the rest of the digitally literate world, I have discovered that I do care. A lot.

THE SHAPE OF THINGS TO COME

Hugh doesn't have a favourite font.

"Not font," Hugh says sharply. "Typeface."

Within the language of printers, I stumble and grasp as stupidly as a two-year-old. I thought font and typeface were interchangeable. After all, doesn't my Mac refer to its assembly of typefaces as a font collection?

"What's the difference?" I ask, the apprentice humbled before the master.

"Easy. A face is what you see. A font is what you use."

Easy for him, maybe. He can tell by the puzzled look on my face (not my font) that his explanation has done nothing to clear my confusion. He ambles over to a tall cabinet and pulls out the top drawer. It is divided into dozens of small sections like a jewellery box or a cattle pen, each one heaped with metal letters. He waves his arm across the drawer.

"This is all Garamond, the typeface for *The Paradise Project*."

The studio is so compact that, without taking another step, he turns and lifts a wooden frame from his worktable. Inside the frame are lines of metal type, the first few paragraphs of my opening story, "Root." He fingers a capital letter *E* out of his Garamond drawer and holds it up beside the frame.

"You see? Each letter is a metal block, with the character in relief on one face of the block. It used to be carved and now it's cast in a mould, but forget about that for now. The important thing is, this is the typeface—the face of the type that makes an imprint on paper. When I choose Garamond as the typeface for a project, I have to buy metal blocks of different point sizes: 10 or 12 or 14 point for the text and 18 or 20 point

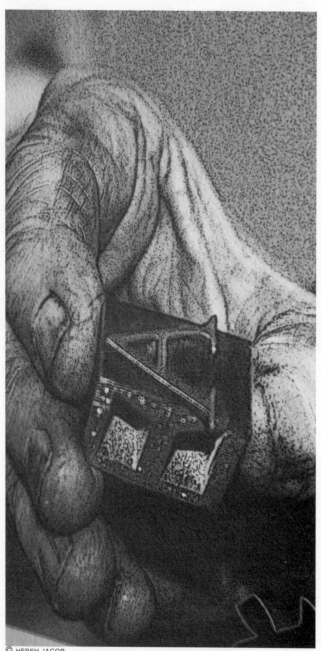

for titles. I'll also need faces of different weights: bold, medium, and light. And I'll need italics, too. *Garamond Italic* is a font. **Garamond Bold** is a font. Garamond 12 point is a font. Garamond is the typeface. The fonts of a typeface all reflect the same basic design principles."

I get it now. A typeface is the design of a particular alphabet. A font is a collection of characters—capital letters, lowercase letters, numerals, and punctuation marks—rendered in one particular size and style. A typeface will be available in several different fonts.

Today, typeface is delivered as a digital software file that can be adjusted to any size in the formatting menu. A stroke of the keyboard converts a letter to *italic* or **bold**. When my son Erik and I discuss the typeface for the digital version of *The Paradise Project*, I suggest ITC Serif Gothic.

"I like the ligatures," I say, trying out my new language.

"Oh, you can turn ligatures on and off," Erik says, airily dismissing ligature as a criteria. He has been working as a book designer for years, specializing in digital books and winning awards for his work. "I think we want a font that's modern, but understated, not too literary—sorry, by that I mean romantic—something clean and very legible at a small size. A typeface with some presence to it."

My son throws face and font around indiscriminately, as is accepted in the digital world. Surely I can be forgiven for confusing the terms. Hugh disagrees. The minute I step inside his studio, I am in his world—a place where face and font are apples and oranges. In the digital world, Apples aren't oranges, they're computers.

On one essential point, however, Erik agrees with Hugh when he says, "Typeface speaks volumes for a book. Not that it changes the meaning of the words, but it gives a completely different feel to them."

I see that. A typeface can make words seem shouted or whispered, they can be prissy and old-fashioned or lippy and modern, quiet or fun or both. Computers may have made us more aware of the existence of typefaces, but their power is still largely subliminal.

My son can choose from an almost limitless array of typefaces: 1001FreeFonts.com alone offers 28,320 fonts/faces for free.

Hugh has six: Garamond and **Bodoni** in **Roman** and *Italic* in three sizes; Caslon in roman and *italic* in four sizes; Bembo in roman and *italic* 12 point; Elegantis in 36, 48, and 72-point roman; Goudy Old Style in open face (an engraved line along the left side of the letter prints like a white shadow); and a sans serif called **Twentieth Century** in 12 point. He also has ten drawers of wooden type that he hasn't yet identified.

When he chose Garamond for the main text of *The Paradise Project*, he did so because the 14-point **Bodoni** is too heavy. The great British designer William Morris agrees, referring to **Bodoni** as a "sweltering hideousness." Twelve-point Bembo, Hugh says, is too light. And apparently, sans serif doesn't suit my writing.

"Serif is more formal, prettier," he says, grasping for words to articulate what is, for him, a gut instinct. Serif type is footed, which means it has an extra stroke that finishes off the line at the bottom and sometimes at the top of a letter. Serifs were developed by medieval scribes to fix a problem endemic to writing with pen and ink: the pressure of the pen falls on the end of the stroke and ink is inclined to drag, so the end of a letter was often ragged and sometimes blotchy. Scribes took to bracketing the letter in the direction of the stroke to finish it off neatly. Then, to balance the letter, they added a stroke to the opposite side, too, and, presto, the serif was born.

SERIF   SANS SERIF

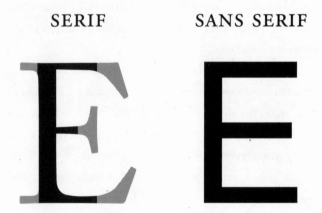

The English word was originally "ceref," probably from the Dutch *schreef*, meaning "a line or stroke." You can hear the word "script" in there, too. Ceref didn't become serif until 1841, although, curiously, sans serif (which incorporates the French *sans*, meaning "without") was coined earlier, in 1830.

My husband has been known to toss aside a book

set in sans serif with the comment, "I can't read this. It's obviously a piece of fluff."

I like sans serif. I appreciate the way the letters stand apart, as if on tiptoe, leaving breathing space between them, each consonant and vowel having its individual say. The British call the square-cut sans serif typefaces grotesques: wildly formed, of irregular proportions, boldly odd. I'm a little put out that Hugh doesn't think this is suitable for my stories, which are experimental— as wild and irregular as I'm likely to get.

He bustles out of the studio and crosses the deck to his house, returning a few moments later with the only book he has ever set in sans serif, *Where Do I Start?*, based on emails his daughter sent to him about her work with drug addicts and street people on Vancouver's downtown east side.

"In the emails, words are spelled wrong, periods are missing, and what the hell are commas anyway? I went through the text and cleaned it all up and then I reread it and said, 'Hugh you really screwed that up!' It wasn't *real* anymore. It was just a piece of work. So I took the text back to how she wrote it, and I chose a sans serif typeface because I didn't want it to look pretty, or formal, or literary. The writing was raw. I wanted the typeface to be raw, too."

Grotesque, in the wildest, boldest sense of the word.

Garamond, on the other hand, reminds me of very precise, old-fashioned handwriting. Hugh points to the distinctive *e* and *a*, marked by what he calls a "small bowl." The uppercase *W* looks like two *V*'s overlaid, instead of one distinct letter. It is a serif face, which doesn't surprise me. Hugh is a fan of footed typefaces; he likes the way the serifs help the eye connect the letters. He says the long extenders and top serifs have a downward slope, although I can't see it. The variation in stroke width, he declares, is minimal.

"I chose Garamond because it has a very honest face," he says. "It's natural-looking. It's not trying to be something else." He winks at me. "Besides, I have a lot of it, so I can set several pages at once."

Garamond is widely thought to be the most readable typeface when printed on paper. When I first started teaching online, I held fast to my typewriter faces, insisting that students submit their work in Times or Courier, until a fellow teacher called me a dinosaur. Indeed, computer manufacturers had already decided on the most readable onscreen faces and made these the default fonts: Helvetica in Mac and Arial in Windows.

Today, Helvetica and Arial users may be the dinosaurs. Half a century ago, when computers were first developed, the low-resolution screens didn't have enough pixels to display details of a typeface. The feet on serifs tended to break up and disappear. As Tobias Frere-Jones, one of the great contemporary type designers, declared, "Some of the world's greatest typefaces were quickly becoming some of the world's worst fonts."

It wasn't long before new typefaces were designed specifically for digital applications, with features that would have been impossible with metal type: tight kerning (the spacing between characters), characters that extend over or under adjoining characters, a wide variety of weights and, most important, a single design that covers all point sizes.

A recent study of onscreen readability found no significant difference in reading speed or reading comprehension among scores of test subjects who read text set in four different typefaces, including both serif and sans serif: Georgia, Times, Verdana, and Arial.

Despite that, the consensus among designers seems to be that the fewer details a font needs to convey a character, the more readable it will appear on a broad range of screens, which means that digitally, sans serif typefaces still edge out the serifs.

"There are trends in typography, like everything else," my son says, "and that influences what people see as best practices. In the early '90s, there was a real us-and-them thing about digital and print, so the digital designers were all using sans serif, no caps anywhere. Now everyone is using Gotham, no bells and flourishes, strictly utilitarian, but in a few years we'll be looking back and saying, 'Oh that's so 2015.'"

His font of choice is a serif. "Sans serif is a little abrupt and awkward on the brain. I've read studies that show the eye reads serif faces better, both onscreen and on the page, because the swoop of the foot of one character leads to the swoop of the next." He's channeling Hugh.

"I like Chaparral because it has a gentle slab serif: a bit of curve on the beginning of the serif, then squared off. It has a chunkiness to it, a little more aggressive, a little more masculine, but with lovely ligatures." I grin and he grins, too. "A nice and easy typeface to read."

High-resolution screens offer more typographical choice, but at the same time the proliferation of devices for reading onscreen has made a designer's job harder. A typeface may be read on a phone, a tablet, a laptop, or a desktop computer, and, as my son points out, each of them might be anywhere from a year to ten years old. "And remember, a font will look slightly different depending on whether you are using Windows or a Mac operating system." He shakes his head. "It's a designer's nightmare."

TYPECAST

I'm teaching at Sage Hill, a writing retreat in Saskatchewan with limited Internet access, when my son and I finally connect to discuss the guts of the ebook version of *The Paradise Project*.

"Are you looking at it on your iPad or your phone?" he says. "You should try it on as many devices as possible." Soon I have both the original print version and his new edesign side by side.

"The apostrophe is odd," I say for starters. "It looks like it's added later, no space for it between the letters. Look at 'he'd' on page 4."

"Not there," he says. "That's the thing about ebooks: your page 4 won't be mine. What font are you in?"

I check. The electronic file offers eight faces, as I stubbornly insist on calling them. My son may be ambidextrous when it comes to face and font, but I'm sticking with Hugh.

"Original. The face you designed it in, I guess."

"Switch to Georgia."

I do and the apostrophe corrects itself.

"Okay, I'll fix that," he says. "Anything else?"

"I don't think so."

I feel my son withdraw. I've failed some test.

Finally, he says, "I thought you'd say, 'Wow! That's amazing. It's a thousand times better.' But you didn't. And that's okay."

"I didn't know what I was looking at." It's a poor excuse, but it's the truth. My face-recognition skills are clearly at a low level, my apprenticeship with Hugh notwithstanding. I peer at the face my son has chosen for the ebook, swivelling back and forth to the print version. Slowly, I see it: the descenders slender and elegant, not curved like a Victorian spoon handle; numerals that sit up on the line beside the letters instead of drooping below; concise italics and roman that, even at 9 point, are beautifully legible; drop caps to open the sections and chapter titles in a soft pearl grey. I play with the other faces, then with type size, making the text tiny, then big enough for the half-blind. No matter how I manipulate the text, the flow is perfect, the design still elegant and readable. He's right, I should have exclaimed with joy.

"I'm a firm believer in making text as accessible as possible. I don't want a bunch of fancy codes that only a new device can read. But the thing about the latest ebook software is that you can lock in special fonts and page views. You can see it exactly as the designer intended it to be read."

"Sounds like ebooks are going back to letterpress."

He laughs. "In a way. Except that you can still change the typeface back to Helvetica and jack the whole book up to any size type you want. But you're right, the days of us-and-them, digital-versus-print, are long gone."

There it is again: us and them. I was among the first of my friends to get a computer: I wrote my early books on a Commodore 64. Wayne, on the other hand, was among the last to go digital. I tease him mercilessly about being a stick-in-the-mud. He calls me a flibber-tigibbet, grasping at every shiny new thing, each of us smug in our early adopter/Luddite roles. Back then, the distinction between past and present was clear: you either had a computer on the desk and the lingo on the tongue—RAM, hard drive, floppy disk, high-res—or you didn't. But now that everyone from eight- to eighty-year-olds is plugged in, that line in the sand serves no purpose. I see the same thing here at Sage Hill, when the twenty-something program assistant spins vinyl on a real record player, Bluetoothed to his speakers: the past is no longer uncool, it's embedded in the present.

Maybe that's how we know we're coasting down the other side of a paradigm shift, by the way the pieces are settling into place. I can finally admit that I love Courier, that after a day of writing onscreen, a paper book in the hand feels oh so fine. Such choices don't say a thing about how stuck in the dark ages I am or how cutting-edge. It's just Courier. It's just a book.

My son and I talk about errant hyphens. For some reason, pouring the text into the ebook format has preserved end-of-line-break hyphens from the original text, even though the hyphenated words are now securely reattached in the middle of a line. We decide to deal with the problem at the proofing stage.

In the background, I can hear his daughters doing the dishes. He is at his farmhouse in the Northumberland hills north of Cobourg, Ontario; the girls have been riding all week, practising for a jumping competition at the local horse show. Outside my window in Saskatchewan, newly fledged barn swallows chatter and beg, then take off from the balcony to swoop over Blackstrap Lake to the bald prairie beyond. If this were Hugh I was talking to, I'd have to be in the room with him, picking out the apostrophes by hand. It is miraculous that my son and I can consult by cellphone from our various lives, but even so, I feel the miles that separate us.

"Let's look at this together when I get back, okay?"

"Sure," he says. "It'll be done by then. I just wanted to make sure you were okay with the direction I'm going."

"I'm more than okay," I say gently, too late. "And, Erik?"

"Yes?"

"The design is amazing, really it is."

Hugh emails me a scan of a trial page set in 18-point Garamond.

"The type's a bit big," I email back. "Actually, it's a lot on the big side. Is there a reason you want the words so large?"

"I'm like a grade six student required to write a two-page essay. I print big and double-spaced," he replies, adding a smiley face with a wink. "Seriously, I will try a smaller face and then we can live with them both for a while. The smaller face may well reduce the format size and change the artwork. I find that working out the design of a book is much like composing music for an orchestra—everything needs to fit together and complement each other. This is the reason I do trial pages."

Point size is a way of measuring the height of type as it appears on the page or screen. The system has been in use for a long time, with every type manufacturer producing its own version of a point size, give or take a millimetre or two. The advent of desktop computing forced a standard: 72 points to an international inch. Twelve point—roughly 1/6 of an inch tall—is the default size in most digital word-processing programs. It is also the requirement for many grant applications and publisher submissions. Not coincidentally, 12 point was also the size of the type on the typewriters I grew up with.

A point is 1/12th of a pica. In other words, 12 points make up a pica. Six picas make an inch.

Which part of a piece of 12-point type is 1/6 of an inch high? None of it. It's the body that is 12 point, the square within which the letter sits. We never see that outside margin, just as we never see the "em," the virtual quad within which a digital letter sits.

If you think size doesn't matter, take a look at the current lawsuit between Microsoft and Apple. The issue is Apple's trademark of the term App Store, but what's interesting is that one of Microsoft's complaints is that the Apple brief is not only too long, it's in too small a font size!

Twelve point is not the most comfortable size for reading, and it's not the most common size either. Nearly every book, newspaper, and magazine you read is set smaller than that. Cost is a consideration: the bigger the point size, the more paper is required to print the words. But slightly smaller type is also easier on the eyes for those with normal vision. In print, the optimal size for body text is somewhere between 10 and 12 point. Even so, legal disclaimers and forms granting power of attorney are often required by law to be in 12-point type. This is no guarantee of readability, as not all 12 points are created equal. For instance, 12-point Avenir is much smaller than 12-point Cambria.

On digital screens, the optimal type size for reading is fifteen to twenty-five pixels (12 point is roughly sixteen pixels). In the early days of computers, poor screen resolution meant that type had to be fairly small or it would break up. That's no longer the case. In fact, for most people, digital text needs to be slightly larger than the same text read on paper because our eyes are generally further from what we are reading.

When Hugh returns from the next Wayzgoose, he tells me he showed around the trial pages set in 18 point and everyone agreed with the fellow who said, "I like it. The type block has good texture and justified on both right and left it makes a strong statement."

Hugh is armed. "Saying a typeface is too large may be based on a subjective tradition of right and wrong," he goes on. "It's as if, because everyone else uses a certain type size, we don't want to appear to be different so we fall into line and that's how we develop cookie-cutter books. You might try looking for a good use of a large face."

Is he right? Have I been conditioned by reading some 8,000 books set in 12-point type to think that this is the right size—the only size—in which a printed word must be read? And maybe it is. After all, print books today are the product of 500 years of refinement in form and function. I try to think of a book published in large print, other than those produced specifically for the visually impaired. I can't.

And the truth is, it doesn't matter what I think. Hugh is on a roll.

"As you know I always write the colophon in the first person in an effort to take responsibility for the artistic quality of the book. To take this responsibility I need to have artistic control. That is not to say that I won't accept suggestions or consider requests. We will work this all out, but as you can tell I prefer that we are both out front with one another."

In other words, back off.

A few days later, he sends me trial pages set in 12-, 14-, and 18-point Garamond. "Consider the visual statements rendered by each size. I will do the same and I'm sure one will rise to the surface and the others will sink."

Choosing the type and the paper for *The Paradise Project* has been a tandem process. The summer was taken up with Emily's endpaper experiments and her visits to my garden, so it is October, the air already crisp, when Hugh sends me "Stone" set in 14-point Garamond, as if a decision had been made.

The title is flush left, set in *Garamond Italic*. The text of the piece is set in roman, justified left and right. The words roll over onto a second page, where two turtles squat between words.

I write back immediately. "The 14 point is perfect."

Hugh's Garamond is old. He found it half a century ago in the same place he found his first press: in a back shed behind a local print shop that was slowly going out of business.

At the time, Hugh was editing a quarterly journal for the Canadian Association of Prosthetics and Orthotics. The journal was printed at Hanson & Edgar, a local printer, then mailed out to orthotics professionals across the country. "A small, select group," Hugh says wryly. At the printer's, he caught a glimpse of an old, retired proofing press, abandoned and filthy in a back shed. Poking around, he found archaic trays and tools, drawers filled with type.

"'I'll take that,' I said. 'And that, and that!'" Hugh gleefully recalls, all but hugging his rescued type cupboard.

No printer is satisfied with just one typeface. The holy grail is an exquisitely beautiful, legible, distinct alphabet that draws the eye irrevocably to the printed page, but in the meantime, in pursuit of perfection, they collect a variety of faces. One of the first that Hugh added to his stash was Goudy Old Style, designed by Frederic W. Goudy. All but forgotten now, Goudy was a household name in print shops in the first half of the twentieth century. From 1915 to 1940, he drew more than 125 distinct typefaces, including the inside type for *Life* magazine. Goudy Old Style, he claimed, was inspired by the lettering on a Hans Holbein painting. His biographer, Peter Beilenson, calls the face "a happy blend of French suavity and Italian fullness, marred by the supposed commercial practicality of shortened descenders."

Beilenson makes type sound like wine.

Goudy was a bit of a renegade. He drew all his typefaces freehand, without a compass, a straight-edge, or a French curve. "Printing is essentially a utilitarian art," he said, "yet even utilitarianism may include distinction and beauty in its type forms. To meet the demands of utility and preserve an aesthetic standard is the problem I set myself."

He took his inspiration from the artists of the

Renaissance. "The old fellows had the good ideas," he said.

Hugh grins. "That's the quote I like best from Goudy."

The financial and marketing benefit of a distinctive typeface design was clear from the beginning. The first patent on a typeface was issued just fifty years after Gutenberg invented his press. And the very first design patent issued in the United States was for a "new and improved printing type"—U.S. Patent DI.

In Canada, perhaps the best known type designer is Carl Dair. When Hugh was in his thirties, he came across a magazine called *Wrong Font*, the brainchild of Carl Dair and Bill Poole, the man who published Hugh's first and only book. Hugh never met Dair, who died during a flight from New York City in 1967, but the designer's spirit was very much part of Hugh's early initiation into typography and letterpress printing. He shows me a first edition of Dair's book, *Design with Type*, in which Dair sets out his Seven Typographical Contrasts—size, weight, form, structure, texture, colour, direction—as a way of designing and critiquing type. Originally published in 1952 and revised in 1967, the book is still in print, a classic introduction to the notion of contrast in design.

Dair studied metal type and hand-punching at the Enschedé Foundry in Haarlem, Netherlands, where he created a silent film called *Gravers and Files* that documents one of the last great punch-cutters, P. H. Radisch. In 1967, for Canada's centennial, Dair was commissioned by the Governor General to create a new and distinctively Canadian typeface. The result was Cartier, a serif based on hand-lettering that has become what some call "our national type."

That notion is not as old-fashioned as it sounds. In 2014, Sweden created a national typeface called Sweden Sans. The starting point was the Swedish flag, a yellow Scandinavian cross on a blue background, in use since Gutenberg's day. The designers developed "mood boards" with different fonts and pictures, drawing heavily on old Swedish signs from the 1940s and '50s. Then they started sketching to the music of Bob Marley and contemporary electro beats. Six months later, **Sweden Sans** was unveiled: a basic sans serif to be used on all government materials.

Designers are working on typefaces to brand other nations. Corporations are getting into the typeface-as-brand act, too. In 2014, Amazon was criticized for launching its Kindle Voyage without bothering to add fresh typefaces to be viewed on its new screen. Lack of choice was one thing, but the ereader still force-justified every line, without hyphenation, creating great gaps between words. As one blogger lamented, "Amazon has invested all of this effort in improved reading technology only to find itself completely at sea when it comes to typography. A device that's dedicated to words on a page, one with a screen this beautiful, deserves better type options."

The following year, Amazon unveiled **Bookerly**, an exclusive font for Kindle devices, designed by one of the world's top typemeisters, Dalton Maag. Developed specifically for digital reading, the font is described by Amazon as "warm and contemporary ... inspired by the artistry of the best fonts in modern print books ... hand-crafted for great readability at any size," claiming it "outperforms other digital reading fonts to help you read faster with less eye strain."

Unsubstantiated claims aside, it is interesting that even the great Internet warrior, Amazon, refers back to traditional print technology to boost the reputation of its digital type. Designers, it seems, have always kept a keen eye on the rear-view mirror. In 1502, the designers of the very first patented typeface modelled it on the lovely, flowing script of Petrarch, who was writing 150 years before.

Erik sees digital typography going in a different direction.

"Check out Titillium," is all he says.

Titillium was born in 2012 at the Accademia di Belle Arti in Urbino, an Italian city in the foothills of the Apennines near the top of the boot on the Adriatic side. It began as an assignment in the Fields of Vision course offered as part of the art school's master's program. The project: to collectively create a family of fonts that would be open source, shared freely with the world through a web platform. Each academic year, a fresh crop of a dozen students works on the project, developing the face further so that now it is available in several fonts: light, roman, *italic*, sans serif.

Graphic designers are asked to send images of how

they've used Titillium for a growing database of case histories. Type designers with a yen to amend or revise the face are invited to co-operate with the student team or to develop their own versions of a character. Three years into the project, this innovative exercise in collective creativity shows no sign of slowing down.

I think of the definition of a camel: a horse designed by committee. This isn't exactly typeface by committee, but it's not individual innovation, either.

"It's the way of the future," my son says.

Meanwhile, when Hugh needs an accented vowel, he creates the piece of type himself, sawing a groove into the body of a vowel and inserting a short length of 2-point lead to create á, é, or í. He's also been known to create his own diphthongs or to tighten the kern (the spacing between letters) by filing down the body of one letter so the next one can tuck in close.

"If I don't have it, I make it," says Hugh. "What else is a person to do?"

CHARACTER STUDIES

I learned to print in grade one. I loved the slender blue lines, the dotted line that held the bowls of the vowels, the faint lines above and below that set limits for the ascenders and descenders, the red margins that defined exactly where to start and stop. At the top of each page was a sample letter. "Trace the letter first," Miss Goetz would say, and I'd grip my fat red pencil. I'd track the loop and slide until I was sure I got it, then I'd carry on along the line, drawing the letter again and again, each identical to the one I'd traced. I don't remember when it dawned on me that what I was doing wasn't drawing, it was writing.

I had already fallen in love with words. Putting them together was like a party in my mouth. Words like filigree or Dumbo could make me laugh just from the contortions of my lips. I don't know when exactly my mouth connected to my eyes and I could say the words I saw, but I do remember the first time I held the point of a sharpened pencil to the page and traced that bulbous *a*. Suddenly, the letter wasn't only in my eyes and my mouth, it was in my arm, my hand, my fingers; in my tongue that stuck out of the corner of my mouth; in my body leaning against the sharp edge of my desk; in my bum that lifted up off the seat; in my toes in their brown Oxfords that didn't quite touch the floor. My whole body was wrapped up in that *a* and in the *b*, *c*, and *d* that followed and in all the words I've written since.

In time, we learned capitals, then cursive. Cursive and capitals go back to ancient Romans, who carved letters in stone using square-shaped capitals for inscriptions and emphasis. Cursive or "running" characters were reserved for correspondence and less formal documents.

In the fifth century, the squared-off capitals were modified and rounded with lighter ascenders into so-called rustic writing. The letters were large, much larger even than my grade one printing.

Economy shaped the letters that seem normal to

us now. As parchment became more difficult to procure, the size of lettering shrank, becoming even more compact as scriptoriums worked to produce books en masse. Capitals are too slow to print by hand in any quantity. Small characters are much faster, which led to a new style of writing called minuscules, as opposed to the large majuscules. Under Charlemagne, the Caroline minuscule became the most influential in Europe, a revival of the rounded, open Roman cursive.

In high school, I had a British pen pal. As much as I enjoyed her stories of England in the early days of the Beatles, it was her handwriting that I looked forward to. My characters sloped like chubby shrubs caught in a steady west wind, but hers spiked up and down, sharp and assured, sometimes leaning back ironically. Everyone I knew—my mother, the aunts who sent birthday cards, my teachers, my friends—wrote with the same chubby cursive hand. The unfamiliar shape of my pen pal's letters confirmed that beyond my small town in Southwestern Ontario, other worlds flourished.

At one time, exquisite calligraphies spoke subtly of national character: Lombardic, the national hand of Italy; Merovingian, the national hand of France; and Celtic, the national hand of Ireland. Mechanical movable type did away with all that. Cartier and Sweden Sans notwithstanding, typeface is not generally national, and it's not personal. I could love my hand-printed *a*, but a machine-printed *a* is anonymous, generic.

And maybe that's an advantage. At my school, the kids with pretty penmanship were considered "good at school" in general. The students who were less coordinated, slow to connect eye with hand, fell behind. Today, cursive writing is no longer taught in most schools; kids use computers to write their essays. No blotted copybooks to frustrate the student and irritate the teacher. Nothing to stand in the way of the meaning of the words.

Given all the variations in writing, formal and informal, personal and business, even national, where did Gutenberg turn for the shape of his alphabet? The Romans, of course, which is to say, the Italians, who in their formal writing had preserved the roundness of the Roman alphabet, never succumbing to the extreme angularity of northern European Gothic writing. And so fifteenth-century Italian handwriting became the standard for the printed word in Gutenberg's day. Half a millennium later, roman (the upright fonts) and italic (the sloping fonts) are still the standard.

Gutenberg's first type was based on manuscript forms because that's what fifteenth-century readers were used to. Otherwise, the printed version wouldn't look like a real book. Before long, however, the printer unchained himself from the scribe. One letter shape was as easy to print as another, so the focus shifted from letters that were easy to write to letters that were easily read.

Punch-cutters further streamlined the alphabet to make it easier to produce in lead type. Practicality won out over beauty. With handwriting, each *a* a person writes is unique, distinct in subtle ways from every other *a* that person has written. With a printed character, each repetition is an exact and faithful facsimile. In making the transition from the human hand to the mechanical press, however, aesthetics were not entirely ignored. As movable type was being developed, the illuminated manuscript was reaching its peak of perfection, providing an exquisite model for the printer's art. In a similar way, the best of today's mechanically printed books are providing a high aesthetic standard for digital type.

Typeface design is barely part of the conversation when Erik and I discuss the inside design of the ebook version of *The Paradise Project*.

"We choose the typeface, but the reader can change it, and they can make it any size they want. That's the beauty of ebooks," he says.

As a writer, I believe in the saying that a book isn't finished until it's read, until the explosions that go off in my mind are set off in a new way in the mind of the person reading my words. Now, a book isn't fully designed, either, until it is in the reader's hands, until they've gone to Settings and adjusted the face and font to suit themselves.

In the digital world of endless scrolling, my stories can be as long as I want them to be. Print, on the other hand, is a zero-sum game. The space for words on the page is finite. In the eworld, I can blather on unchecked, making additions and subtractions and substitutions to my heart's content, right up until the ebook is "published" and beyond. In traditional publishing, there inevitably comes a moment when the editor says, "Stop!"

I used to beg to make changes in the typeset text of my books, only to be told, No, it would affect the line length or the turn of the page. Sitting in Hugh's studio, I finally get it. I'm proofing a typeset page, wincing at words I'd love to replace, but I say nothing. I know first-hand the work involved in picking out the bits of type, repositioning them again. Hours and hours. I swallow hard and move on, setting my sights on misspellings and only the most grievous grammatical errors.

Months later, when I prepare the text for the digital versions of my out-of-print books, I breathe freely again. When I come upon an infelicitous phrase, I try this word and that, choosing the best one I can think of, not the one I was content with all those years ago when I first wrote it. Already there are collaborative writing platforms, including Wikipedia, where a person can nip in, pulling out words, adding others, mixing them up, the notion of text suddenly organic, fluid, as endlessly free-flowing as a river.

A THOUSAND WORDS

I contrive for Hugh to meet Erik at Christmas. "We'll come to the studio," I tell Hugh. "I'll bring the Grand Girls."

Hugh is on to me. "You want to get him hooked, that's the idea, am I right? Once printer's ink has entered his veins, he'll become immediately addicted to these desperate activities."

My son started sketching and painting as a young boy. By the age of twelve, he was producing accomplished oils. By nineteen, he was in Berlin, apprenticed to the provocative figurative painter Attila Richard Lukacs. As a mother, I was worried sick. As an artist, I was more jealous than I dared to admit.

When Erik returned from Berlin, he found a gallery to represent him and had show after show. His paintings were selling well enough that he could live from his art. He married a designer, they had a baby girl, and bought and renovated an 1880s row house in Toronto, all within a year. He was twenty-five years old.

In July 2001, the gas company sent a notice to its Toronto customers saying that if there were old gas lines in a house, the company would remove them free of charge provided they were contacted within a month. My son and his wife were eager new homeowners; they called almost immediately. Early one morning, a gas man showed up. They directed him to the pipes. A moment later, the house was engulfed in flames. The gas man had cut into a live pipe with a Sawzall and sparked a firestorm. He bolted up the stairs and turned off the main gas line before he collapsed on the grass. My son and his wife grabbed their baby and fled. The fire department arrived within minutes, but it was too late. The young family lost almost everything.

For Erik and his wife, their life divided into BF and AF: before the fire and after. As well as all their furnishings, their wedding presents, and photograph albums, Erik lost the paintings he'd been developing for two upcoming shows. He lost the file that held the names and details of all the paintings he had produced up to that moment. And he lost his boxes of stimulation, the bits and pieces that would have inspired his paintings of the future.

He hasn't painted much since. Ten years after the fire, the insurance claim was finally settled. For the lost paintings, he received time and materials in compensation for works he had presold for $3,000 and more. When I ask him why he doesn't paint, he says, "I don't know. It just doesn't seem important anymore."

He has lost heart. Hugh is all heart. I can't wait for the two of them to meet.

Hugh has been pondering the possibility of illustrations since he first proposed publishing *The Paradise Project* nine months ago. He was his own first choice.

"I wasn't the world's greatest speller, and my printing wasn't great either, and I didn't really read books until I moved to Kingston when I was twenty-seven or so, but I was always able to draw. I was good at that," Hugh says. It's about as boastful as he gets.

The first book to come off Thee Hellbox Press, *A Letter to Teresa*, is illustrated with linocuts of aboriginal dancers and portraits. Underneath the text itself are soft, pale ochre images inspired by the rock paintings and petroglyphs of the Great Lakes first peoples: birds, spiny-backed fish and animals, human figures, boats, teepees, and turtles.

Hugh made these floating images not by cutting them into wood or copper or linoleum, the traditional block-printing materials. Instead, he used contact cement to glue a thin sheet of medium-density, closed-cell, cross-linked polyethylene foam to a piece of plywood. Using a surgical scalpel, he carved into the foam, removing everything but the image. The foam-topped block was set in the press a bit higher than the type to account for compression.

"I wanted to produce images with fading edges, a softer image than I could produce with hard-edge lino blocks. A ghost image. I called them soft-block prints. As far as I know, it's the only new method of image reproduction since linocuts."

He refined the technique further in a print he titled "Free at Last," published in commemoration of Martin Luther King Jr.'s "I Have a Dream" speech, delivered on the steps to the Lincoln Memorial in 1963. The print was Hugh's 1985 contribution to the Wayzgoose Anthology, an annual collection of work from Canadian letterpresses. To create the effect of skin on the portrait of an African-American, Hugh sandpapered the foam, exposing the cellular structure, which traps more ink, darkening that part of the image.

Hugh has been talking about making soft blocks for *The Paradise Project*. He sends me an early trial of "Stone," printed over three soft-block boulders in shades of yellow and orange. I'm not enthusiastic. Nothing more is said about soft blocks or illustrations until a month later, when he tells me he has approached Gerard Bender à Brandis, a well-known Canadian bookwright and engraver.

"I received a long letter from Gerard, handwritten with a proper square-nib pen," Hugh tells me in an email. "He is a magnificent engraver, especially of botanical prints, and he is in favour of us using some of his existing blocks. His offer comes with a lot of conditions, which I can meet, but rather than using black wood engravings, my preference leans to using multicoloured objective abstract prints. I think this brings life and depth to the pages, not that they need it, but to celebrate the text."

Hugh has assumed there will be pictures. Me, I've never been comfortable with the phrase "a picture is worth a thousand words." Why a thousand? Why not five words or fifty or five thousand? Can a picture really replace my words? For Hugh, words and pictures amount to the same thing: lines to be inked and printed on a page.

Erik's visit goes well. He likes Hugh and loves the press. At art college, he studied printmaking with George Walker, famous now for his wordless books of wood engravings: *The Wordless Leonard Cohen Songbook*, *The Life and Times of Conrad Black: A Wordless Biography*, and, most recently, *Trudeau: La vie en rose*. I see a new spark in Erik's eyes.

Hugh plans to make a trip to Toronto to look for cover stock. "I'll wait until Erik has a chance to read the manuscript. Then perhaps I can meet him for lunch and we can conspire against you. (<;)- Did you notice that I use a hyphen on my smiley face as the petite tail of my beret?"

In early January, Hugh sends me a list of promotion points for *The Paradise Project*. "I was starting to self-intimidate regarding the potentially high price of the book, however once I made this list I'm reassured that we have a unique object that may well be under-priced." The stories, the endpapers, the Salad paper, the hand-printing and hand-typesetting are all on the list. And now, Number 6: ten engravings by Erik Mohr.

LINE O' TYPE

In high school, I wanted to be a journalist. I lived near Stratford, Ontario, and, every summer, the newspaper there took on a fourth-year university student as an intern. In grade eleven, I applied. In grade twelve, I applied again. When I applied after first-year university, the editor finally hired me.

My first day on the job, he led me through the newsroom, introducing me to women reporters who smoked and wore red lipstick and sportswriters with fedoras stuck on the backs of their heads, cigars fuming in glass ashtrays beside their Underwoods. I was in heaven. After I'd met the writers, he ushered me down a narrow hall to a dark, greasy room where men sat hunched on stools in front of clanking machines.

"Linotype," the editor yelled.

I nodded, my hands over my ears. My boyfriend, who would soon become my first husband, was an artist. He had just finished a series of linocuts. I assumed the machines had something to do with linoleum.

"Line-o-type," the editor shouted, spelling it out.

The compositor handed me a scrap of paper and mimed that I should sign my name, which I did. He tapped out the letters on the giant keyboard that sloped in front of him. There was a clattering, then whirrs and clunks as giant gears turned then ground to a stop. He opened a flap and pulled out a shiny, two-inch slug of lead, the mirror image of my name in bright italics, a quarter-inch high:

Merilyn Simonds

Every word of every article in the entire newspaper, all my reviews of plays, my profiles of actors and voice coaches and prop mistresses, my infamous piece that used the f-word, a joke the compositor and I played on the night editor who failed to catch my profanity so that it went uncensored into the breakfast nooks of the town's matrons—every word I would write that summer would be typed into these behemoth machines and cast into lead slugs that would be fitted into the press and printed with smudgy black ink onto newsprint.

I loved the smell of that compositing room, a dark, smoky, inky scent. A muscular male musk that made writing seem important: not the feminine outpourings of fancy fountain pens on blue-lined paper, but words forged in hot lead by the clatter and stamp of brawny men with tattoos on their arms and rollies hanging from the corners of their mouths, the air bruised with ciga-rette smoke and words I wasn't supposed to understand.

I had no idea so many hours and so many hands touched every letter I read in books, newspapers, and magazines. From Gutenberg's day until the 1880s, every individual letter of type was put in place by a human hand, the way I would learn to set type in Hugh's shop. Then in the 1880s, Ottmar Mergenthaler, a German watchmaker living in Baltimore, Maryland, invented line casting, which sped up the process exponentially. (Apparently he got the idea from the wooden moulds used to make *springerle*, German Christmas cookies that I stamped out by the dozen all through my sons' childhoods.) The operator types a line of text into the seven-foot-tall machine. At the top of the machine, waiting in their narrow channels, are matrices—brass units impressed with characters on one face—that drop down in order as the line of text is typed. The operator checks that all the letters are correct, then pulls a switch and the line of type slides over to where molten metal is injected, casting the letters in a line. A line o' type. The metal cools on contact with the matrices and the line of type is ejected to the galley tray. An arm swings down and collects the matrices, each of which is coded with a particular blaze that ensures it will slide into its correct channel at the top of the machine. Several lines of type are assembled in the galley tray, and when that's full, the tray is taken to the proofing area, locked in a proofing press, and printed to check for errors. When the page of type is completely error-free, it goes to the press for printing.

Thomas Edison called the Linotype machine the eighth wonder of the world. It could set type six times faster than the human hand. Typesetters were afraid they'd lose their jobs, but, instead, the demand for print exploded once books, newspapers, and magazines could be produced so quickly and cheaply.

Mergenthaler wasn't the only one looking for a speedier way to set type. At about the same time, James Paige developed the Compositor, financed by Mark Twain, who had started out as a printer and was a science and technology buff, a friend of both Edison and Tesla. Twain patented three inventions of his own, including an "improvement in adjustable and detachable straps for garments" (a surrogate for suspenders) and a history trivia game. He sank $300,000 into the Compositor, the equivalent of $8,200,000 today, drawing on his book royalties and his wife's inheritance. A more complex machine—the Compositor had 18,000 moving parts compared to the Linotype's 5,000—it was made immediately obsolete by Mergenthaler's invention. Paige lost all his money and Mark Twain filed for bankruptcy, accepting an around-the-world lecture tour to pay off his creditors. On his return, he wrote the travelogue *Following the Equator*, published in Britain as *More Tramps Abroad*.

The print shop's loss was literature's gain.

HERDING CATS

The pieces of the puzzle that is the printing of *The Paradise Project* are coming together at last. The manuscript is with Erik, and he is working on a series of linocut images to float under the text. Nothing is happening fast enough for Hugh. He's as jumpy as a flea on hot type. He doesn't want Emily to start work on the endpapers until the size of the book has been determined, and he doesn't want to close the door on that until Erik has produced some drawings. All of which means Hugh is on idle, itching to start setting type.

His emails natter at me with questions I can't answer. "I'm not sure how Erik wants to place the blocks on the page. Do we print the linocuts first, like soft blocks, then have the text overlap them to give the page depth and colour? This would mean printing the blocks in light colours and that might bother Erik. Do we wrap the text around them? Do we place them on separate pages? Do we place them at the beginning or the end of the text? The inclusion of illustrations may alter the number of pages, so I can't even go ahead and order the paper."

It is the end of February before the three of us can meet. My life is complicated by a renovation disaster that has forced Wayne and me to move out of our house for six weeks. The fellow smoothing the basement floor must have reversed the exhaust fan on his sander: within seconds, the house filled with fine silica dust that settled on our clothes, our food, the papers on our desks. The rooms look like Pompeii after Vesuvius blew. I have a festival to attend in Mexico. What with Pompeii and Mexico, I am home only two days that month. Finally, in the last week, I get a missive from Hugh:

"I hate to be the bug, but if we are intending to launch *The Paradise Project* in June of this year I need to get started post-haste, as I will have between 400 and 500 hours of work to do before June 1, when the books go to the bindery. Forgive my aggression but 'herding cats' sometimes requires a whip."

The process with the ebook couldn't be more different. Erik and I determine a publication date, and he sends me a work-back schedule that clearly identifies all the tasks chronologically. He is his mother's son. I suggest a few changes and, within the hour, a revised sked is in my inbox.

Is this a mark of efficiency, or do the two technologies demand different philosophies of production? Digital production renders certain decisions unnecessary or ridiculous. The number of copies is limitless. The size is infinitely flexible. The price is preset. There is no paper to select and order. No ink. No press. No bindery. I am beginning to wish letterpress printing were as simple.

Finally, the three of us meet by email to thrash out the details of the Thee Hellbox edition. Together we decide that Hugh will print 300 copies, to be sold at $150 each. Hugh and Erik come up with a size of 5 1/4 by 10 inches, and I agree to the content: sixteen stories and ten linocuts. When I suggest printing single broadsheets of the shortest flash fictions to sell separately, Hugh bristles.

"I distribute the type after printing each page, so we can't do something like this as an afterthought. I think I will pass a new Barclay's Law: 'Authors, in particular those who are mad, must be obliged to spend a day or at

least a morning setting type so that they have an understanding not only of what it means to set type but also
what it means to experience the joy of this activity.'"

Clearly, I still have a lot to learn.

I'm just the writer. I used to think that was important,
that the entire scaffolding of the publishing world was
built on the foundation of the written word. Now that
I am deep inside this architecture, I see that I'm just
another two-by-four, doing my bit to keep the edifice
from collapsing in a heap.

I spend the next week tweaking the stories, juggling
them into an order that is aesthetically as well as narra-
tively pleasing. These flash fictions are oddities, some of
them so short they can hardly be called stories. I decide
to work from the ground up, ordering the pieces the way
nature orders a plant: "Root," "Tendril," "Petal," "Seed,"
"Fruit." At the end of the book, the larger landscapes of
"Stone," "Garden," and "Earth."

"I finished putting the manuscript together today," I
write to Hugh early in March. "I am weak-kneed with
delight that you are publishing these little fictions. I
love them dearly."

When I finally send Hugh the finished manuscript,
it is almost a year to the day since he first approached
me with an offer to publish the book. I'm embarrassed,
but he makes a joke:

"I can't wait to dine out on my story of having to
wrench your 'child' from your bosom after being obliged
to wait a year. I can see the remains of the umbilical

cord still attached. Please be assured that your 'baby' will be safe in my hands."

SLOW READING

Before the Linotype machine, an army of people set the type for the world's books by hand one letter at a time. For 250 years, from the time of Gutenberg until the late nineteenth century, this was how it was done, and it is how I am about to set a page of *The Paradise Project*.

Hugh has rerun his calculations: he has to work eight hours a day, Sunday to Sunday, to meet a June launch.

"It will be tight," he says.

"I can help," I offer, thinking of something Hugh said to me shortly after we met: "I love setting type because it's slow reading—it gives me an opportunity to think."

I read too fast. Twenty years ago, I strode into my local daily newspaper office and asked to review a book. I was fed up with my tendency to skip over a page like a stone in search of a horizon, splashing up a sentence here and there. "I want to read every word," I said to the books editor, and for a while I slowed down. Terrified of making a fool of myself, I read every word.

I blame my speed habit on school, university in general, and my nineteenth-century novel course in particular, which demanded I plough through thousands of pages every week. Now it occurs to me that people who lived at the time those novels were published must have read them differently. How long would it have taken my great-great-great grandmother to read Proust? And if I were a friar reading an illuminated manuscript, each word drawn by hand, surely I would read that differently yet, the words traced in my mind as slowly as a scribing pen.

I rarely review books now, and my reading has resumed its breakneck speed. There are times when this seems like a good thing. Along with making an ebook of *The Paradise Project*, I am bringing two out-of-print works—*The Convict Lover* and *The Lion in the Room Next Door*—back as ebooks. I don't have Word docs of the final, edited manuscripts of these two works, so I have to read my digital file alongside the printed book, making corrections as I go. The work is demanding; I can't make any mistakes. I set a time limit as a kind of marathon challenge.

This is how my onscreen days unfold: shifting from file to file to email to browser like a cross-country runner clearing hurdles, striving for agility and efficiency but, above all, speed. At the end of the day, I open a paper book, panting.

I need the slow reading lessons that typesetting will teach.

HAND TRAVEL

Hugh slides a drawer out of the type cabinet and sets it on the table in front of me.

"California Job Case," he says as if introducing me to a friend.

The wooden tray with its dozens of compartments looks familiar. I have one just like it, sloped in my closet to display my motley collection of earrings, bracelets, and other baubles.

"Historically, the common letters and the capitals were kept in two separate cases," Hugh says. He never misses an opportunity for instruction. "The capitals were in an upper case, which explains the name. The other letters were in the lower case—you're smart, you get the idea. When typesetters started moving around, shop to shop, the capitals and common letters were combined into one case for easier carrying."

I peer into the compartments. "But the letters aren't in alphabetical order," I exclaim, shocked. "How is a person supposed to find them?"

"That would be too much work." Hugh grins devilishly. "Look: the letters most often used are the handiest."

Over four centuries of manual typesetting, dozens of different cases were developed as printers tried to find the configuration that was easiest and speediest to work from. Eventually, the California Job Case, developed by printers in San Francisco, became the standard. Its proponents claimed it would reduce "hand travel" by more than half a mile a day.

The California, as Hugh calls it, has eighty-nine compartments of varying sizes. Numerals and symbols are across the top. Lowercase letters are on the left; capitals on the right. The most frequently used lowercase

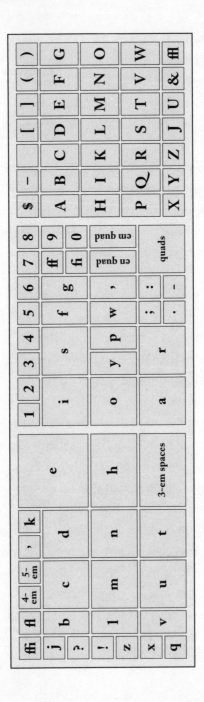

letters—*u, m, c, d, e, i, s, o, a, r*—have the biggest bins, arranged roughly in a semi-circle directly in front of the typesetter. Less frequently used letters—such as *j, z, x, q, w, f, g*—are farther away, tucked in the smallest compartments.

Only the capitals are in alphabetical order, with two exceptions. *J* and *U* were not used by early English printers so their compartments were tacked on later, after *Z*. Spacers of various widths are scattered about, some on the upper left, some on the lower right. Spacers—known in the trade as quads, short for quadrats—are square blocks of blank type, with the printing face inset so it doesn't take any ink. Quads are used to create paragraph indents and the spaces between words and to fill out a line of type. The most common is the em quad. The em quad gets its name from the letter *M*, which in most typefaces is as wide as it is tall. For example, if the type is 10 point, the em quad will be 10 points high and 10 points wide. The other spacers are based on the em quad. There is a five-to-the-em spacer, a piece of lead a fifth as wide as the *M*; four-to-the-em; three-to-the-em; and the en-spacer, which is half as wide as it is tall, the dimensions of the letter *N*. Hugh uses three-to-the-em spacers between words and four-to-the-em spacers between sentences.

Then there are the ligatures. The word comes from *legat*, which means to bind. In a ligature, two or more letters are joined as a single glyph. "Glyph," I have to admit, is one of my favourite words. I discovered it while accompanying an expedition of archeologists to the Mayan ruins at Bonampak and Yaxchilan on the border of Mexico and Guatemala. The code for the Mayan system of writing, which consists of pictorial glyphs carved in soft stone, had just been broken. I learned to read the blocky images of jaguars, serpents, and hook-nosed women with ropes piercing their tongues. When Hugh says "glyph" in his tiny garage-studio in Kingston, the small word reverberates from the metal letters in their bins across continents and millennia to the Mayans, to Asia, and to ancient Egypt, binding the world in seconds.

For me, ligatures are delightful, subtle reminders of how mechanical printing is linked to handwriting, a kind of human-machine meld. What is cursive writing, after all, but word after word of ligatured letters? Medieval scribes, in an attempt to speed up the copying of manuscripts, started combining characters in what we now call "scribal abbreviation." For example, if letters with bowls (*c*, *o*, *e*, *a*, *b*, *d*, *g*, *q*, and *p*) followed each other, the facing edges of the two bowls would be superimposed, as in œ or æ. Similarly, the verticals of characters such as h, m, and n might also be combined. One of the most common ligatures, the ampersand (&), was originally made by joining *e* and *t*, which spelled *et*, Latin for "and."

At the time Gutenberg was developing movable type, a manuscript might have hundreds of these scribal abbreviations. Because his movable type was based on handwriting, it also included many ligatures, which made mechanical printing easier, since one block could replace two or three. In the twentieth century, ligatures fell out of favour as designers and printers leaned towards cleaner, more modern lines. When computers came along in the 1980s, ligatures all but disappeared. Early software couldn't produce ligatures on command, and most of the new digital fonts didn't include them.

As hand compositors went the way of the dodo, so too did ligatures. But there is a happy ending to this story. The rise of book artists and bookwrights, a revived interest among young designers in classic alphabets and old books, and the increasing support of computers for languages other than English, many of which still include ligatures, have restored to life the lovely tradition of hooking letters together the way we used to hook our little fingers together to make a wish.

Poking in the ligature bin, I remind Hugh of the first time we met, when he waved his ligatured bookmark under my nose.

"I couldn't believe it!" he says, still stunned by what he sees as an unforgivable designer's oversight. "The typeface they chose for your book didn't have a single ligature. I'm not sure how many people in the world would pick that out."

To correct the error, he had set the *Convict Lover* bookmark in Caslon, named for William Caslon, an early eighteenth-century gunsmith and typeface designer famous for his ability to carve his perfect punches freehand. Caslon established the first English national style in typeface. Ironically, the first version of the United States Declaration of Independence was printed in Caslon. Hugh chose it for my bookmark because the *c* and *t* in words like convict were joined.

"Like manacles!" he'd grinned as he dropped a pile of bookmarks on my signing podium at the Penitentiary Museum.

& is a common ligature, as are *Th*, *st*, and *fl*. In fact, *f* is the most commonly ligatured letter. On the wall of his studio, Hugh has a limited-edition poster called *Ligatures*, which he printed with wooden type to celebrate the anniversary of the Abecedarian Project, now more than forty years old. (It promotes early childhood education as a way of overcoming the disadvantages of poverty.) Hugh used lowercase letters to spell out a lovely aphorism that contains three double ligatures followed by two triples. Just so everyone gets it, Hugh printed the five ligatures in red.

A hundred years ago, a skilled typesetter would have been able to "read" such a text as it was being set by a fellow typesetter, simply by watching where he reached for his letters. I suppose a sharp observer could tell what I'm typing, in much the same way. My computer keyboard, like my typewriter keyboard, is not laid out in alphabetical order: it uses the standard QWERTY format, with letters arranged according to principles of speed and efficiency, just like the California case.

When I prepare *The Paradise Project* manuscript for ebook publication, I simply type the words into a Word document that Erik pours into an EPUB file. The program automatically justifies the margins and sets the spacing between words. It adds hyphens in exactly the

LIGATURES

saffron

fireflies

baffle

traffic

We created this poster to dovetail with Hersh Jacob's ABCedarian
Celebration using a circa *1890* Chandler-Price press and wooden type
on felt laid paper to feature ligatures only used with letterpress printing.

The poster is limited to *37* copies of which *3* are marked Hors Commerce
HC1-HC3 and *34* are numbered. This is copy number 23 .

Hugh Walter Barclay and Faye Batchelor

Thee Hellbox Press, Kingston, Ontario

right places. If I misspell a word, it underlines my error with a squiggly red line. I am cosseted and corrected and jollied along by a technology that makes me better than I am, stripping away every mistake, every evidence that I am all too human.

The hand no longer travels very far to typeset a book. But I wonder, what is lost in giving up the journey?

OUT OF SORTS

My head hurts. I feel as though I've been dropped onto another planet, one where the citizens speak a language I recognize, although the words all have unfamiliar meanings.

"This is a clean case," says Hugh.

Not very, I think, surveying the messy heaps of metal letters. The heaps are called "sorts." When a typesetter runs out of a particular letter, he is "out of sorts." I have lots of letters and, still, I'm out of sorts.

"In a 'dirty' case, the letters are mixed up. If I spill a case, I've 'pied the case.'"

I prop one of *The Paradise Project* stories in front of me. My job today is to set "Shoot," a story based on a scene I witnessed one spring sitting by the window of the restaurant where Hugh and I like to meet. When we began this project, Hugh offered me an 1827 appren- ticeship contract that demands I start at six thirty every morning, chopping wood to build a fire to warm the shop by the time the journeymen and the Master (that would be Hugh) arrive at eight o'clock. The contract guarantees long hours and poor pay. I'm a writer, I told him, I'm used to that.

Hugh is eager to get started. Erik hasn't finished the lino blocks—the images have to be printed first, with the words printed over top—but he has sent a map of the book, so we can typeset the pages that have no illustrations.

Hugh brings me a galley tray, an open-ended metal tray that looks like a small cookie sheet. On it are the tools of the trade I'm about to learn.

"This is a composing stick," he says, handing me what looks a bit like a Scrabble rack with a fixed barricade on the right and a sliding one on the left, near the handle. "Note that the stick's name has its origin in early newspapers, where the owner would compose the stories." Hugh winks at me, always happy to take me down a notch or two. "Who needs these pesky writers anyway?"

He adjusts the left side of the composing stick to the length of the line he has decided on for the inside pages, then he lays down a thin length of lead called a 2-point line spacer. A spacer like this will separate each line of type.

To create the first paragraph indent, he sets an em spacer into the stick. Holding the stick in his left hand, he picks out the letters of the first word with his right.

"See this notch?" he says, upending the letter *I*. "There's a nick in the bottom edge of each piece of type. That lets you know by touch that you've got the bottom. You can feel the notch when you pick the type out of the case. Turn the nick down, keep the face up." His right hand feeds type to his left thumb, which slides the letter or spacer into place and holds it fast. His hands glide and swirl over the California case in a dance, right hand leading, left hand following a heartbeat behind.

He makes it look simple, even with his gnarled knuckles and his perpetual hitchhiker's thumbs, bent by arthritis. Read a line of text; pick out the letters one by one; drop them into the composing stick. How hard can that be?

What isn't clear to me until he hands me the stick is that I will be working upside down, right to left. I squint at the text, then squint at the case of letters, spelling each word standing on its head. How on earth did da Vinci do this, writing 13,000 pages of notes in that mirror script?

It was March

I can't figure out why Hugh calls this slow reading. It's slow all right, but it sure isn't reading. The words in reverse dissolve into indiscriminate letters, devoid of meaning.

Twenty minutes later, I'm finally at the end of the first line. It wasn't as hard as I thought. The trick of reading upside down has come back to me from my days as a journalist, when I used to read the notes on a person's desk while sitting opposite them in an interview. But I have a problem. Hugh has designed the text to be justified both right and left, which means the words have to fill out the line on both sides, with a three-to-the-em spacer at the beginning and another at the end. These are the immovable stops and starts of every line, and there simply isn't room for the final *r* in the word "outdoor." If I remove the entire word, or even half of it, the letters will slosh in their trough. If the text was ragged right, I could drop "door," put in a hyphen, and add spacers to the end of the line, but that's not an option.

"This is the fun part!" Hugh exclaims.

I was wondering when that would start.

"You are using a three-to-the-em spacer between words and a four-to-the-em after a period or a comma, right? But we have five-to the-em and even narrower spacers. So take out some of those three-ems and four-ems, and set in thinner or thicker spacers, whatever you need to make the line look good. Be creative! You know about that, right?" He winks.

It was March, still too cool for out–

I put an extra space between each word. It's too much. I backtrack. I've read the damn line so often it feels trampled and torn. And what a lousy line it is! I hate it. I wish I could rewrite the whole thing, but I've already invested an hour getting these twenty-eight letters into place.

"Keep going! Keep going! We don't have all day! Well," says Hugh, "we do have all day, but let's get at least another line out of you."

Finally, the first line is tight. Hugh hands me the long, thin 2-point spacer to separate the lines, and I start on the next one. I'm getting used to where the common letters are in the California case. I can almost imagine a time when my fingers will reach for them as blindly as they reach for computer keys. Then, at the end of the second line, another crisis: a long, unsplittable word, one that can't possibly fit, and if I push it to the next line, this one will be as gap-toothed as a second-grader.

"This is where I invoke Barclay's Law #46. I think that's the number," says Hugh with a grin. He has been hovering at my back, clearly waiting for me to arrive at this impasse. A cruel teacher, he delights in not warning me of the obstacles littering the path ahead. "Law #46 states that, to take up slack in a line, a pressmark matching the weight of the type will be inserted between words, usually following a comma or period. I have been known to use two or three pressmarks on a page."

Hugh's pressmark is a stylized image of a turtle. Thirty-five years ago, he and Verla visited the petroglyphs near Peterborough, Ontario, the largest concentration of aboriginal rock carvings in Canada. At the time, the carvings were at the end of an unmarked dirt road: over 900 images carved more than a thousand years ago into a limestone shelf. Figures writhe across the surface, a fanciful bestiary of turtles, fish, leaping and browsing four-legged creatures, shamans, solar symbols, boats, humans, and geometric shapes. The site is sacred to the Ojibway people, who call it *KinoomaageWaapkong*, "the rocks that teach."

Now the site is part of Petroglyphs Provincial Park. A protective building has been built over the carvings, but when Hugh and Verla saw them, the carvings were part of the landscape, the sun shining down on the rocks, the wind rushing, an underground stream burbling up now and then, the four elements of earth, fire, air, and water all stroking the senses. Among the glyphs, Hugh noticed a stylized turtle.

"The turtle is fundamental to Ojibway mythology," says Hugh. "In their story of the Great Flood, it was a turtle that offered its back to Waynaboozhoo to bear the weight of the new earth. In fact, Ojibway and other First Nations people call North America Turtle Island because of its shape—Florida is one hind leg, Baja California is another, Mexico is the tail."

Hugh carved his own version of the petroglyph turtle in several sizes, and a friend cast them, creating a handful of pressmarks that live in the California case alongside the letters, numbers, and punctuation marks. He fingers one out of the case now and drops it into the too-wide gap between 🐢 words on my composing stick.

"There! Problem solved!" Hugh exclaims. "You see, the turtles not only bridge unavoidable gaps between words, they block rivers, too."

"What's a river?" I say.

"Blank spaces that run down the page. Books these days are running with rivers!"

He pulls a book at random from the stack on a side table. "Unfocus your eyes so all you see is black text on white paper. Notice the white rivers? That's what happens when wide spaces between words line up, one after the other. Machines can't fix that. Not even computers. But we can."

Ebook software can, too, but I take his point. Word spacing is key. When I was writer-in-residence at Green College, one of the graduate students was writing her PhD dissertation on spaces between words in the Arabic language. The run-on nature of Arabic sentences, she theorized, slowed the adoption of the printing press and the advances it provoked. In ancient cultures, reading was oral and words flowed together: it was up to the reader to separate out the words and convey the breaks through breath and cadence. It was Irish scribes in the seventh and eighth centuries who first separated words in their manuscripts, a practice that took 300 years to spread to Europe.

One of Gutenberg's challenges was to mimic human script with his press. Today, when we print or write longhand, we instinctively vary the spacing between our words. The width of each letter might vary, too. We squeeze the words or stretch them out in order to make them fit the line. To duplicate this, Gutenberg had some 290 characters in his type cases, almost four times as many as Hugh, every letter cast in a variety of widths.

"Gutenberg realized that his new adventure had to be as pleasing to the eye as books written by hand. In my opinion, our attention to aesthetically pleasing typesetting has decreased since Gutenberg and has been all but obliterated by the digital age." Hugh goes off in a huff.

I return to my composing stick. The next two lines go smoothly. Even so, it has taken me two hours to set four lines of type. If I really were a printer's apprentice, I'd be sent back to my hovel in disgrace by now.

I show my work to Hugh like an eager puppy with a chew toy, waiting for a pat on the head. Hugh's brow furrows.

"Did you proofread each line as you finished setting the type? The composing stick doesn't come with spell-check."

"You didn't tell me I had to proof as I go!"

He grins, a master of tough love. "Typesetting offers a lot of options for making mistakes. You can place a letter upside down, leave a letter out, insert an extra letter. You can put in a wrong letter or leave a word completely out or put the same word in twice. You can use a wrong font." He enumerates the possible errors on his fingers. "Congratulations! You have committed most of these sins in your first four lines!"

I'm used to proofing pages, not lines, to scribbling a manuscript with corrections and letting someone else make it right. I look back over my work and, sure enough, midday has three *d*s, I've dropped the comma after "terrace," and the *e* in "children" is upside down.

That upside down *e* looks familiar. Before we started

The Paradise Project, I commissioned Hugh to print mementoes for the authors we invited to Kingston WritersFest, a literary festival I founded. Just before the mementoes were to be delivered, Hugh sent me a message: "I have made a single copy of the WritersFest Keepsake for Wayne that will have the *e* in your name upside down. Don't tell Wayne about my devious plan. I think he may enjoy that little touch."

Hugh toppled his *e* in whimsy; I committed my sin in ignorance.

"What do I do now?"

"You rip it out!" Hugh says as gleefully as my mother did when I sewed my first zipper in backwards. "Use your bodkin."

I've used a bodkin as a needle to pull ribbon through lace, and I know a bodkin as a small dagger from reading Shakespeare, but a printer's bodkin is neither needle nor knife. Pointed like an awl, with a rounded wooden handle that sits sweetly in the palm, the bodkin is a kind of pick for extracting letters from set type. Clearly, I'm not the first person to make a mistake: in this business, errors have their own special tool.

I lift out the extra *d* and the errant *e* with my bodkin. Adding the comma is more troublesome. There are no spacers I can safely remove to make room for it.

"If you can add spacers, you can take them away!" Hugh shows me how to replace the three-em spacer with a single em. "Bingo!"

I pop out spacers and shift them around, breaking up the nascent rivers.

The winter before, Hugh and I visited Queen's University Special Collections to view their reproduction Gutenberg Bible. "You remember how the word spacing was seen as very narrow slits of white? No rivers anywhere? That's what we aspire to."

He looks at my paltry four lines of revised text. "Good! Good!"

I feel a ridiculous rush of pride. I could have entered these four lines of text into a computer file in about forty seconds, but there is more to this typesetting business than speed and efficiency. A peculiar alchemy has taken place. The heavy burden of my errors and ignorance has been transformed into a glow of satisfaction. My few lines, at last, are worthy of Gutenbarclay.

Hugh is an erratic teacher: here one minute, gone the next. I could have got out my laptop and watched an instructional video on compositing made by the California Vocational Foundation, complete with background music that sounds like it was lifted from a 1950s drama. *Perry Mason* maybe, or *Dragnet*. The muscled young man in the checked shirt slips type into his composing stick with all the dexterity and pride of a hipster showing off his Android skills.

Without the help of the checked-shirt man, however, it takes me the better part of two days to set a page of text. I've used two turtles. Three words in italics. Four hyphens. Made countless mistakes.

I proof and proof and proof again. When I am pretty sure every letter is where it should be, no more and no less, I show the block to Hugh.

"Uh-huh, uh-huh, uh-huh," is all he says.

THE STONEMAN'S IMPOSITION

When I've set seven lines, Hugh shows me how to unlock the movable edge of the composing stick and slide the type into the galley tray, pushing it up into the far corner in a firm block. By the time I have thirty lines set—one full page—the block of type bears a passing resemblance to a page in a book.

"Ready for the next step?" Hugh asks, and I nod with anticipation, a perpetual five-year-old. "Time to lock up."

He sets the open side of the galley tray up against the sheet of glass on his work table, eyeballing glass and metal until they are perfectly level, then he slides the block of set type from the tray to the glass.

Four "chases" lean against the wall beside his press. He selects one and lays it over the block of type. The chase holds the type and is inserted into the press where it will be inked to print the page. Chase, Hugh explains, is a British corruption of the French word *châssis*, which means frame. Printing is studded with these verbal delights, corrupted tidbits of European languages that travelled to England with the printing press.

The process of locking the type in the chase is called imposition—as opposed to composition, which, in Hugh's world, refers to the setting of the type. (In my world, composition is the writing of words and sentences and paragraphs.) Historically, imposition was done on a large, flat stone, and the person who imposed the words was called the stoneman.

Hugh is the stoneman. He selects some "furniture" from a sloping cupboard beside his type cabinet: assorted rectangles of hardwood that look like the blocks we made for our sons to build ramps and garages for their Hot Wheels cars. The thin slats of hardwood that look like lathes are called "reglets," a word probably derived from the French *règle*, meaning both "groove" and "rule." Hugh arranges the furniture and reglets to fill in the empty spaces around the text block until it sits square and tight within the chase. Then he inserts a small "key" into the quoin, a word I've used often in Scrabble although I didn't know it meant "corner," from the French *coin*. This makes sense: as Hugh tightens the quoins on two sides of the chase, the type is pushed tightly against the opposite corner.

"All locked down?" I say.

"Locked up," Hugh says. "Locked down is for prisons."

Hugh twists the quoin key, tightening each quoin in turn, then hands me the empty composing stick. "Keep at it, Apprentice!" he says, chuckling merrily as he returns to the press.

INTO THE HELLBOX

I set a few more lines, but I am too slow for Hugh. He fires me, which is a relief. I can spend hours at the computer happily inserting a comma and taking it out, but

corn

were swept bare.

they said, and the

pped forward.

dog

she sniffed. No

in even a false

thmod? An olive

Too smelly. Too

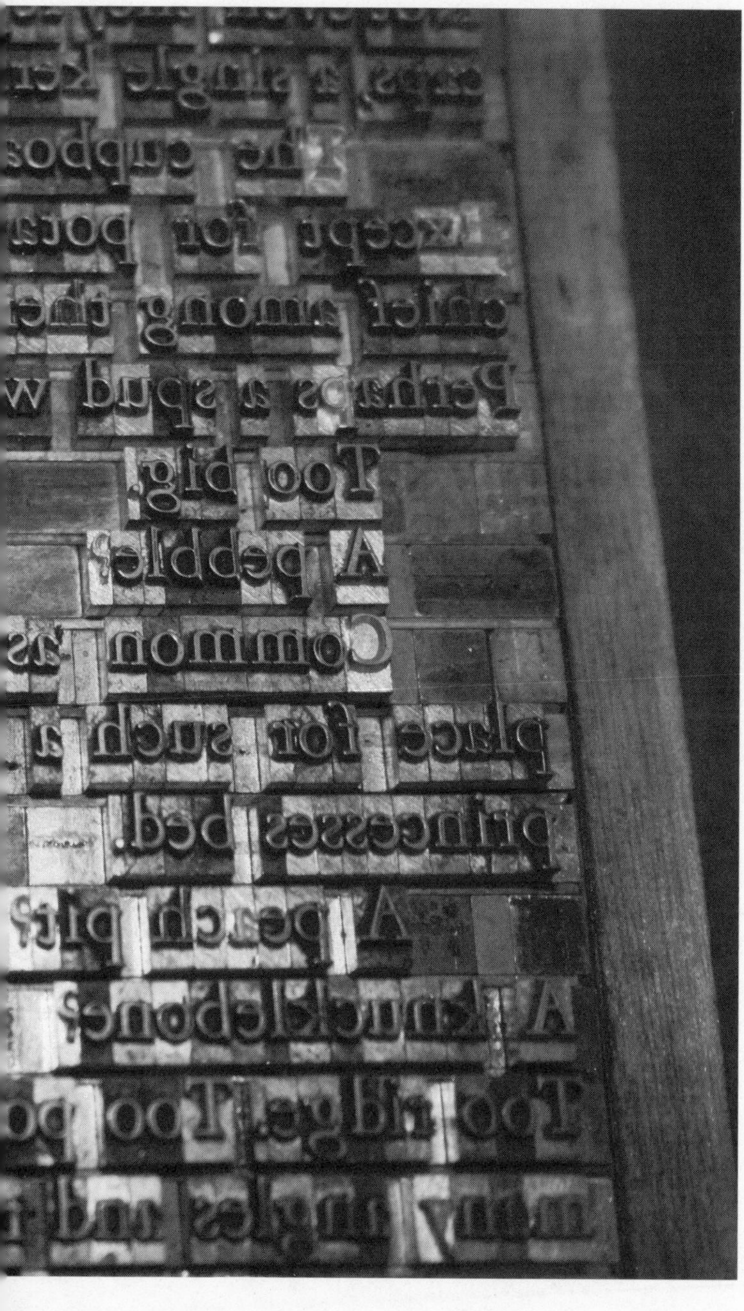

A single ker

he suppos

Except for pota

chief among the

Perhaps a spud w

Too big,

A pebble?

Common as

place for such a

princess's bed.

A perch pip?

A knucklebone?

Too ridge. Too po

an angles and r

to pick out the letters physically, whether for practical reasons of spacing or because Stupid Merilyn has been at it again, drives me to distraction.

Hugh carries on until all four chases are locked up, or down, I forget which. Every so often he sends me an email, complaining that I use too many commas, or have such an affection for *H*'s that he has been forced to buy more type.

"What happens next?" I ask when I see the four chases lined up neatly on the glass. The studio has always struck me as dirty and disorganized, but the better I get to know Hugh, and the closer I look, the more I see a different kind of order, measured and controlled, exerted by the process itself.

"Now I print," says Hugh. "I don't have enough type to set more pages."

I had the idea that the type for all the pages of the book would be set at once. I realize now how ridiculous that would be. Imagine the number of *H*'s Hugh would have to buy!

"So what do you do with these?" I wave my hand over the four pages. They look so permanent, each block of metal letters fixed within its frame.

"After I print them, I distribute the type back into the case."

It reminds me of the sawdust carpets the people of San Miguel de Allende, Mexico, make each year at Easter. Several kilometres of cobblestone street are covered with coloured sawdust, laid down in exquisite images of Christ, Mary, and other icons of peace and spirituality.

Families work from dusk until dawn to finish the carpets so that the feet of the pilgrims returning to town will never touch stone. By eleven in the morning, their night's work is smudged beyond recognition; then the sawdust is swept up by street cleaners. The ephemeral rugs exist only in the photographs I take as I walk. In the same way, the type we have just set will exist in this particular configuration only on the printed page.

When I return a few days later, Hugh is hard at it, disassembling my sentences, letter by letter, as carefully as he set them. He stands in front of the open drawer of Garamond 14 point and pitches the letters and spacers into their proper bins. It is a meditative task; he seems to hardly notice me.

Suddenly he turns and pitches a letter into a cookie tin with a winter scene pressed into the side, a gaily trotting horse pulling a sleighful of laughing children.

"What's that?" I ask.

"The hellbox!"

I assumed the name of his printing enterprise— Thee Hellbox Press—referred to thinking outside the box, the box itself being some kind of hell. But no. Hellbox is the container where typesetters traditionally toss their type after printing. It was left to the apprentice, the printer's devil, to pick out the letters from the hellbox and put them back in the type case, surely a hellish job. Because Hugh has only temporary—and in my case, incompetent—devils, he distributes the type himself, reserving the hellbox for broken and damaged type: *T*'s and *I*'s with a serif snapped off; a *P* caught in the edge of the press and bent to a curve; vowels that have been used so often their faces are slick and round.

"The thing about type is that it has no tolerance. It has to be absolutely flat, or it won't print. I can't tell you how many times I've had to pull out a lowercase *i* because the dot didn't show. It was there, all right, but it was worn down below the level of the rest of the letter."

In Gutenberg's day, worn and damaged type would have been melted down and recast. I assume Hugh ships his back to a foundry somewhere.

Hugh laughs. "I've had the same hellbox since the beginning of time and it is only half full. I've told my executors to ship it to a foundry but to make sure it's remade into lead type, not bullets!"

Hugh named his press after the hellbox of type the printer handed over when Hugh hauled away the old hand-operated press that gave him his start back in the '70s. The Hellbox Press: that's how the name is spelled in his first book, *A Letter to Teresa*.

"It was Bill Poole who suggested, with tongue in cheek, that I call it Thee Hellbox Press so my press didn't get confused with all the other Hellbox Presses. (<;)-"

Hugh likes to think of himself as one of a kind. A rebel. He draws his role models from the ranks of innovators and revolutionaries. Johannes Gutenberg, Martin Luther King Jr., Che Guevara.

"There is a quote that we think was uttered by Che in 1959 when his soldiers entered Havana. 'We don't know where we are going but we can't turn back.' In my mind, it not only takes courage to make a statement such as that, it also invites generations unborn to take up the cause. I think it also speaks to our cause."

I'm not sure if he means *The Paradise Project* or the survival of letterpress printing. Maybe it doesn't matter.

"Press on!" Hugh exclaims, punching his fist in the air. "Joy is the objective!"

INK
INK
INK
INK

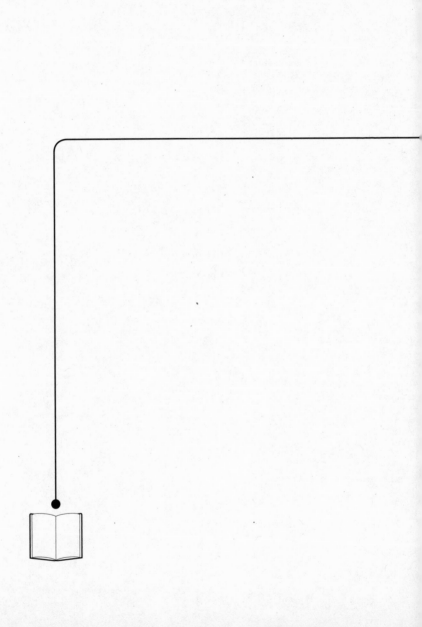

BLOOD INTO INK

In the photograph, the woman is naked except for black brogues and argyle socks held up by leather sock suspenders. She sits splay-legged on a stool, an antiquarian book the size of a ledger propped open between her legs. With one hand, she turns a page. In the other, she holds a long feathered quill. Her eyes are closed in ecstasy, and her head tips back as she dips the quill deep into her wide open mouth.

This photograph sits on my desk and has done so through three houses and almost as many decades. It was taken by Dianne Whelan, an Ottawa photographer who was a friend of my older son's girlfriend. She sent it to me as a thank-you postcard. Once, when I thought

I'd lost it, I tracked down the photographer and bought three more, just in case. A lifetime supply.

The photograph could be an illustration of something T. S. Eliot once wrote: "The purpose of literature is to turn blood into ink."

Hemingway supposedly said something similar—Writing is easy. You just open a vein and bleed—except that if he actually did say this, he was quoting a 1949 newspaper column in which Walter Winchell interviewed "Red" Smith, a popular sports columnist of the day. When Red was asked if he found it difficult to churn out column after column, he replied, "Why, no. You simply sit down at the typewriter, open your veins, and bleed."

Even then, it was not a new idea. Nietzsche, in his philosophical novel *Thus Spake Zarathustra: A Book for All and None,* published in the late 1880s, makes a similar allusion to blood as ink in the chapter "On Reading and Writing":

"Of all that is written I love only what a man has written with his blood."

Could blood, physically and chemically, be used as printer's ink? Lovers down the ages have spilled a little blood and dipped in their pen nibs to sign their names in a lasting pledge of love. Ever since Tom Sawyer, and probably before, novitiates have been signing their names in blood to join a gang. The Scottish Covenanters signed their call for a Presbyterian Scotland in their own blood, wearing red neckerchiefs as their insignia (the genesis of the term redneck, which originally meant a Scottish dissenter).

The Dutch poet and journalist Ruud Linssen took the metaphor literally and printed his entire *Book of War, Mortification and Love* using his own blood as ink, to stress the voluntary suffering that is the theme of the essays. First, he very considerately had his blood tested "to avoid innocent people getting exotic diseases by reading a book." When his blood was declared fit, vials of it were removed by a doctor. Linssen gave the vials to an experimental printer. Months of experimentation followed in an attempt to overcome the primary obstacle: the blood, which is water-based, refused to mix with the oil-based printing ink. In the end, Linssen's blood was freeze-dried to remove every last drop of H_2O, leaving behind a pure blood powder that was mixed with oil to create ink for the offset press. (The typeface the printer used was Fakir.)

Every time I am with Hugh—every single time, without fail—at some point in the visit he'll thrust his fingers towards the crook of his arm as if he's holding a syringe. "Time to get my fix," he'll say, which means, time to get back to the press. He and Vladimir Nabokov would have gotten along. "Ink, a drug," Nabokov writes in his 1947 dystopian novel, *Bend Sinister*.

I look at my photograph, at the naked woman dipping the quill into her mouth, and I understand, at last, my attraction. Ink may be in Hugh's blood, but my life-blood flows in every word I write.

"It all sounds good to me," says Hugh. I have just laid out what I think we can accomplish today: choose the ink, okay the images, set up a timeline. "However, I am a little worried about riding with a woman who is picking up a chainsaw."

It is early March, and we are on our way to our first formal meeting of Team Paradise Project. I picked up Hugh just before noon. We are due at Erik's farmhouse in the rolling hills of Central Ontario just after lunch. It's not a farm, really, although that's what city people call a hived-off acreage like his, with an old farmhouse, a barn, and a scattering of outbuildings, testimony to the actual farmer's attempts to make a living from cows, then pigs, then chickens, and, finally, small-engine repair. We live on a similarly much-reduced former farm further east. It's spring, time to cut wood: I need our chainsaw back.

I'm feeling querulous. I'm not looking forward to spending three hours in the car with someone I barely know, even after a year. And I'm concerned, just a little, about bringing my son into the project. I mentioned in passing that Erik was a painter and *bam!* Hugh anointed him Team Artist.

This book project is running ahead of me, and I'm struggling to catch up. I'm used to an editor, a copy editor, the predictable unfolding of production. Decisions about typefaces and paper stock and illustrations and how many books to print and where to sell them: that's always been someone else's business. I don't mind being involved.

In fact, I usually insist on voicing an opinion, and I am looking forward to knowing more about the innards of publishing through this project. But no editor? I feel as though my father has just taken his hand off the seat of my bicycle, shouting, "Keep pedalling, you'll be fine."

Like almost every writer I know, I have little faith in my own words, and when I look at my son's block prints, no faith whatsoever in my ability to assess whether they are brilliant or complete bunk.

Erik is feeling tentative, too. "I know you want me to have the freedom to express myself, but I would love to hear what you think of the images," he says gently, opening the folio of sketches. "Not that I will change them," he adds with a smile. The old one-two.

We are sitting at a table in the red-brick farmhouse he gutted last year, stripping it down to its essentials. The place isn't quite dressed again. Shreds of green-checked wallpaper wave from the kitchen walls and the plugs hang precariously from a post, but we don't pay them any attention. We're here to work. Hugh fans colour swatches over the Salad paper he has spread on the red-checked tablecloth. We narrow the colour fan to show only strips of green, every hue from pale pea to deepest jade.

My eyes go directly to a soft spring green. Erik is fingering a muddy olive. My heart sinks. Hugh nods enthusiastically.

"Uh-huh, uh-huh, uh-huh," he says, bobbing his head up and down. "That's good. That'll work."

I say nothing. I trust my son. The two of us have worked together before. When he was thirteen, we visited ruins in the Yucatán jungle. I wrote a travel piece about the trip and the magazine illustrated my story with his watercolours of Mayan glyphs. When he was twenty, he painted the cover for my first book of stories, *The Lion in the Room Next Door*. He has his father's surname, so the publisher who hired him didn't realize he was my son. When he called me with the news, he asked if I was cool with the idea. "Sure," I said, "but we're both professionals. If I don't like it, I'll say so."

Now he is telling me that this muddy chartreuse is perfect for the images that will lie beneath my words.

"Like ghost images," Hugh says.

"Exactly!" says Erik.

They are speaking the same language, a lexicon of colour and design that is foreign to me, although I can appreciate the sound of it, its cadences.

I push back my chair.

"It's up to you," I say, throwing up my hands, just a little.

They both stare. They aren't used to me having no opinion.

"Really," I insist. "You decide. This is your bailiwick. I have nothing to contribute."

I've been wrong so often, I know enough to keep my mouth shut, although I haven't yet learned to do it graciously. My son leafs through the folio, showing us sketches for the block prints he will carve. I struggle to disguise my shock. I had imagined delicate plants twining through the pages, a vision that was dispelled weeks ago by the first sketch he emailed to Hugh: scissor blades slicing through a stalk.

"Secateurs," I wrote back. "A plant cutting is made with secateurs, not scissors."

"Hey! I'm the artist!"

"Right. I just thought you'd want to know. For accuracy."

"It's not an illustration."

"Of course not. The scissors are great."

He changed them to secateurs, now in a big brawny hand that reaches up from the bottom rim of the page. The drawing is muscular, vaguely threatening.

But it's a *paradise* project, I want to tell them. All the people in these stories are making a paradise, their own Eden. However misguided we may think they are, it's an honest impulse, deeply human. A positive thing.

"I took the theme of tools," Erik is saying. "The things people use to make their paradise."

I make encouraging noises, but in my heart, I'm not convinced that these images won't overpower my words, shift their meaning. I'm not used to competing for a reader's attention. Won't it be confusing?

A story, to me, has always been a pure object. A thing that exists apart from me. Pre-exists, in fact. As a writer, my job is to find it, give it shape, walk the reader through it in a way that will show it off in its best light. Not the prettiest light, but the most authentic, the most effective, which sometimes means taking the most dramatic path and sometimes the softest, subtlest one. I've written sixteen books. So far, nothing has shaken that socks and underwear in his drawers in the same way in each place so that if he closed his eyes he would hardly know he had moved.

He always took a small cutting of the purple-fruited plant. The transport of vegetative matter across national borders was frowned upon, he knew, but tourists carried more potent seeds wedged in the soles of their shoes, of that he was quite certain. Besides, he assured himself, it was only one plant.

No matter where he heeled it in, the cutting prospered: in the lush loam of Sri Lanka, the red lime dust of Cuba, the dark volcanic scrapings of Iceland. It rarely bloomed the first year, though it would put on growth rapidly, sending up stalks in such profusion that his back garden, wherever it was, would be transformed into a familiar grotto. In the second season, the lovely purple fruit would set and he'd spend his evenings bathed in the indigo light glinting off its strange translucent skin.

He was a man who never looked back. Country to country he travelled, leaving his small, considered mark on conception. Design, printing: it's all in service of the story, isn't it? By which I mean the words. My words.

Now the story is no longer mine to tell. Erik is telling it through his images. Hugh is telling it through his choice of ink and type and paper, and the way his turtles are set into the page. I thought I understood collaboration, but the truth is I thought of this project as my stories, with embellishments by others. It's only now beginning to dawn on me: we're all in this together.

A few days later, I get an email from Hugh. "I just returned from dinner at Swiss Chalet, where my mind was focused on Erik's work, which I find totally outstanding. One of my personal tests for artwork is being able to recall the work to my mind's eye long after seeing it. I can do this with every piece Erik sent in his email.

"I think you will agree," he goes on, "that our interviewing and reviewing the work of the other twenty candidates was time well spent and that we have made the proper selection in Erik. (<;)- Oh! and all the paper has arrived, hoping for ink tomorrow."

IT ISN'T EASY BEING GREEN

Type gives shape to words, pressing letters into paper, crushing the fibres to make an impression. But it is ink, flowing between the banks of those curves and lines, that makes type—letters, words, sentences—visible.

For Hugh, the transformation is a miracle, one he takes very seriously.

In choosing the ink colour for a text, he rarely resorts to default black, which is the colour of the words in all the books on my shelves. Indeed, in all the books I've read throughout my life, a fact that only now hits me.

I get it: the first inks were made with the cheapest and handiest colouring agents, which just happened to be black—lampblack, graphite, charred bones—but why hang onto the darkness when modern chemistry can paint us rainbows?

Hugh agrees, but when he is about to print a new project, he doesn't impulsively grab the tin of colour that reflects his mood of the day, which is my guiding principle when I change the colour preferences on my laptop screen. He chooses his colours to reflect the text. When Jack Layton, the leader of the New Democratic Party of Canada, died, Hugh printed an excerpt from Jack's final letter to his supporters. "My friends," it begins in deep NDP orange. "Love is better than anger. Hope is better than fear." When Hugh printed "The Bridge," a poem by Shaun McLaughlin, a twelve-year-old Irish boy killed by an IRA bomb, he chose purple for bravery.

Hugh loves colour. He especially loves red. You wouldn't know this from looking at him: he wears sombre working-man clothes, mostly blues and browns, although I suspect this is not so much an aesthetic preference as a practical one, given that he is a widower who spends most of his time around ink.

"It was Verla who pointed out that I didn't use enough colour," Hugh tells me. He doesn't talk much about his wife, not because he has forgotten her, but because, even after a dozen years, he still feels her loss so sharply that his eyes well up at the mention of her name.

Verla was married before she met Hugh. She contracted polio as a young woman, which left her paraplegic. She lived with her first husband in his old family house behind the Kingston Vinegar Works. One day, the factory caught fire and she was trapped inside the house. She wasn't harmed, but the fire department insisted her husband build her a wheelchair ramp. There wasn't much money, so a neighbour built it for them. After that, to supplement the family coffers, Verla knitted sweaters and socks to sell. That first marriage dissolved long before she met Hugh, but she loved knitting so much that she carried on throughout her life. Eventually, Hugh bought her a loom and she took up weaving. When he set up his private orthotic practice, she finger-wove privacy screens, scenes of birds and landscapes. "Beautiful things!" Hugh exclaims, tears in his eyes. He still wears the sweaters she knit for him, unravelling now at the wrists, and on special occasions the sashes she wove on her small lap loom.

"When I began to print books, she complained that I was afraid to use colour, which was probably true. She spurred me on to experiment."

Not all his early experiments were successful, however.

"When I printed *The First Paradise, Odetta*, back in 1985, I used a lighter brown ink because I thought it made the text a little softer. I was a neophyte printer and the pale brown text drew a lot of scoffing from my letterpress printer friends at Wayzgoose. They said it was too hard to read."

After that, Hugh embraced bolder colours. He is especially fond of rubification, the official word for making things red, from *ruber*, the Latin word for the colour. *Rubrica* was red ochre. In the thirteenth century, "rubric" was coined to refer to the directions in a religious service, which were written in red, as were important days on the calendar—red-letter days. Red was used so often in medieval manuscripts for headings, running titles, and initials, that people assumed their books would be black and red, like the Bible I read as a girl, the words of Jesus as red as freshly spilled blood.

One might say that Hugh is rubicund, inclined to redness. He uses the colour to excellent effect on his "Saffron Fireflies" ligature poster, the bright red *fft* and *ffi* bursting out from the shadows of black words.

Colour printing came of age in the nineteenth century, when printers started using multiple colours in illustrations, especially in children's books. At first, each ink was individually mixed, but eventually systems were introduced that could produce every conceivable colour simply by overprinting the three basic colours—cyan, magenta, and yellow—with a bit of black to add richness to the hues.

Much research has been done on the readability of different colours of ink as they appear against various backgrounds—red on green, blue on yellow—but little attention has been devoted to the readability of one colour of ink as compared to another. If purple, black, and orange is each printed on white paper, which is more legible?

This hasn't been an issue since printing was mechanized and black was adopted as the universal colour for text ink, but in Gutenberg's day, when inks were ground for each project, colour may well have been a topic of conversation. And today, when readers can choose any colour for the words on their computer screens, why aren't we talking about the relative merits of grey, black, and mauve?

As the colour theorists like to point out, the real issue with reading coloured text is contrast, not the actual colour itself. Paper is never absolutely white, and even black ink is never absolutely black. How a person sees white, black, or any other colour will depend on the light shining down on the paper.

Nature doesn't deal in absolutes, but technology does. Pure black on pure white may not be possible with ink and paper, but it *is* possible on a digital screen. Even so, pure black and white are almost never used because backlighting makes the contrast so hard on the eyes. On ereaders, the background "paper" is almost always off-white, and the "ink" is off-black or dark grey. This is easier on everyone, but especially on dyslexic readers, who can be particularly sensitive to brightness, which for them causes words to swirl and blur together.

People who grew up with digital readers are used to a lot more colour in their text. I expected to discover that the colour choices were intentional, the result of years of readability research, but no. Why is Facebook blue? Because its co-developer, Mark Zuckerberg, is red-green colour blind. Blue is the colour he sees best. And why are hyperlinks typically blue? Because Tim Berners-Lee, one of the primary inventors of the web, was working with Mosaic, a very early browser that displayed web pages with black text on a dismal grey background. The most intense colour available at the time that would stand in contrast to the black text was blue. Hyperlinks have been blue ever since.

Hugh, of course, doesn't play the practicality game. He doesn't care which ink is cheapest or easiest to procure or quickest to clean up or even the easiest to read. He doesn't play the personal-preference game, either. If he did, all his books would be printed in red. But no, he chooses the ink for *The Paradise Project* the same way he approaches every other element of the printing process: by selecting a colour that is organic to the text.

Paradise is gardens, so of course the images must be green. The stories are rooted in the soil, so the ink for the text—no question—has to be an earthy brown. Precisely which green and which brown has yet to be determined.

How can I not love this guy? For him, as for me, it all starts with the words.

BOXCAR COLOUR

Hugh buys his inks from Boxcar Press in Syracuse, New York. Boxcar can premix ink to any number on the

Pantone scale, a colour-matching system developed in the late 1950s by a young university graduate, Lawrence Herbert, who was hired part-time at a print shop. Passionate about chemistry, he took it upon himself to systematize and simplify the company's stock of pigments and the production of their coloured inks. Within a few years, he had bought the company for a song, renamed it Pantone—"all colours"—and developed the familiar Pantone Guides: cardboard strips printed with related samples of colour and bound into the fan deck still used by most graphic designers and printers.

Boxcar can make ink in any Pantone colour or a printer can mix it himself. Sixteen hundred distinct hues can be produced from just fourteen colours of ink. Even the six basic colours—warm red, reflex blue, yellow, and transparent white for mixing, plus printing black and opaque white—will produce a few hundred colours.

"I don't have the full complement of fourteen, but I have more than the starter kit," Hugh boasts, but when he checks his stock, the old inks are skinned over like cold cocoa.

That wouldn't happen if he used the rubber-based inks Boxcar recommends for general letterpress printing.

"It's true the rubber-based inks don't dry out. They let a printer leave the press open longer. The ink can stay on the press overnight and still be good to print in the morning, no problem. The bad part is that when a page is printed it can take days or even weeks to dry, so you can't stack the printed pages. And I sure don't have enough room to print hundreds of copies and lay them out! I tried that once and ended up using a heat gun to blow them dry."

He picks up an old poster he printed with rubber-based ink and another printed with oil-based colour. He has that gleam in his eye that tells me we are getting to the crux of his love affair with ink.

"See that? The rubber-based inks are matte. Dull." He holds up the other sample. "Here, lift this up to the light. Not like that. Flat to the light," he says, whipping it out of my hand and giving it back, tipped at the proper angle. "See how it shines? That's oil-based ink."

He goes for the glitter every time. I wear rhinestones on my T-shirt: I'm a glitter fan, too.

"Sure," he answers before I ask. "I have inadvertently mixed oil-based and rubber-based inks and it is like mixing oil and water," he says. "I just swear a bit at Stupid Hugh, throw it out and clean the press and start over."

Oil-based colours are brighter and set up quickly, which means Hugh can stack pages as they come off the press. But if he leaves the ink on the press overnight, he'll have a royal battle on his hands to clean the rollers. And they skin in the can. Every time he starts a new project, chances are he'll have to buy fresh stock, which he does now for *The Paradise Project*: a fresh starter kit of six basic colours plus a few empty cans to hold the particular colours he'll mix.

I expect Hugh to be the sort of seat-of-the-pants printer who mixes his coloured ink by eye. And it's true: if he's printing what he calls an ephemeral—a small-edition broadside or one of his famous Christmas keepsakes—he admits he sometimes mixes a colour right on the press. Most often, though, he uses the formula that Pantone supplies.

"I have a metric weigh scale in which I can measure to the one-hundredth of a gram. If the formula calls for six parts green and twelve parts white, I estimate how much ink I'll need for a print run and then scoop out with a knife a weight of thirty grams of green and then add sixty grams of white, making a total of ninety grams. I mix them together with a slightly bent 1/8-inch rod spinning in a 1/4-inch drill."

The Paradise Project is one of the biggest projects he has printed: it will take a lot of ink. For smaller projects, he's just as likely to dole out the prescribed amount of each colour with a set of kitchen measuring spoons, working the colours together with a knife on a piece of glass on his work table.

The ink he scoops out of the cans is as thick and heavy as *dulce de leche*. His technique for hand-mixing looks a bit like scrambling eggs: the knife moves smoothly through the ink, then under and over, under and over, working and reworking until the pigments are thoroughly blended and the new colour is uniform.

"Mixing is a bit of a crapshoot because the hue of the paper will influence how the colour looks on the page," Hugh says, scooping the dark, earth-coloured ink into a spanking new ink can. "I always do a trial run, especially when I'm overprinting, because the colour underneath will affect the colour of the over-print, too."

A few days later, Hugh calls me into the shop. It is

time to decide on the precise green and brown for the printing inks. "Bring that husband of yours," he adds. "We need all the eyes we can get."

He has printed trials of one of Erik's images in the muted chartreuse that the two of them liked, and in the soft, spring-like hue that appealed to me. Over the images, he's printed words in three different hues, from dark olive to a rich oxidized brown that looks like the roan-coloured soil of Brazil, where I grew up.

The three of us peer at the pages intently. The results are clear. The next day Hugh sends out a gleeful email to Team Paradise Project:

"Erik, just so you are in the loop, Wayne, Merilyn, and I agreed that the lighter image was a wallflower saying, 'I hope that Hugh Barclay, the good-looking fellow, doesn't ask me to dance,' whereas the darker image was shouting, 'I am!' We all agreed that the ink colour you picked was best."

The chartreuse is perfect, just a shade darker than the Salad paper. The colour is named for a liqueur that has been made at the cathedral in Chartres, France, by Carthusian monks since 1737, following instructions written down in 1605. Its natural hue is the yellow-green of summer apples. The loamy brown of the text seems to have been dug from the same orchard. The words don't hold the image down like a grate, as I feared. Rather, it's as if the image has come alive and is muscling up through the fibre of the paper, pushing the words into view, bringing them to life.

I'm glad I kept my mouth shut.

When I found the letters that became the basis for *The Convict Lover*, they were a chaos of loose papers spilling out of tins across my attic floor. It was ink that helped me put the pages back together into discrete letters. Blue ink pilfered from the warden's office. Orangey-brown ink the convict made himself from boiled-down vegetables or walnuts he found by the quarry. Black ink from charred lamp wicks, or iron filings from the workshops, or soot scraped out of the stoves. For every letter—some of them twenty-five pages long—a new batch of ink that he stole or made from whatever he could find.

I have never made ink, but my sons have. They would beg me for lemons, squeeze the juice into a jar, and write their messages on paper that they'd rub over a light bulb until the heat browned the lemon words into being. Watching the words emerge reminded me

of something Vladimir Nabokov wrote, "The pages are still blank, but there is a miraculous feeling of the words being there, written in invisible ink and clamouring to become visible."

When the boys grew older, they added a little honey to give their lemon-ink the viscosity of the real thing. When they moved from detectives to medieval knights, they tried making ink from nails soaked in vinegar, combining the nail juice with boiled-down black tea.

Remembering this makes me wonder, *What is ink anyway?* Chemists define ink as a colloidal system of fine pigment particles dispersed in a solvent. Colour doesn't come into it. Neither does liquid.

Ink is much older than the paper we apply it to. Even before 2500 BCE, people were making black inks from a suspension of carbon (usually lampblack) in water, stabilized and thickened with egg white. The vehicle for modern inks can include a host of other ingredients: pH modifiers, humectants to retard premature drying, polymeric resins to impart binding and allied properties, defoamer/antifoaming agents to regulate foam efficiency, wetting agents to control surface tension, biocides to inhibit fungal and bacterial growth, and thickeners or "rheology modifiers" to control ink application.

I have just rounded up all the inks in my office. Apart from my husband's eight antique pottery ink jars, all of them empty, I have twelve bottles and four inkwells, all containing inks of various colours and in various stages of dehydration: the usual Sheaffer, Skrip, and Waterman inks for my fountain pens, a fabulous Stone blue-black ink from England that for some reason has never dried up, the Victor Hugo ink I bought in Paris that is now the consistency of old window putty, three wax-sealed bottles of ink I bought from an ink-maker in Siena, Italy—black, blue, and sepia—and the small square bottle of turquoise ink that Margaret Atwood gave to each of the other nominees when she was named Author of the Year by the Canadian Authors Association. My antique travelling letter-box from Pittenweem, Scotland, where my five-greats grandmother lived before she emigrated to Canada, has a small glass inkwell set into one end of the case, the desiccated dregs still visible.

When I was in school, being allowed to write with ink meant you'd left your puny childhood behind. In grade one, my desk had a hole in the upper-right corner, but it wasn't until grade six that the hole was fitted with a glass inkwell. By the time I got there, however, no one was writing with straight pens dipped in ink. The Bic pen hit North America the year I turned ten. The next year, ballpoint pens replaced inkwells in my grade six classroom.

It wasn't until I wrote *The Convict Lover* that I learned to love the straight pen. I chose it as the tool for my first draft for the same reason that Hugh chose Salad paper: because it fit what I was doing. With the straight pen in my hand, my sentences grew longer, my thoughts allowed to roam as long as there was ink in the nib. In the same way, writing on a typewriter chops my sentences into fragments. Onscreen, however, physical limits fall away: there is no pen to scratch the paper, no nib to run dry, no pencil point to flatten. I can write sentences and paragraphs as long I want. That's always been true, of course, but for me, the writing instrument and the ink that flows from it act on my mind to make the words come out differently.

The ink that flows from our pens—writing ink—accounts for only a small percentage of the ink that is produced today. Over ninety percent of manufactured inks are for printing, made not with liquid and soluble dyes but with oil or rubber and insoluble pigments.

Originally, even printing ink was made with water. The Koreans and the Chinese brushed their wooden characters with Chinese ink and pressed the blocks onto mulberry pages. The ink was thin and black and pooled on the type, where it was sucked up by the tissue-like paper.

In Europe, medieval scribes also used water-based ink that they kept in inkhorns fitted into holes in the sloping tops of their wooden desks. The ink itself was a solution of tannic acids from gallnuts mixed with ferrous sulfate and thickened with ground-up gum arabic. This replaced the earlier carbon-based ink. Iron gall ink soaked into the parchment, unlike carbon ink which could easily be rubbed off. Iron gall ink was shinier, too, giving words on parchment their inimitable gloss.

But whether made from iron gall or carbon, these water-based inks simply wouldn't stick to metal type well enough to avoid splotches and blurs on the stiff rag paper of fifteenth-century Europe.

Gutenberg needed an ink that would retain its

viscosity both on the slick metal surface of the type and against the extreme pressure of the press; an ink that would dry quickly enough that pages could be stacked, but not so quickly that the ink became tacky on the press; an ink whose viscosity and colour would remain consistent throughout the printing of an entire book.

At the time, painters were just beginning to work with the new medium of oil paints, which gave a depth of colour and light to the paintings that would become a trademark of the Renaissance. Oil paint dries by oxidation, the oil reacting chemically with oxygen so that it gradually changes from a liquid to a gel and finally becomes hard.

It is impossible to know which painter first mixed his or her pigments with linseed oil—the new medium arose more or less simultaneously in northern Europe and Italy—but certainly the Flemish artist Jan van Eyck was an early adopter. So, too, was Leonardo da Vinci, who mixed oils and tempera—pigments combined with a water-soluble binder, usually egg yolk—for *The Last Supper*. By 1500, tempera had all but disappeared as a painting medium, lingering on in frescoes. The new painting medium was so widely adopted that paintings on canvas were soon referred to simply as oils.

Gutenberg must have been aware of these developments. Printers and painters belonged to the same guild. They would have known what each other was up to. Painters worked on illuminated manuscripts and they worked with engravers, too, the same men who were making the moulds for Gutenberg's type.

It wouldn't have taken Gutenberg long to realize that the water-based inks used by scribes had no staying power on his new press. A look at the painters in his guild-hall would have given Gutenberg his solution: ink made with oil.

This switch from water- to oil-based ink seems a slight and obvious change, but it may well be Gutenberg's most important contribution to printing. The typeface can be exquisitely carved, the paper like velvet, the words themselves the breath of angels, but they all count for nothing if the ink won't stick.

The pigments used for printing were the same as those used for painting. Black from carbonized bone, burned without oxygen to a crisp ebony, then ground in a mortar and pestle. Or from lampblack, made by burning linseed oil in a lamp then placing a clean dish over the flame, carefully brushing off the soot that collects. Cennino Cennini describes the process in *Il Libro dell'Arte* (*The Craftsman's Handbook*). Written fifty years before Gutenberg invented his press, the book is still in print today and available digitally at Project Gutenberg. To get the deepest black imaginable, a printer had to commit to some serious bone-grinding. Cennini doesn't pull any punches: "grind this black for the space of half an hour, or an hour, or as long as you like; but know that if you were to work it up for a year, it would be so much blacker and better a colour."

Black from bones, blue from the semiprecious Asian gem lapis lazuli, red from cinnabar (once believed to be the blood of dragons), the colours ground to a fine powder and mixed in perfect proportion with oil: these produced the first printer's inks. My arm gets tired grinding a few flax seeds in a mortar and pestle; I can hardly imagine the muscles on the young men who apprenticed to the work. Or the young women, for Cennini advises that the grinding of lapis lazuli, the perfect blue used to paint the Virgin Mary, "is an occupation for pretty girls rather than for men; for they are always at home, and reliable, and they have more dainty hands. Just beware of old women."

(Given the laborious grinding required for printing inks, it seems amazing to me that power grinders weren't developed until the early 1800s, especially given that specialized ink-makers were in business almost as soon as presses were running.)

As impressive as a year of grinding sounds, the real key to good printing ink was the oil. Pure linseed oil was the gold standard in Gutenberg's day and still is. The oil was heated and subjected to prolonged boiling at a high temperature to produce a varnish with the viscosity to carry the pigment and withstand the press, as well as the ramped-up appetite for oxygen that would convert the ink from a gummy substance to one that was solid at room temperature.

For those who have seen a Gutenberg Bible, the difference is clear: the blacks so rich and glossy they might have been printed yesterday. His ink was good. According to Martyn Lyons in *Books: A Living History*, Gutenberg's recipe was lampblack mixed with varnish and egg white. He got his spectacular results with fastidious grinding, no doubt, but historians postulate a secret ingredient, too. A Roman army physician in the first century recommended adding to the ink the "urine of an uncorrupt boy," and indeed Cennini specifies *not* to grind red "lac" with urine, implying that urinating into the ink was common practice, and in this case, to be avoided.

The inky problems Gutenberg faced and overcame were legion. The lampblack had to be roasted to degrease it. If he wanted coloured inks—and he must have in order to produce a book up to the standard of the scribes—he had to grind the minerals until the particles were consistently fine as dust. The oil had to be exactly the right viscosity and the finished ink identical in colour and texture from batch to batch within each project. And that was just the beginning. How much pressure was needed to get the ink on the paper without smearing it or leaving blank spots? How much ink had to be applied to the press to produce a good image without filling in the bowls of the *e*'s and *c*'s and smudging the page?

Without varnish, the pigment wouldn't stick to the type and without its drying properties, the advantage of a mass-producing printing press would have been lost. But the varnish-making stage of the ink-making process was lengthy and risky, given that oil, when heated, can spontaneously combust. It was such a dangerous undertaking that twice a year the printer and his apprentices would travel outside the town walls to make ink, turning the foray into a party with free-flowing schnapps and bread rolls fried crisp in the boiling oil. Linseed oil is edible—in fact, it is prescribed as a nutritional supplement—but rolls deep-fried in print-er's oil? I make a mental note never to tell Hugh this bit of ink history or he'll be boiling up vats of the stuff, one more way to get printer's ink into his blood.

I tap four letters on my computer keyboard.

WORD

Three seconds. It is easy to take this simple gesture for granted, to forget that for half a millennium, hun-dreds of men and women cracked their skulls trying to solve the problem of making words visible, transferable, indelible.

I squint at the screen. My *WORD* is visible and transferable, but how indelible is it really?

BEACH BALLS & GHOSTS

I can easily imagine grinding sheep's bones, inking rollers, and watching varnish burst into flame. But I'm stumped by the electronic micro-wizardry that makes the words I type on my keyboard appear on a computer screen.

If you are reading this book on a dedicated ereader such as a Kindle or a Kobo, the letters are likely made visible with E Ink. E Ink stands for electrophoretic ink, which isn't just ink; it is both paper and ink rolled into one.

E Ink was developed at the MIT Media Lab. Xerox has a version, too. In both cases, the ereader "ink" is made up of millions of little capsules, each one filled with tiny pigmented balls that float in an oily substance. I try to imagine them as the manufacturers suggest:

think of the capsules as clear beach balls filled with thousands of white Ping-Pong balls suspended in a blue liquid. Okay, I can do that. If I look down on the beach ball, onto the white Ping-Pong balls that have all floated to the surface of the liquid inside, the beach ball looks white. If I hold the ball above my head so that all I see is the liquid, the ball looks blue.

In an ereader display, these teeny-weeny "beach balls" or capsules are suspended between two sheets of super-thin plastic that are divided into cells like 3D graph

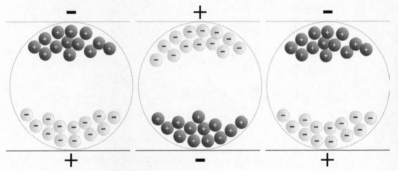

paper—about 100,000 balls fit into every square inch of ereader display. Each cell is wired to microelectronics in the plastic sheet that control whether the capsules have a negative or a positive charge. This charge determines whether the Ping-Pong balls inside the capsules are submerged or floating, creating patterns of light and dark that appear as letters, words, and sentences.

That's how the ink in an ereader works. However, if you are reading on a tablet, a smartphone, a computer, or even a flat-screen television, the words are made visible through LCD (liquid crystal display) technology. Liquid crystals sounds like an oxymoron, but the crystal in question normally exists in a state somewhere between a liquid and a solid: I imagine something like a slushie. Even a small increment of heat will make the liquid crystal truly liquid, which is why a computer screen goes wonky when left out in the sun.

LCD technology has been around for a long time by contemporary standards: about forty years. Basically, on an LCD screen, words and images are made up of millions of tiny blocks called pixels (picture elements), each of which is effectively a separate red, blue, or green light that can be switched on or off very rapidly to make a moving colour picture. (On original iPod screens, the pixels were black and were either switched on or off, creating a black and white screen.) The liquid crystals control the passage of light through the screen. When voltage is applied, the transformed crystals block the light and that pixel appears dark. It's actually much more complicated than that, but like the beach balls, this gives a rudimentary sense of how the technology works.

In geek chat rooms across the Internet, there is a running debate about which is superior, E Ink or LCD display. The E Ink used in ereaders, for the moment at least, only comes in black. It's slow to refresh, which means that each turn of the "page" on an ereader can leave a ghost image of the previous page on the screen for a few seconds. On the plus side, E Ink actually looks like ink. Weirdly, it appears to have depth and texture. Almost like the real thing.

LCD technology comes in all the colours of the rainbow. In the last ten seconds I've changed the words I'm writing on my laptop from turquoise to orange to lime-green. If black is too harsh, I change it to charcoal, or dove grey, or boot-leather brown. This technology effectively shifted decisions about colour and intensity from the designer's hand to the reader's.

Those who love ereaders claim that E Ink is easier on the eyes, but the claim doesn't stand up in the lab. When fatigue or eye strain is measured, there is no difference in the effect of E Ink and LCD displays. The age of the device does matter, however. Old-model, low-resolution LCD screens cause more eyestrain than newer, high-resolution LCD screens.

But how do both of these ways of getting words onto digital screens stack up against the dark chocolate ink that Hugh is printing onto our cream Salad paper? The most obvious difference is that once Hugh's ink hits the paper, it's there forever.

Well, maybe not forever. Hugh boasted that the oil-based ink he buys from Boxcar will last 500 years, but he also told me that, years ago, he printed a passage from Kahlil Gibran's *The Prophet* and hung it on his office wall, facing south. The title was printed in red above black text. After several years, he noticed that the title had disappeared. When he looked closely, he could see tiny peelings of red ink dusting the bottom of the frame. Given enough time, ink will flake off, it will fade, its permanence an illusion.

How long will E Ink last? Trying to predict the

longevity of a new technology is a mug's game, but early claims that ninety percent of E Ink displays would last more than ten years under typical conditions have proven true. The Sony LIBRIé ereader, introduced in 2004, was the first to use E Ink. In 2015, those E Ink displays were still going strong. By then, seventeen million ebook reading devices had been sold with E Ink displays.

It boggles the mind to think that all the words I could ever write will fit inside an ereader. The little coloured Ping-Pong balls just keep rolling around inside those teeny beach balls, endlessly rearranging themselves into new words on command. No cinnabar to flake off the page. No smudges, no stains. No physical substance with a set of needs and requirements, a life of its own. No ink to get into the blood. Only beach balls and slushy crystals. Only ghosts.

ON TRIAL

You can't hide anything from ink. It is like the teacher with eyes in the back of her head who can see the boys making spit-balls, the girls passing notes. Nothing is safe from its scrutiny. It shows up every flaw in the type: the missing tittle above an *i*, one side of a *t*-cross snapped off, a bent *s*, a worn-down *D*, a river of spaces streaming white down the page. A little lazy at pounding the type flat into the chase? Ink will make your sins manifest, printing only the words that rise up above the others. It is ruthless in its lack of forgiveness: every irregularity in the press bed, in the chase, and in the individual letters of type has to be fixed before ink will flow every word onto the page.

"I'm quite sticky about setting type because I am just that anal," says Hugh. Even so, inevitably there are mistakes, errors that are hard to catch when reading the type itself, set as a mirror image of the page. This is why printers run proofs, trial pressings of each page in a standard black ink. The proof shows up mistakes in the spelling and grammar, but it also reveals deficiencies in the type that need to be corrected for the ink to do its work.

Proofs are scanned by Hugh and his proofreader, Faye Batchelor. I can tell I live in a small community when the circle closes: Faye was Erik's elementary school art teacher. When he came back from Berlin after his apprenticeship with Attila Lukacs, Erik had a show of paintings in the gallery where I launched *The Lion in the Room Next Door*, with Karl and his musical friends providing the ambience. Faye was there. She bought the best painting Erik produced in Berlin. I was jealous. Last year, when she moved into a smaller house, she handed the painting to me, and I handed it on to Erik. Round and round.

"Faye keeps me straight on nuances like repeating words or using a wrong font when I set type," says Hugh. She also checks for damaged or bent type that doesn't take the ink as it should. "We're both concerned with maintaining the standard of the press, and this requires constant vigilance: removing all typos, controlling the negative spacing, and having the same amount of inking and pressure on each page. The standard we have set is high and mostly we meet it, but we're never perfect."

Hugh enlists me as a proofreader, too. Working with a writer who lives an hour outside town flummoxes him at first—how will he get the proofs to me?—but then he hits on a solution.

"I always thought I would need to mail the pages to you for proofreading and this would mean the type-setting would be at a standstill until the dogsled reached Upper Oak Leaf Road and I'd be twiddling my thumbs until you got back to me via email to say all was okay or that I had left out a comma. However, after watching an ad on TV, my brain finally clicked in and I saw the pos-sibilities of using a scanner to email the typeset proof to you. I feel bad about not feeding the sled dogs, but time marches on."

What is the almighty rush? I think. When my books are commercially printed, and when I make the ebook, too, I receive the entire book to proof with a few weeks in which to accomplish the task. Surely Hugh is just being persnickety. But on the day I deliver the first set of page proofs to his studio, I understand. I find him standing by the press, staring vacantly at the platen, watching the ink dry before his eyes. All his chases are tight with type. His work is stopped. He can't set more type until these four pages are inked and printed, and he can't do that until Faye and I call in our corrections. It may have been obvious to everyone but me, but at last I get it: *The Paradise Project* will be typeset, inked, and proofed four pages at a time, as if it is made up of fifteen thin little books.

"It's about time," says Hugh, grabbing the pages from my hand. "I was about to dock your pay!"

He drags a stool to his worktable with one hand and with the other, pulls a chase towards him. He finds the right proof and unlocks the chase.

"Don't worry," I say, backing towards the door. "I'll let myself out." He is already picking at the letters with his bodkin.

"Yeah, yeah," he mumbles, waving a hand at me. I'm not sure if he's saying goodbye or dismissing me like a lord with much more important things to do.

CHASE KISS

Hugh is mixing the dark chocolate brown ink we've chosen for the text. Eighty percent cacao, I'd say, melted in a *bain-marie*, one of my favourite cooking gizmos, just a simple ridged ring of aluminum that sits in a pan of simmering water.

Cooking and printing aren't that far apart. With an old kitchen knife, Hugh scoops two dollops of rich, dark ink onto the disc of the press. The ink looks black, but I know from the hours we spent comparing colour chips that this is not black, which is all colours, but rather Pantone 497, a darkness that approaches black through a spectrum of magenta and yellow with nary a drop of blue.

The disc being inked is the size of a pie sufficient

for a family of eight. It is made up of two parts: an inner circle and an outer ring, both perfectly, exquisitely flat. Hugh flips a switch, and the disc moves towards vertical at the same moment that a lattice of rollers rises up to lick across the surface, smoothing the dollops of ink into two streaks. Up and back, up and back. Each time the disc moves towards the rollers, the outer ring shifts a few degrees in one direction and the inner circle rotates a fraction the opposite way so that the rollers lick a different part of the surface with each pass. Within seconds, the entire disc is slick with ink, damp and glistening, but still the rollers lick, lick, lick with admirable persistence.

In Gutenberg's day, the ink was spread by a press man holding a leather pouch filled with rags. He'd rock the pouch over ink slathered on a stone, then he'd rock it back and forth over the type.

"Definitely an acquired skill," Hugh says. The first book he helped print—his own collection of poems— was printed on a simple flatbed press, not unlike the one Gutenberg invented. Hugh inked his poetic type by hand using a small roller called a brayer.

"Getting even coverage and the proper amount of ink for each impression took practice," he grins, "and yielded more than a few seconds."

He has turned off the motor. The rollers are still. He leans over the press, inserts a piece of thick, creamy paper just so, and gives the flywheel on the press a turn with his hand. The inked disc rises to vertical, the rollers pass over it and, on their downward stroke, smear ink over

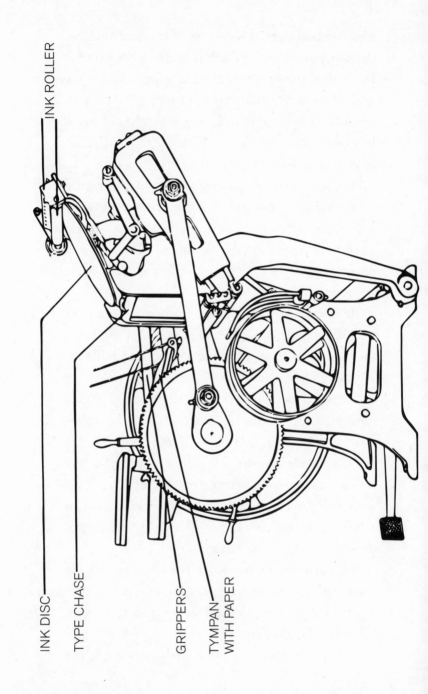

INK ROLLER

INK DISC

TYPE CHASE

GRIPPERS

TYMPAN
WITH PAPER

the bed where my words are set in mirror image in the chase. Then, in a movement as smooth as Fred Astaire, the inked type moves forward, the paper moves forward, too, and they meet—*smack!*—a quick, chaste kiss that springs them apart, my words transferred to a piece of paper that can be picked up, read, passed hand to hand, folded into an envelope, mailed around the world.

"Too much ink," Hugh grumbles, swiping his fingers across the letters. They don't smudge, but some of the *e*'s are filled in, and so is an uppercase *W*. Hugh wipes down the type, turns the flywheel again, and prints another trial page. The two look identical to me.

"Much better!" he exclaims.

WORDS, ONLY WORDS

Hugh, the printer, looks over at Erik, the painter. They are standing on opposite sides of a small table strewn with squares of paper and gobs of ink in shades of yellow, green, and chartreuse. Behind them, hunched like a gargoyle, its flywheel an unlikely red, sits the printing press. All morning they have been inking Erik's woodblocks, setting them into the press, pulling proofs, cleaning off the blocks, trying again.

"Your blocks are super," Hugh says, puffing with pride as if he'd carved them himself. "If we can get exactly the right colour, they'll become ghost images. That aspect appeals to me. And I like the way you start some of them off the page. Of course, the page size will vary slightly because we rip them from the large sheet, and the deckle adds a-whole-nother dimension."

I'm listening in like an eight-year-old allowed to sit at the adult table. Erik has brought along what he calls a flatplan, a thumbnail layout of all the pages, showing the approximate length of text for each story, with the position of the block prints appearing as pale ovals at the bottom of roughly every other spread. He emailed it to us weeks ago, so that Hugh could start typesetting pages that had no images. Now, the two of them peer at the flatplan, discussing gutters.

"If we run the artwork for the quarter title over the gutter it will end up on page 16, but if we skillfully cut the block and print the first part on page 1 and the remainder on page 2 the image will appear to cross the gutter," says Hugh.

"Neat!"

"It will take a bit of planning, but what else is new?" Hugh casts a glance in my direction and smirks. "Wouldn't it be nice if we had an easy job like a writer?" Yesterday he sent me a quote he found on the website of Library and Archives Canada: "Authors don't write a book, they write a manuscript that is made into a book by others."

I read it like a slap on the wrist.

How much of a book are the words on the page? The answer comes easily to me—all of it! The stories in *The Paradise Project* have been gestating for years. I wrote the first one a decade ago while I was working on *The Holding*. I'm not a poet, but now and then an idea stops me and out roll the words carrying an image so succinct and polished that I think, *Maybe this is what a poem feels like.*

"Stone" was like that, a thread that spooled out, not a break in the words, although the story spans a hundred years, coursing through the tension between a man and nature, a man and a woman, and within the woman herself, all of it unfolding in just thirty-nine lines. The piece has hardly changed since that first laying down of words.

An easy job like a writer. The words make me cringe. It *is* an easy job, at least on those days when the words are lining up, compliant and raring to go. Even when they aren't, when I spend hours lugging commas from here to there, shovelling in new phrases, axing them out again, prying words apart, wedging in fresh ones, even then what survives looks easy. The better the writing, the easier it looks. An art, as Shakespeare said, that conceals itself.

So I feel guilty, with this easy job of mine. No ink under my fingernails, no dangerous flywheels or finger-grabbing clamps, no boiling oil or noxious fumes. I have to admit, words are just the start of this paradise project of ours, the seed in the soil, the glint in the eye.

The same might be said of Erik's images. When he delivered them to the print shop this morning, Hugh was excited but cautious.

"One never knows until the ink is on the paper," he warned.

Ink, the final arbiter.

Hugh loves to overprint images. To his mind, it gives the writing depth. He prefers obscure or abstract images.

"Abstracts give the reader the opportunity to interpret the image in a number of ways, none of which have a right or wrong answer. If you wrote a poem about a house with a mountain in the background and I made a print of the house with a mountain in the background, I am really saying to the reader, 'I know you are stupid so I thought I should draw you a picture of what the poet is trying to tell you.' I'm sure you agree that would not be a good idea."

Hugh has illustrated several of the books he has printed, most often using the soft block technique he developed, overprinting the images again and again in a process called reduction printing that can create a multicoloured image with just one block.

"Let's say I start with a square block. I print the entire square in a light yellow. Then I reduce the block by cutting away a section, say a triangle, and ink it again with a different colour, say, blue. When I print the page again, the blue overprints the yellow, except where the triangle was cut away. That's yellow. Then I reduce the block further by cutting out a circle. I overprint the page again, this time using purple ink, creating a three-colour image of a yellow triangle and a blue circle on a purple background."

When Hugh first showed Erik his soft blocks, I think he was secretly hoping the young artist would adopt his technique. But Erik is a traditionalist. He carved his images into thin pieces of lino that Hugh glues onto backing blocks of composite hardwood.

Hugh and Erik test-print the images alone, then with an overprint of text. When they are satisfied, Erik cleans the linocuts and stacks the blocks neatly in order under Hugh's work table, ready for the press whenever Hugh is.

Three years later, I go looking for those blocks.

"I have no idea where they are," Erik says. Hugh just shrugs when I ask. For men who love to work in the three dimensions of the real world, they display a curious disregard for material objects.

Neither remembers trashing the blocks.

"I normally leave the ink to dry on the blocks when I'm finished with them, so they can't be used again," Hugh says. "I never deface them. I couldn't do that."

"Mind if I rummage around in your workshop?"

"Go crazy," he says.

I find half a dozen buried in the rubble under Hugh's work table. Another four are propping up one end of a sheaf of long paper. Two more are hanging out with the soft blocks on top of the type cabinet. One is missing. I find it weeks later in Hugh's living room, under a pile of books. I feel like a rescue dog, saving victims of an avalanche. Now Erik's blocks stand among the books on my office shelves, *madeleines* of my toil in the fields of Gutenbergia. For Christmas, I frame one for Erik beside the test-page printed with that image.

When Erik designs the digital version of *The Paradise Project*, I insist on including the images. But there is no way to print text over an image on an ereader screen. The Ping-Pong balls inside those beach balls are either black or white. No tonal shading, no floating images, no hope of adding depth to a page. In the end, Erik positions his linocuts as small icons that begin each story, which is lovely, but it's not the same.

"But look!" Erik says. He clicks on the image, and it looms as large as in the printed book.

Still, on the digital page, my words stand alone, the way I thought I wanted them to be. But now I miss the image rising up from under the words.

Hugh has ruined me.

SAVING GRACE

A week after the image trials are done, I walk into Hugh's studio and find him cleaning up. Garbage bags sit plumped on the floor. The counters are swept clean.

"What's going on?"

"I'm straightening up. I do this every few years, you know."

I open a garbage bag and peer in.

"There are proofs in here! The first pages of my book!"

"Yes. So?"

"What about archives?"

"What about them?"

I think Hugh must be teasing me. He isn't.

"They're just proofs," he says. He stops what he is doing and stares at me with genuine puzzlement. "It's okay, don't worry, we have those pages printed. We don't need that garbage."

To him, a proof is just a way station, one of many along the path to a finished page, which is all he really cares about.

I am pulling out the crumpled papers smeared with ink from the filthy rags he's tossed into the bag.

"This breaks my heart, Hugh."

I mean it. I can't throw anything out. My basement is stacked with boxes of letters and photos and mementoes from my parents, my husband's parents, my long-dead aunts and uncles, my grandfather's wedding tie, his christening outfit. If a thing is old, if it has no apparent practical use, if there is a word scribbled anywhere on it, my sisters ship it off to me.

"We need these, Hugh. How will anyone ever know how we got from there to here?" I gesture wildly from the type in the hellbox to the pages stacked on the drying counter.

"From where?"

It's me who is speaking a foreign language now.

"There. Wherever we started. We'll keep the end result, but what about the process?"

I still have the deck of cards I made when I was ten, each back coloured in a blue and red design, each front copied from my parents' bridge deck. I have that Linotype slug with my name in italics from my first visit to the compositing room when I was a cub reporter in Stratford. I have every draft of every story I have ever written.

"The process is over!" Hugh exclaims, waving his arms as if to make all the garbage bags disappear so we can end this ridiculous conversation. "The trial is finished! Move on! We've got work to do!"

But I'm hauling paper out of the bags, salvaging what I can, tossing the rest down around my ankles until the floor is adrift with pages.

Hugh stands there, hands on hips, shaking his head. "And I thought you would come in shouting, 'Oh boy! Look how clean the floor is!'"

I rummage under the counter and in the back corners until I find a decent-sized cardboard box.

"This," I say with all the firmness I can muster, "is the archive box. Don't throw anything in the garbage. Throw it in here. Understand? I want all the proof sheets. All your scribbles, all your notes, your tests, your smears of ink." I want to ask him to date the pages he saves, but even I know that is asking too much.

"All of it, understand?"

Hugh nods meekly, but I catch his smirk. I'll be lucky if anything ends up in the box I've neatly labelled in block letters, *ARCHIVES*.

And maybe that's okay. When Erik and I make the digital book of *The Paradise Project*, there is no paper to save. We work through the design issues digitally, sending PDF after PDF back and forth. I label all the versions and save them in digital folders, along with the final PDFs, but I will never have the pleasure of pulling out fresh manila files that I label in black ink, *PARADISE PROJECT EBOOK*. I will never line up the banker's boxes on our storage shelves. I will never pass the files and boxes into the hands of Heather, the Queen's University archivist who backs her van up to our door every few years to haul away another load of boxes.

Will I ever print out those digital files? Probably not.

And the odd thing is, as much as I was desperate to salvage those crumpled proofs, I don't really care about the digital files. They don't seem real to me. Interesting, yes. Valuable, maybe. But not real.

ONE-OF-A-KIND

The Chinese have a proverb: "The faintest ink is better than the best memory."

In *The Paper Garden*, Molly Peacock describes how, in 1773, Mrs. Mary Delany made her famous paper mosaics of garden flowers. She'd start by painting a background sheet of paper flat black, then paste on the petals, stems, and other plant parts that she cut from either white paper or sheets she'd painted herself, sometimes shading in another colour after the cut-out petals were glued down.

How well these paper-flower mosaics have survived depends to a large extent on the kind of pigment she used. Where she used a pure black pigment, the backgrounds are relatively smooth and unblemished. But sometimes her pigments contained impurities such as copper. And sometimes, in a rush to finish or feeling an economic pinch, she would stretch her paint by mixing in iron gall ink. We know now that iron gall acidifies paper, drying it out, crazing the paint. Whatever economies of the moment she enjoyed, they were gained at the expense of her legacy.

Expediency and economy over quality: it's a compromise I've made a thousand times. Buying the slightly limp grocery-store lettuce instead of walking the extra five blocks for fresh, plump heads at the farmer's market. Choosing the cheap and cheerful skirt that won't last out the season, the dollar-store notebook with pages that suck up ink and drool it out, turning periods into puddles.

I came to Hugh's studio thinking that ink was such a small and insignificant part of the printing process that it hardly warranted a conversation. Why not thin it out with iron gall? Buy the cheapest on the market? Who will notice? Who will care?

I should have known the answer: Hugh will.

I lounge against the work table as he mixes up enough chocolate ink to print 300 copies of every page of *The Paradise Project*. It's not as much ink as I expect.

"Each two-page spread uses up about one-thousandth of a gram of ink," he says. "When you think of the power, the beauty, the drama that can be conveyed using a thousandth of a gram of ink, it is quite amazing, at least to me. After forty-five years, I am still amazed every time I see a printed page emerge from the press."

The amount of ink on the disc decreases slightly with each impression. During the printing process, Hugh will have to watch the ink coverage closely and replenish it when the impression begins to fade.

"Because of ink," Hugh says, "every page is just a little bit different."

The idea stops me in my tracks.

When I hold one of the books Hugh printed, I assume that it is exactly the same as every other book in that printing. I assume that my first-edition copy of Michael Ondaatje's *The English Patient*, published by McClelland & Stewart, is exactly the same as yours. After all, isn't that the point of Gutenberg's invention: the exact and speedy replication of a text? I open the pages of a book firm in the belief that the text I am about to read is identical to the text that every other buyer of this book is reading. I see what they see. Our experience is the same.

"When I put a book together," Hugh goes on, "I select the pages that match in terms of the impression of the ink on the paper."

He muses on as if this is an ordinary conversation. I am reeling. Once again, Hugh has blasted my assumptions to smithereens. Large press runs on commercial machines may produce identical copies, but each page that rolls off Hugh's press is infinitesimally different from the one that came before it and the one that will come after. The type is the same. The paper is the same. The press is the same.

The poet and book designer Robert Bringhurst says that writing is the solid form of language. But Hugh has taught me otherwise: the solid form of language isn't writing, it's ink.

PRESS
PRESS
PRESS
PRESS

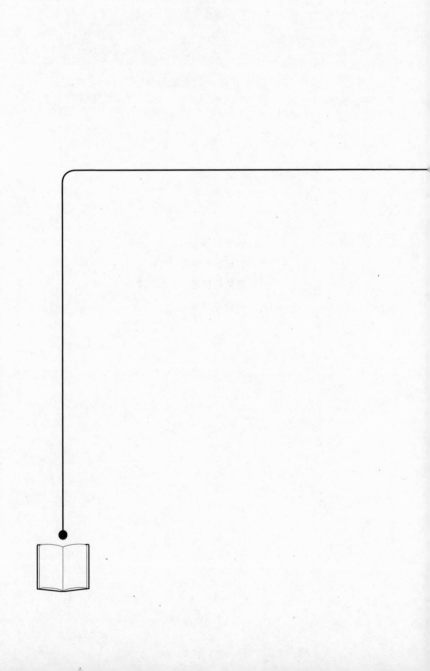

NO SMALL POTATOES

When my boys were young, every year in late November, we'd choose half a dozen of the biggest potatoes from the bin in the cellar and cut them in half. The boys would draw a candy cane or a fir tree or an alien with a star on the flat side of the potato, and I'd cut away everything but the picture, leaving it in raised relief. They'd take turns pressing their half-potatoes on a green or red or purple ink pad, then rock the inked flesh against a piece of folded card. Again and again we'd shift the cut potatoes from ink to paper until the table was covered with red aliens and green candy canes in a forest of purple trees.

That's how I thought the printing of *The Paradise Project* would proceed. We'd get all the pages typeset, stack up all the paper and the tins of ink, then get down to it, printing all 300 copies of its sixty-plus pages at one go. It would be a long day, sure, but it would be over all at once.

If I was learning anything from my time with Hugh it was that, more likely than not, my assumptions were wrong.

GUTENBERG'S PRESS

For its first 300 years, the printing press was not considered the brainchild of Gutenberg. Johann Fust and Peter Schöffer were credited as the inventors, with Gutenberg mentioned in passing as their "associate." In fact, Fust and Schöffer were Gutenberg's financial backers, and while they didn't invent the press, it's fair to say that the press would not have come about as soon as it did without their support.

Gradually I've come to understand that the printing press wasn't one invention, it was a series of problems that had to be solved: getting paper that would take an impression, type that could be easily interchanged and reused, ink that would stick to metal yet dry quickly. By comparison, developing the press itself seems relatively straightforward.

Presses of one sort or another have been in use for millennia. Over the years, I have owned a flower press, a laundry press, a butter press, a cookie press, a French press for coffee, and a cider press for apples. Basically, a press is any apparatus that applies pressure, especially downward pressure, in order to compact something into a smaller, denser, flatter form. In the process, liquid or juice is often expressed.

Once the printing press took hold, it hijacked the word so that now printing presses are simply presses, as in "Stop the presses!" The word has even come to stand for the entire profession of journalism, as in *Meet the Press*. It is interesting to note that the word "expression" dates back to 1460, about the time the Gutenberg Bible was being printed. The original meaning of expression was "to represent in words or symbols." Later, the word came to mean something closer to "produce." A French press expresses coffee. A printing press expresses words.

Once he developed type and ink, Gutenberg could have simply laid a piece of paper over the type and rubbed. The Chinese and Koreans had been doing that for centuries.

But the rag paper made in Europe was stiff and thick. Rubbing wouldn't have worked. The letters had to bite into the paper to create the indentations to hold the ink, and that required pressure.

Historians speculate that Gutenberg got the idea for his press from the wine presses he must have seen in Mainz and Strasbourg, both cities located in the great wine-producing valley of the Rhine. Mechanical wine presses had been in use since Archimedes invented the screw, a marvellously simple machine that provides the force to draw two surfaces together. Early Greeks and Romans used a screw press turned by slaves or oxen to lower a stone into a vat to crush grapes, the juice running out a bottom spout. Olives were pressed for oil the same way. In the middle ages, the screw press was refined by adding a basket made of spaced wood slats bound together by metal rings. Grapes would be loaded into the basket and a heavy horizontal stone disc screwed down into them until juice poured out through the gaps.

The cider press that Wayne and I used every September to turn bushels of apples into a hundred litres of juice operated on exactly the same principle. Our stone house was situated in the remains of a century-old apple orchard. We'd dump fall apples into the hopper of the press, where they'd be chopped into mash that fell into a stave bucket below. When the bucket was full of apple mash, we'd position it under a metal screw that lowered a heavy wooden disc into the fruit to press out the juice.

By the time Gutenberg was working through the problems of reproducing words on paper, screw presses were being used for things other than fruit juice and olive oil. They stamped patterns onto cloth. And they pressed paper to remove moisture from the rag mush, flattening the page. I peer at the paper press in the background of Jost Amman's illustration of an early paper mill in his *Book of Trades*, published in 1568. It looks remarkably like the printing press in his illustration of a printer's shop.

Gutenberg needed the horizontal pressure of a paper press, but with a lot more force. And the pressure needed to be absolutely consistent if he was to get an impression of every letter of type across the page. He also needed a sudden "elasticity"—a sharp, hard, quick meeting of paper and type to avoid the smudging that slow, uneven pressure would inevitably produce. He also needed a way of changing the paper fast. After all, the point of the exercise was to better the speed of the scribe's pen.

The printing press Gutenberg developed could do all of these things. The type was set into a frame on a perfectly flat granite or marble surface. The stone was mounted on rails so that it could slide quickly into place under the press and back out again. The type was inked with an ink ball, then a sheet of paper was laid over it. A hinged frame, called a tympan, held the paper in place. This was topped with a frisket, a frame of parchment that protected the margins of the paper from being sullied by the press.

The stone with its topping of paper was slid into the press under a heavy horizontal metal plate—the original platen, the part of the press that provides the weight to press the inked type against the paper. A lever released the screw to press down quickly and heavily, causing the type to impress the paper and the ink to transfer. The second the platen touched the paper, the lever drew it back up. After the page was printed, the stone was slid out, the frisket and tympan lifted, the printed page removed and hung up to dry.

The process took two or three skilled craftsmen: one to ink the type, one to fit the paper in place, and one to lower the platen. A good team could print a page every twenty seconds.

I imagine Gutenberg as a man made in the same

mould as Hugh, pulling proof after proof, holding pages up to the light, trying to figure out what went wrong when the type failed to impress the page or when the impression was too light or the ink drooled and eddied on the paper.

To get an even distribution of ink, both the platen and the stone had to be absolutely flat and parallel to each other. But even with a perfectly true, heavy screw press, the paper was still too hard to take a good impression, which led to Gutenberg's trick of dampening every other sheet and pressing them together for a few hours until the moisture distributed itself evenly.

No one knows how long he worked to perfect all the elements of the mechanical process, but according to three separate medieval writers, the bugs were worked out by 1440. At the age of roughly forty-five, Gutenberg finally had a working printing press.

HUGH'S PRESS

A print shop collapses time. Hugh is standing at his press, a machine that has a platen with a tympan, a press bed with a chase, and an ink plate with rollers and a giant hinge that brings all three—paper, type, and ink—together in a swift intersection that Gutenberg would recognize as a process not much different from his own.

Hugh was also forty-five when he got his first press: an eight-by-twelve-inch Chandler & Price. He tells me it was built in the late nineteenth century as a "jobber" for printing invitations, stationery, and such. Harrison T. Chandler, an Illinois banker, and William H. Price, the son of a builder of printing presses, had become partners in the early 1880s for the purpose of building a high-quality workhorse platen press to service the rapidly expanding printing industry.

For 350 years, printing presses had not advanced much from the simple wooden hand press that Gutenberg invented. But in 1800, the metal Stanhope press was introduced: faster and more durable, it had a large plate that allowed a printer to ink an entire folio—four pages of text printed on one sheet of paper—at a go. In 1811, the London *Times* acquired a steam-driven press that could print 1,100 sheets an hour, ten times as much as a hand-press operator working at top speed. Mechanical presses proliferated: by 1880, there were a hundred different platen presses on the market, most of them lightweight, awkward, even dangerous to operate.

In 1884, Chandler and Price introduced their famous jobber press, manufactured in Cleveland, Ohio. It wasn't an original design: they used the expired patents of George Phineas Gordon, an actor-turned-printer who invented a jobbing press. He called it the Franklin press, claiming that Benjamin Franklin had revealed the design to him in a dream, but it has since been known as the Gordon Jobber.

Instead of the common "clamshell" design, where the platen was hinged at the bottom to receive a piece of paper thrust between the type and the inked surface, the Gordon design had a vertical press bed on a long hinge that brought the platen and paper up to the inked type so the two were parallel. The Chandler & Price variation was powered by a small quarter-horse-power motor, although some models came with a foot-operated treadle. The company advertized its press as "strong, reliable, simple," and it became instantly popular. By the turn of the twentieth century, the company boasted there was at least one Chandler & Price press in every print shop in every town in America. It maintained its status through the '30s and '40s and survived even when other platen printing press manufacturers went under, victims of the boom in offset printing that took hold in the 1950s. When Chandler & Price closed its doors in 1964, it was the only American company still producing a hand-fed, flywheel-driven platen press.

Chandler & Price produced some 100,000 printing presses over the ninety years they were in business, and they were as much a fixture in small Canadian print shops as they were south of the border.

Hugh's Chandler & Price came from Jackson Press, a large Kingston print shop. When we first met over *The Convict Lover* bookmark, Hugh told me his press was built in 1890. We are well into publishing *The Paradise Project* when I grow curious about the provenance of his press. I email him for the serial number so I can check the date of manufacture.

"I didn't even know it had a serial number!"

"Look on the front edge of the press bed."

Der Buchdrucker.

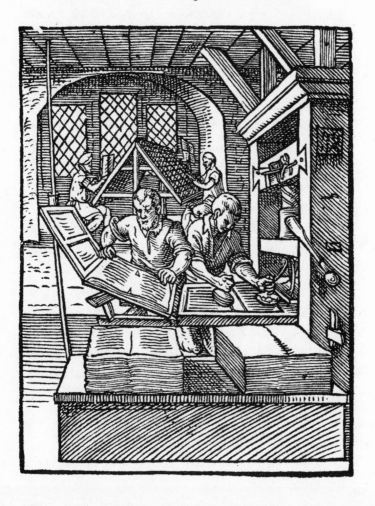

Within minutes he gets back to me. "I found it! The serial number is 50108."

Chandler & Price introduced their New Series of platen press in 1912. The Old Series was more ornate, with a high base, a curved-spoke flywheel, and curlicue castings befitting a Victorian machine. The New Series was plainer and heavier, with a lower, more utilitarian silhouette. Its flywheel was smaller, and the flywheel spokes were straight: more Edwardian than Victorian. The whole machine was painted black with natty gold pinstriping.

The New Series begins at number B-50000. Hugh's press is number B-50108, which makes it the 108th Chandler & Price built according to the new, improved design.

Although Jackson Press was the largest printer in eastern Ontario, nothing survives of the original owner of Hugh's press except a lovely old red-brick building, in the heart of downtown Kingston, that still bears its name. The press closed its doors in the early 1970s, but Hugh didn't buy his press directly from Jackson.

"At the time, Faye was going around buying up letterpresses from the print shops that were closing down and selling them to schools. She bought one of the Jackson Press jobbers. She lived down the street from me, and after the press had sat in her basement for a year or two, I bought it from her."

The same Faye who has been proofing the pages of my book.

Faye's brother, a big, strapping lad, and Hugh muscled the press up her basement stairs. This was no mean feat: the Chandler & Price weighs over a thousand pounds. Hugh took it apart and ferried the pieces to his house on a wagon, depositing them in the corner of his orthotics office where it sits today, fully restored, the braces and orthotics gone, replaced by reams of paper, drawers of type, and pots of ink.

"The press was in terrible shape," Hugh recalls. "I brought it to the point where it was usable and printed on it for several years, then I rebuilt it a second time, making some modifications. Now it produces excellent letterpress images."

The Chandler & Price was not, strictly speaking, Hugh's first press. In the mid-1970s, when Hugh was pursuing a career as an orthotist, his daughters brought a note home from their principal at Lord Strathcona Public School, inviting parents to get involved in extra-curricular activities.

"I went over the next morning and told him I would like to start a print shop with the children. The principal rolled his eyes and said, 'Oh, that's a good idea. But you'll need a press.'"

At the time, Hugh was editor of the journal for the Canadian Association for Prosthetics and Orthotics (now Orthotics Prosthetics Canada, which publishes a journal, *Alignment*). In the early 1970s, when Hugh was editor, the journal was printed by one of the few surviving Kingston printers, Hanson & Edgar. He asked if they had an old press they'd be willing to part with for a good cause. They gave him a rusting Vandercook #2 proofing press, along with several drawers of old wooden type and a type cabinet he spied in a back shed.

"I came back to the school the same day and said, 'I have a press and type. Now I need a room.'"

The principal showed him an empty classroom, and within a couple of weeks Hugh had a group of keen grade six students returning to school one night a week to learn how to operate a printing press.

"I think I was looking for an excuse to buy a press," Hugh grins, "but I was also looking for an opportunity to teach open-ended problem solving, to create a situation that would allow the kids to open their minds to new ideas that don't have a right or a wrong answer. I didn't want to use intimidation as a motivator, the way it's used in conventional classrooms. When we sat down at a table to meet the first time, I didn't sit at the head. I always used a different chair. And I had them call me Hugh, rather than Mr. Barclay, because I called them by their first names. It meant something to them. Some of them still stay in touch, forty years later!"

Hugh and his band of neophyte printers named their venture Bubble Gum Press. Their first project was *The Wrapper*, a magazine written and printed by the kids under Hugh's guidance. They started out with great expectations: a bimonthly printing of 100 copies distributed to parents and friends who could buy a subscription for 50 cents. Their motto: *Don't spend your money on the gum—just buy* The Wrapper.

"We never knew when we might finish an edition, so in the colophon I always included a phrase like,

'Published in the month of melting snow.' I think it would be neat to include such a phrase in your book, since we don't know exactly when I'll get it finished."

"How about 'Published in the month the peonies fade'?"

"Consider it done!" Hugh crows. Why don't I learn? Hugh picks up suggestions like live grenades and tosses them onto his agenda, no time for second thoughts.

Bubble Gum Press eventually printed stationery, Christmas cards, and thank you notes as well as the magazine. Every issue of *The Wrapper* was an exercise in innovation: poems and stories were solicited from all the kids at the school, and selected by a student editorial committee, which eventually included one of Hugh's daughters. Faye Batchelor was an advisor. One issue was accordion folded, printed on both sides. One was a six-page "menu." One had tipped-in block prints. A note in an early issue promised: "*The Wrapper* will make use of different materials and formats, in an effort to give our subscribers and ourselves the benefit of new experiences." That sounds pretty serious, but every issue was infused with the quirky, irreverent wit Hugh exudes. How the kids must have loved him!

On the wall above Hugh's Chandler & Price hangs a framed print of a girl running. One evening, one of the young Bubble Gummers, Elizabeth Southall, drew the figure on the blackboard, turning the chalk this way and that so the limbs were thick, then thin.

"I looked at it and thought, Jesus, that is great!" Hugh made a tracing of the blackboard drawing and, at home that night, transferred the drawing to a piece of lino mounted on an eighteen-by-fourteen-inch board. The next week, the kids printed the image on the proof press, inking it in one colour and daubing the thick parts of the line with a second colour. They did fourteen printings, every one a different colour. Hugh has #11 hanging on his wall. At least one of them was Elizabeth Southall's entry into the poster contest for the 1976 Olympics.

Hugh closed the door on Bubble Gum Press in 1978, when his spare time suddenly evaporated. After a decade of working as an orthotist at Frontenac Rehab Centre, then Kingston General Hospital, he had decided to strike out on his own.

"I remember driving home thinking I was crazy to try running an orthotics consulting business on my own, then I saw a dump truck ahead, listing to one side, with old tires and a beat-up box. I said to myself, *If that bastard can run a business, so can I!*"

The old proofing press lay abandoned in his basement, but Hugh couldn't resist the call of ink in his veins for long. Every so often, he'd drive the 350 kilometres to Grimsby, Ontario, to spend a weekend typesetting and pulling prints at Poole Hall Press. Two years later, in 1980, he finally gave in to the urge and bought the Chandler & Price from Faye for $500. Twelve months later, almost to the day, the restored Chandler & Price printed the first Hellbox Press book.

"I promised that press it would never be required to

print anything that was not an art form. To my knowledge, I have kept that promise."

WHAT FOLLOWS NATURALLY

Hugh and Verla were married in 1968. Shortly before the wedding, they bought a building lot in a new subdivision in what was then the outskirts of Kingston. They'd looked at houses, but each one needed such extensive alterations to make it livable for Verla that they decided to build. They hired Verla's cousin, an architectural technician at Expo '67 in Montreal, to design a house especially for them, with wide halls, and windows low to the ground so that Verla could see outside from her wheelchair. By the time they were married, the house was far enough along to move in, although Hugh spent another five years on the finishing touches. He built kitchen cupboards out of teak, designing them to accommodate Verla's chair. When it came time to choose hardware, he wasn't satisfied with the prosaic chrome hinges and knobs available in the shops. He borrowed a forge and made all the iron knobs and hinges himself.

When he quit the hospital and went out on his own, he converted the garage to a two-room office: a small space in front to meet orthotic clients and conduct his business, and a shop behind where he built the orthotics that would turn the profession on its head. It was here that he developed the invisible scoliosis orthosis and the tilting wheelchair, and it was here that he tore apart the old Chandler & Price and put it back together again. Seven years later, in 1988, he sold the orthotic business and went full-time into tilt-wheelchair manufacture. It wasn't until that enterprise failed and Verla died in 2003 that the garage became a full-time print shop.

Hugh's press didn't come with an instruction manual. There *were* no instruction manuals. Presses like his were run by printers who would have learned how to operate and maintain the machines in trade school or during their apprenticeship. In fact, Chandler & Price presses were such a mainstay of the printing industry that the textbook for training printers, *The Practice of Printing* by Ralph W. Polk, used a Chandler & Price as its teaching model.

By the time Hugh came along, the letterpress print trade was all but dead. There were no typesetters or pressmen, as all the commercial shops had switched to offset printing, essentially an image-based, lithographic process. Hugh had no idea how a press came apart or how it went back together, but he learned in his usual way: by doing. I can't help wondering what would have become of him if he'd been born into the digital age, where dismantling doesn't get you anywhere except face to face with an inscrutable motherboard.

"Taking the press apart and putting it back together was duck soup. Building and rebuilding things has always been second nature to me. And it was just a matter of time before I figured out how to adjust the ink film and the pressure to produce a good impression. You know, you don't need a PhD to run one of these things. I'm sure

I made mistakes, but all that is just part of the learning curve."

As far as I can tell, Hugh has always been like this. In 1957, he was working as a car mechanic in Belleville. His friend Johnny Meyers had been in a car accident in high school that injured his lower spine. He'd been fitted with long leg braces at Sunnybrook Hospital in Toronto, one of Canada's best rehab hospitals, but he wasn't happy.

"The braces weighed eight pounds," says Hugh. "Imagine dragging that around with every step! Johnny asked me if I could make him something lighter. Fibreglass was just coming in and it looked like it had possibilities, so I took some time off work and developed the first moulded orthosis."

He tosses this off as if every twenty-three-year-old leaves their job to help a friend, inventing a new orthotic device in the process.

Hugh had no experience with either mould-making or fibreglass, but lack of knowledge has never stopped him.

"I found a book that showed how to make plaster moulds for small decorative articles. Based on that information, I constructed a three-sided box on a wooden door, which I laid across two sawhorses in my basement. I filled the box half full with plaster of Paris, and then had Johnny sit in it so his legs were half immersed in the slurry. I used liquid soap as a parting agent and poured the top half of the plaster mould. I was cleaning up the pails when I heard the door break.

Johnny was trapped in the mould. I found a big screw-driver and pried the two parts of the mould apart. His legs were beet-red from the heat given off by all that plaster, something I hadn't anticipated. We decided not to tell Johnny's mother about this episode. (<;)-"

Young Hugh salvaged the mould and created a single fibreglass-reinforced orthosis with knee joints and locks. The whole thing weighed eight ounces. Three years later, Johnny was working for the March of Dimes as a fundraiser when he heard that the Frontenac Rehab Centre in Kingston was looking for a bracemaker. He urged Hugh to apply. The minute he was accepted, Hugh dumped his job as a car mechanic (once again), figured out how to get some training at Sunnybrook and SickKids hospitals in Toronto, and started on a twenty-year career as an orthotist.

Hugh attacked the press with that same confidence in his ability to solve whatever problem might arise. Luckily, the press had no breaks in the frame that would relegate it to the scrap heap. But the rollers were worn down to nubbins and the press bed could no longer hold a chase in place. He found a machine shop to mill new rails for the press bed and fashion ends for new rollers to ride the rails. The press had a motor, but it also had a foot treadle that he hooked up until he could recondition the motor. After putting the press back together, he repainted the body a shiny black, converting the horizontal arm to a sunny yellow and the flywheel to a bright red. Then he learned to operate it the same way he learned to rebuild it.

If I ever wondered how an orthotist becomes a printer, I found my answer in Hugh's youth. At ten, he built himself a workshop in his parents' basement. At twelve, he designed and built his own sailboat. By seventeen, he was working as a mechanic. At twenty-two, he built one of the fastest go-karts on the continent. At twenty-three, he invented a new kind of leg brace.

He winks at me. "Doesn't it follow naturally that in midlife I would become a private press printer?"

DANCES WITH DEVILS AND BEARS

Letterpress printing comes with its own quaint lexicon. Compositors were called "monkeys"; the boys who did menial jobs like distributing type from the hellbox were "devils"; the men who pulled the presses were "horses" or, in France, "bears."

"Makeready" is among the most mundane of printers' terms. It means pretty much what it says: the process of making the press ready for printing.

Watching Hugh work through the makeready for printing *The Paradise Project* is like stepping into a novel by H. G. Wells. Gutenberg himself wouldn't have done it much differently.

By the time Hugh is ready to print, he has four locked-up chases leaning against the wall of his shop. In each chase is a block of type, the forme carefully proofed for spelling errors, for good layout, and for problems with the type. The forme was moved into the chase and furniture and reglets fit around it to position the text exactly on the page, with proper margins all around. When everything was tight and true, the quoins were tightened with the quoin key, locking up the chase.

Hugh sets one of the chases on his imposing stone—the glass plate on his work table—and turns the quoin key to back off the quoins a bit. Then he picks up a planer that looks less like a carpenter's plane and more like a big blackboard brush with a padded sheet of canvas stretched across the bottom. He sets the planer across the type and taps it gently but firmly with the quoin key, the handle of which is conveniently shaped like a little hammer. Tap-tap-tap, until he is certain the type is perfectly level in all directions. Then he retightens the quoins and lifts the short end of the chase slightly off the glass. Gently but firmly he presses his fingers against every line of text and every piece of firming furniture.

"You can feel movement if something is loose. If nothing moves, we're good to go."

The principle on which the old press operates is simple enough—rollers rise up over the press bed to ink the chase, a sheet of paper is laid on the platen, and a clamp pulls the two together to transfer the ink to the page—but to get a good print, every moving part has to be level, true, and perfectly aligned. That's what makeready is all about.

Hugh lifts a spring lever at the top of the press bed and inserts the chase, then knifes a daub of ink onto the disc. He turns on the motor and lets the press run, inking the rollers for the proofs.

"Makeready happens in two stages," he explains. When we are talking about the press, he is the soul of patience. I feel less like Stupid Merilyn, more like a straight-A student. "The first makeready proofs are about the ink. The second makeready proofs are about the type."

When the press has run long enough to spread the ink evenly on the disc and the rollers, he slips a piece of bond paper onto the platen and takes a print.

"Now this next part is very scientific, so pay attention. You take the paper off the press and run your finger across the printed image. If the ink smears, there's too much."

He is laughing at me, but I play along, rubbing my finger across the print. It comes away clean. The first makeready is done.

Guide pins along the lower edge of the platen keep the paper from slipping down into the press, and grippers, like long pointy fingers, press against the paper, holding it in place as the platen rises for the print.

Between the paper and the platen is the tympan, which on Hugh's press is a metal frame that clamps down a piece of Mylar. (In Gutenberg's day, it would have been a stretched sheet of strong linen.) If the type isn't biting deeply enough, or if there are pale spots on the proof, the situation can be corrected by packing paper under the tympan.

Hugh prints another proof, lifts the page from the press, and turns it over. The letters are punched so deeply into the paper I can almost read the text in reverse. "Too much deboss," he says. "I like a really light bite. You want to be able to feel the impression on the backside of the paper, but not see it."

At one end of the spectrum is the traditional "kiss impression," in which there is just enough pressure to transfer ink to paper but not enough to create an indentation on either the front or the backside of the page. At the other end of the spectrum, a page can be "bitten" or "punched," creating a visible depression where the type hits the paper and a noticeably raised surface on the underside—an emboss.

Hugh tucks a sheet of bond paper under the tympan. Again and again he checks the impression. He doesn't care where the text ends up on the scrap of paper he's using as a test: he's only looking for the bite of type into paper, ensuring that it is just deep enough, and consistent across the page.

Erik's images have their own makeready demands. The total thickness of the lino blocks is 0.918 inches, the same as the type characters on their matrices. Erik gave Hugh the thin lino carvings and Hugh built them up to the correct thickness, gluing the lino first to a block of three-quarter-inch plywood, then building the thickness to the correct micrometre by gluing thin layers of card stock on the back.

"Erik's linocuts have far more surface area to them than a block of type, so there has to be more ink on the disc and more pressure on the platen."

It would be a minor miracle if the first makeready proofs were perfect, although given Hugh's years of experience they are usually close. The page we are preparing to print still has some dark and light patches, known in the trade as "monks and friars." Hugh positions torn strips of paper under the tympan to build up the light areas. Tearing rather than cutting the paper gives it a feathered edge that contributes to a more consistent impression.

Hugh shoves the wheel away from him, printing proof after proof until he gets the impression just right. It reminds me of sitting in the dentist's chair as she grinds down a newly filled tooth, slipping in that blue paper, having me bite down, taking it away to grind a bit more, then making me bite down again. Trial and error seems such an old-fashioned, imprecise way to find the sweet spot, and yet she gets there, and so does Hugh.

"There's just this one letter causing trouble," Hugh says finally, squinting at the proof.

I blanch at the thought that he might unlock the chase and have another go at the typesetting. But no. He lifts the chase out of the press bed and lays it on its side against the glass. Peering closely at front and back, he locates the *h* that is refusing to print, its bottom hump paler than everything else on the page. He tears off a sliver of Scotch tape and fastens it to the backside of that character's matrix and slips the chase back into the press bed.

"That should do it," he says. He runs another proof. It's perfect. The type has made a distinct but not brutal impression in the paper. The ink settles smoothly into every letter like a maze of shallow forest pools.

"Doesn't this drive you crazy?" I say. "All this fiddly, picky work?" I would have given up hours ago.

"What drives me crazy is to see that *h* not standing up with all the rest. Imagine printing 300 copies of that page and seeing the *h* fading every time into the background."

The makeready has been so intimate, Hugh leaning over the press, stroking the paper, gently tapping the type, that I expect him to pat the press on its flank now that it's done and say, "Good boy!"

"Does it have a nickname?" I ask.

He looks at me blankly.

"The press. We used to call our Westphalia 'Willy' and our little green Datsun 'Esmeralda.' You know, a nickname."

"Like 'Sally,' or 'Bert'?" He doesn't bother to keep the scoffing tone out of his voice. "No. The press is an eight-by-twelve Chandler & Price."

I should have known.

Hugh is leaning over the tympan, measuring it with a ruler. He draws two pale pencil lines, one vertical, one horizontal, on the left side of the Mylar to show where the leading edge of each sheet of paper should sit so that the columns of text will print precisely where they belong. Perfect register is especially important when he is printing the page twice, once with the image and again with the text.

At last it's time for the first running proof: a proof made with the motor running, the real test of what will happen when Hugh is printing this page in its 300-page run. He flicks the motor on and the press rumbles to life. Suddenly, I see the risk in this operation. The C&P has a "dwell"—a brief pause when it's open, enough time to place a sheet of paper on the platen and to get your hands out of the way—which seems like a god-send compared to its nineteenth-century competitors, known in the trade as "snappers" because they opened and closed without a pause. Printers had to be light-fingered or risk losing a digit or two.

Hugh stands in front of the press. On his right is the paper tray, a swivel-arm that holds a stack of fresh Salad sheets, fanned slightly so that the edges stick out for easy picking. With his right hand he pulls a clean page off the tray, and simultaneously with his left he removes the printed sheet from the tympan. The faster the left hand removes the paper, the more time the right hand has to place a fresh sheet.

At maximum speed, his press can print 2,600 sheets an hour. "When I got the press, it ran like a rocket ship!" Hugh exclaims. "I couldn't feed it that fast so I built a jack shaft to gear down the motor." Now, it churns out about 500 impressions an hour, but Hugh isn't aiming for that. He no longer feels the need to prove that he can keep up with a machine. Satisfied with the test run, he turns off the motor and moves even further back in time, to the trusty flywheel and the strength of his arm. He'll be happy to get this print run of 300 pages done in the course of the afternoon.

He sways with the rhythm of turning the wheel, feeding the paper, pulling it out, stacking the printed sheets carefully in front of him so the ink doesn't smudge, pausing now and then to transfer the stack to his worktable so he can carry on. His eyes are staring, a bit glazed. I have disappeared. There's just the thrum of the press, the clack of type, and the intermittent swish of paper and rollers, a syncopated percussion that beats in rhythm with his heart.

PRESS PRINT

What I take for granted:

- That the lights will come on when
  I flick a switch.
- That water will flow when I turn on
  the tap.
- That words onscreen will appear as ink
  on a page when I press Print.

I don't necessarily want to know the workings behind these magical events. Take electricity. "Think of it as water," my father used to say, but that didn't help. I didn't believe there was water flowing through the walls, either. Pressing and turning those keys, knobs, and switches always seems to me to be an act of faith.

Maybe this explains why I thought the digitization of books had done away with makeready. I assumed that once an ebook was designed and locked into a file, all that remained was to upload the file to a retailer's website and wait for a reader to click Add to Cart.

"It's *all* makeready!" Erik exclaims when I proffer my theory. My ignorance is endless, it seems. "Sure, there's no physical evidence—no first, second, third draft, nothing you can write *Artist Proof* on—but just because you can't see it, doesn't mean it doesn't happen."

He sends me the pages of the book as a file that I say is onscreen, but it isn't. The pixelated image of the words is there. The file itself is a knot of code, an intangible, indecipherable Rosetta stone.

Erik and I once stood before three sky-high Mayan stelae, squinting at the columns of glyphs that told the story of Lady Xoc, overseen by the ruler Shield Jaguar, making sacrifice to the gods by pulling a skein of bark cloth through a piercing in her tongue. Blood drips into a gourd-bowl she holds in her hands. At least that's what the archeologist guide told us the glyphs meant. While I learned to read the glyph code, Erik painted the images.

Now he is tilting his laptop towards me so I can see the columns of code for *The Paradise Project* scrolling down the screen. We are in a program called Calibre. Erik used an application called InDesign to create the ebook, then dumped the file into Calibre to fine-tune the code and convert the file to other formats for exporting to retail ebook sites.

What I'm looking at, he tells me, are Cascading Style Sheets (CSS). Every paragraph, every letter (character) in a word, is shaped by its own chunk of code. This is not news to me: I learned a smattering of basic .html to manage the website Erik designed for me twenty years ago.

"This should look familiar," he says. "Books are coded in XTML, which is a smarter HTML. From a coding perspective, ebooks are essentially websites viewed on an ereader. They are built the same way."

Erik explains that the file of *The Paradise Project* contains the code for how my words will be seen. Every time a letter, word, or phrase is bolded or italicized, or a paragraph needs to begin flush left instead of indented, the CSS for that letter, word, or paragraph has to change.

"An ereader is a format for reading what's in a book. The ereader doesn't change what's there, but sometimes it can fail to recognize certain code." I'm starting to get that electricity/plumbing feeling, as if we're talking about faeries and extraterrestrials. "This means that, as well as the basic code, I have to add separate lines of code for specific devices, so that readers looking at the book on Kobo and Kindle and iBooks will all see the same thing."

"So the makeready for a digital book is like setting up the type to run on half a dozen different presses?"

"Exactly."

My brain feels like it is about to explode.

Erik goes on. "For instance, there is no code in Kindle for a drop cap. I love drop caps. I designed them into the chapter openings, but Kindle can't read them. What do I do? Get rid of drop caps? Or be content that Kindle users will have a different reading experience?"

Basically, ebook designers like Erik have to choose one format and design for it, accepting that in other ereader formats the headings might not look the same and the page breaks might fall in different places. Where he can, he adds extra code to correct the anomalies.

For *The Paradise Project*, I have up-to-date Word files of all the stories, so the process of dumping the text into a publishing file goes smoothly. But Erik is also designing ebooks for two of my out-of-print books: *The Convict Lover* and *The Lion in the Room Next Door*. Typically, I write longhand, enter the story into the computer, editing as I go, then I print out a fresh draft for another go-round, repeating the cycle until the piece is as good as I can make it. Over the years, the process has become increasingly digital, until now I spend more time with my fingers on keys than with a pen in my hand. But even my first book, published thirty-eight years ago, has ended up as a computer file. The computer I worked on then is long dead, the file no longer readable. Even if I could read the file, it wouldn't match the printed book: editors and copy editors made their own changes to a manuscript on its way to publication. The writer rarely gets a copy of the final digital file.

To make an ebook of *The Convict Lover*, the pages of the printed book first had to be run through an optical recognition scanner, a machine that reads printed text and converts it to digital code. In this case, the machine needed its eyes checked. On one page alone there were 138 errors. For instance, "the" was consistently read as "die," and "shifted" became "shitted." The text required a very thorough proofread.

For *The Lion in the Room Next Door*, I had digital files of each story, but they were in AppleWorks, a now-defunct word-processing program. Converting them to Microsoft Word was easy, but the new files had to be compared word-for-word with the print edition of the book to catch all the publisher's copy edits.

In the end, I hired my niece, an editor, to proof both books. The files were flawless when she handed them to Erik. Even so, when he poured the text into the book-formatting program Calibre, there were hundreds, maybe thousands, of conversion errors in the EPUB file, including the old hyphenation from the Microsoft Word format that showed up in the new files. Combing out the misplaced hyphens and other errors was a painstaking and irritating process.

The ebook format requires some unexpected changes in the text, too. A table of contents with page numbers seems pointless now: which "page" a text falls on will depend on the point size and font the reader chose and the device it is read on. There is no longer a single page number that can be referenced and found by every reader from Sydney, Nova Scotia, to Sidney, Vancouver Island, to Sydney, Australia.

Erik looks at me with sympathy. "Not pointless. We'll keep the table of contents and link the chapter titles directly to the chapter openings. A reader can quickly skip from the contents to where they want to go in the text, they just won't use page numbers to do it."

Size has changed, too. It is no longer fixed. Before Gutenberg's press, the size of a book was left to the whimsy of scribes or the person who commissioned the work. The *Codex Gigas*, the *Giant Book* (also known as the *Devil's Bible*) is the size of a small table and weighs as much as a sturdy woman; the skins of 160 young donkeys were scraped to create the vellum for its pages. Not taking into account illustrations and embellishments, if a scribe wrote non-stop, 24-7, the *Codex Gigas* would take five years to copy.

At the other end of the spectrum are the thumb-sized prayer books, Bibles, and Books of the Hours that became popular in medieval Europe. Complete with illuminated portraits, embellished lettering, and intricately worked clasps, these miniatures were small enough for a lady to hang from her belt, yet they contained hundreds of pages written in fine script.

During the hand-press period—from Gutenberg up to about 1820—the dimensions of a book were determined largely by the size of page that could be printed on the press. Paper was manufactured in a variety of sizes defined by terms such as pot, demy, foolscap, and crown. As printing and papermaking technology developed, it became possible to print on larger sheets and even rolls of paper. At the same time, experiments were honing in on the optimal line length for reading and the optimal size for holding in the hand—for a novel or biography, for instance, the ideal size is six-by-nine inches. All of this worked towards standard book sizing, although rogues abound. In 2012 the biggest book in the world was declared to be *This the Prophet Mohamed*, made in Dubai, United Arab Emirates. It is the size of a backyard swimming pool. The smallest book is *Teeny Ted from Turnip Town*, written by Malcolm Chaplin and illustrated by his brother Robert, published at Simon Fraser University in Vancouver, British Columbia, in 2014. A thirty-page story, it is printed on a single tablet the width of a human hair and can be read only with an electron microscope.

Erik doesn't have to deal with the far ends of the size spectrum, but his challenge is great enough: to design a book that can be read equally well on a full-size computer monitor and on a cellphone screen smaller than a deck of cards.

When the digital design for *The Paradise Project* is finished, Erik tests the EPUB file across as many devices as he can: desktop computers, laptops, tablets, and phones of various sizes from the major manufacturers. He asks me to try to open the file on all the devices I own, and on Wayne's, too.

"Send me screenshots," he says. "The final, uncontrollable factor is the user, because, in ebooks, the user has control over some of the design elements. What will the design look like if the user views it on a black background with white characters, or a purple background with green characters? What if the user bumps up the text size to 24 point? How does the text size and every variable under the user's control affect the page breaks, the way the text sits on the page? The type is changeable, but I still have control over the spacing and flow. That's what I've been working on—making sure that no matter what the user does, the book will still look good, the reading experience will be everything it can be."

This is the digital makeready, a process just as fussy

and perhaps even more time-consuming than Hugh's makeready on the old Chandler & Price. At least Hugh only has one press to deal with.

"We've let computer programs determine how we see text," Erik says, "but we still have to go in and make sure the program is working correctly and is consistent. In the same way that there are limitations on the machinery that lets people see the words, there are limitations in coding that the designer has to find a way to work around."

Ebook formats are intuitive: they will remove excess, unnecessary coding. But even so, a lot of what Erik does during his digital makeready is to edit the metadata to make sure that the coding not only works, but is elegant. Once he's done everything he can, he runs the file through an EPUB validator website set up by the International Digital Publishing Forum: he uploads the EPUB file, runs a validation on the code, and the program spits out a list of errors. When he validates the EPUB file for *The Paradise Project*, it comes up with solid green checkmarks: no errors. He converts the file to MOBI, which Amazon uses for the Kindle, and sends me the final files. Then, one more format: a PDF for reading on a computer screen.

Many self-publishing authors don't use a designer. The Amazon uploader will convert a simple Word doc quickly and easily to a file that can be launched on Amazon in seconds. The conversion tool at Smashwords, another self-publishing platform, is called the meat grinder, a name that speaks for itself. In the world of Hit Publish, writing replete with typos and redundancies and elementary design is the norm. But readers can tell the difference.

"There's a certain magic to this, a certain finesse," Erik says quietly, almost defensively, yet with pride. "Really, really clean code is a beautiful thing. In the same way that a smooth-running press with a perfect skim of ink on the disc and a perfect bite of type into the paper is, and perfect consistency to the prints even when you look closely at the pages through a loupe—in that same way, you can see beauty and elegance in a well-coded ebook."

The language he is speaking is as foreign as the Mayan glyphs, but at the same time I understand exactly what he means, the way I understand Spanish from the cadence even when I can't translate the words.

Where did he learn to speak this digital language with such ease? Have I raised a nerd?

Not a nerd. A born-again Gutenberg, a next-generation Hugh.

THE BALLET OF THE SIGNATURES

The Salad paper arrives in twenty-two-by-thirty-inch sheets. The book, as Hugh envisions it, will be relatively narrow, with text columns three inches wide and eight inches long. The question is how to get the maximum number of pages out of a single sheet of Saint-Armand paper.

Hugh and Erik toss this back and forth at our first meeting of Team Paradise Project. I'm not really listening. I figure there must be mathematical equations for such things. They are talking about ways of folding and cutting when I throw in my two cents.

"Wouldn't it be nice to have uncut pages," I muse, more an effort to participate than a serious suggestion.

I've used the term incorrectly, I discover later when I cruise the rare-book sites. What I meant was: Wouldn't it be nice to leave the pages "unopened"? When mechanical printing presses proliferated around 1830, among the many inventions designed to speed book manufacture were the paper-folding, cutting, and binding machines. Before that, printers rarely trimmed pages. If large sheets of paper had to be folded to create pages, the book would be issued with the edges untrimmed and the folded pages "unopened," known in the trade as *intonso*. Once the trimming of the fore-edges of a book was relegated to machines, it sometimes happened that a folded page or two was missed. These "uncut" pages are accidental—a delight or irritation, depending on the reader's temperament.

As a denizen of the digital age, I expect every question to have an answer, so I am nonplussed to discover absolutely no online history of page trimming. When Hugh asks, "How long has it been since a book was published in Canada with unopened pages?" I have to say, "I don't know." All I've managed to unearth among the debris of blogs, chat rooms, and Wikipedia entries is a 1918 treatise on paper-cutting machines that bemoans the "lack of information on the subject, either historical or technical."

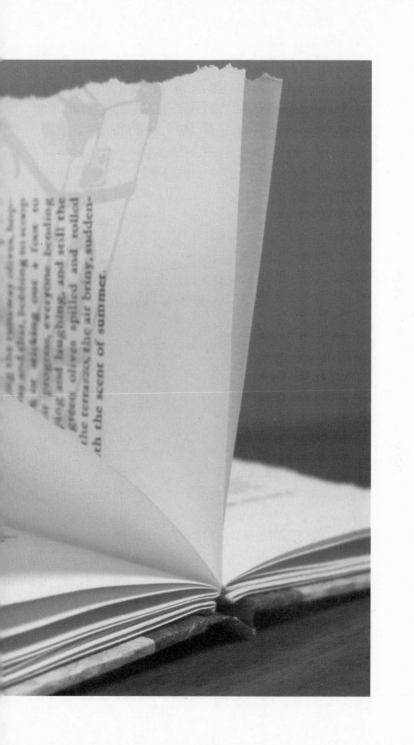

...g the pathway shrub hop-
...and flat, holding to scoop
... sticking out a foot to
... program, everyone leaning
...ing and laughing, and still the
green olives spilled and rolled
the terrace, the air briny, sudden-
...ch the scent of summer.

Hugh is stoked by the idea that it might have been a century, maybe two, since a book printed in English was produced with unopened pages. (Many French books are still published unopened.) Well after midnight on the day of our meeting, he sends Erik and me a message:

"I must fess up and tell you that I went to bed for a three-hour nap after Merilyn dropped me off. When I got up around nine, all the restaurants except Denny's were closed. Good enough for a bowl of soup. After I had eaten, I asked the waitress for a napkin. She left me three, which I folded to create pages, numbering them and sketching out a plan. Eureka! It all works out like a dream."

He has figured out how to cut each sheet of Salad paper into three strips, folding each strip into a *W*—eight printed pages, with one unopened fold in the centre.

"So the unopened edge is in! This will give an interesting touch to the book, in my opinion. We can include a knife and a little note explaining how to cut open the page and let the story out. In order to have two unopened edges in each signature, we should go up to sixty-four pages, which means that Merilyn will need to come up with an additional four-page story to be placed in the second, third, or fourth signature."

There's another wrinkle. He'll save time and aggravation at the fold if he can print two-up: two pages at once. By shortening the column of text a hair, he discovers he can fit two columns in the chase, but there's no room for a page number at the bottom and no bottom margin for the guide pins to grip. By the next day, Hugh has made new guide pins that extend beyond the platen so the page can hang below the chase, creating a bottom margin. And he has moved the page numbers to the outside margins, halfway up.

The final page size of the book will be five and a quarter by ten inches, the column of text 3.33 by 6.66 inches. Because he will be printing two-up, each eight-page fold of paper will go on the press four times: first, he'll fold the paper in half, print a two-page spread, then turn it over and print another two pages. Then he'll open the fold and refold it to show the blank side, and print both of these sides.

Convinced this will work, Hugh starts tearing each Saint-Armand sheet into three strips. He rips dozens before giving up. "I just spent Sunday morning trimming about fifty sheets. At that rate my back will be broken in two days, so I have decided to take the paper to a fellow who has a cutter and have him do the work."

This gives him time to go over his plan. Sure enough, he comes up with one more problem to be solved:

"I must make you aware that each sheet of paper shrinks at a different rate, depending on the amount of fibre in that sheet. The width of the sheets can vary up to a half-inch. This means I have to adjust the position of each sheet on the platen in an effort to keep the pages centred. And this, of course, means I will have to run and feed the press completely by hand."

Oh my god, I think. *My suggestion has become anything but idle.*

Open a book anywhere. The two side-by-side pages are called a reader's spread. Page 2 is beside page 3. Page 36 is beside page 37. Take a book apart, however, and you'll see that page 2 is actually connected through the binding to a page much further into the book. This is called a printer's spread.

When a signature is unfolded to a flat sheet, some pages will appear upside down or backwards. I remember the IQ tests in grade eleven that instructed us to match shapes scattered in different positions across a page. "Just spin them around in your imagination," the teacher said. I couldn't do it. I can't visualize what a dress cut from a pattern will look like, either.

Whatever I lack in spatial imagination, Hugh has in spades. Working from the numbered pages on Erik's flatplan, Hugh figures out a printer's plan, his map for printing words on paper so that when it is folded and stacked, the pages will read like book.

"You may be interested to know that I folded 220 sheets in an hour," he writes in early March. "In total there are 2,880 sheets that require folding three times. All that folding will take forty hours of work not counting coffee breaks."

A few minutes later, another email pings into my inbox. "I miscalculated the folding necessary to produce the unopened pages. I think it is around 14,000 folds but who's counting and moreover who gives a damn."

Here's the math: Hugh intends to make 300 impressions of each of the 64 pages of type plus 300 impressions of each of the 15 images. That's 64 pages of type to set and

47 makereadys and 47 press runs. 14,000 foldings of paper. 23,700 kisses of the platen to the press bed.

Hugh estimates it will take him 400 to 500 hours to print *The Paradise Project* in its entirety. Although I didn't keep track, that strikes me as about the same amount of time it took to write these stories.

PRESS RUN

Hugh starts printing on March 20, the eve of the spring equinox. He aims to be finished by July 15, three weeks after the summer solstice. A quarter turn of the Earth to print a single book.

The first runs go well. Erik makes the trip from Toronto to help Hugh pull the image pages, which have to be done first. That night Hugh writes: "We pulled a proof of each block, then we decided he would run the 300 copies of the 'Tendril' block while I straightened up the place. We went out for dinner and a beer and then came back and ran the 300 pages of the 'Thorn' block. Erik was running the press and could print them faster than I could refold. We finished around ten p.m. and Erik is heading back to Toronto now. He asked me if he should address me as master. I assured him that wasn't necessary. Most Wonderful One would be quite acceptable. (<;)-

"This was the first day in a long time that I haven't had a wee nap. I wasn't pushing myself, I just didn't want to miss anything. We now have six of the forty-seven press runs complete. We are making progress!"

Once *The Paradise Project* is on the press, emails fly fast and furious. For every run of the press, there's a new makeready, which means a proof for me to check, then, when I give the okay on the text and Faye does, too, Hugh has to adjust the ink and the impression and print the 300-page run.

"I have attached a new scan. Oh! And I do know the image is upside down and it needs a wee bit more pressure on the petal side to firm up the weight of the impression. Don't worry. All is well in typesettersville.

"I'm still holding up the press and type until you have a chance to proofread the last pages I sent the other day. I await your instructions.

"Attached are two more pages for you to cast your critical eyes upon. I'm sure you would agree that this suggests I'm not leaning on my oars. My printing plan has saved considerable time to fold and refold the pages and makes better use of the type we have. You see, Miss Barclay worries too much."

His spinsterish alter ego may not worry, but I do. I am not prepared for the pace. I'm getting pages from Hugh every few days in the order they're being printed, which is nothing at all like the order in which they'll appear in the book. It is messing with my head.

By early April, he is signing his emails "The Whip." He nags for the last images from Erik, the final story from me.

"I will be printing the table of contents Sunday. I

need to know the length and placement of the new story so I can include it in the contents. Also relay that information to Erik so he can adjust the flatplan."

On May 2, Hugh confirms the deadline we are working towards. "This is my latest thinking: I will be putting the press to bed in mid-July. You should be aware that I have been known to lie. (<;)-"

The deadline sounds reasonable enough, until Stupid Hugh shows up. He prints all 300 impressions of the image for "Petal" on a left-hand page instead of a right-hand page. He has not only wasted a day of printing, he has ruined 300 sheets of paper, each folded to become eight pages of the book. But Smart Hugh has an idea. The image was supposed to be on the right, on the second page of the story. If Erik agrees, he can fix his mistake by running the block print on the first page of the story instead. This changes how the deckle edges fall: now they will be on the left for the first eight pages of a signature and on the right for the next eight.

"I don't see that as a problem so long as I carry the system through the book," Hugh declares. "As a matter of fact, I like it better that way!"

Hugh has taken to writing long Sunday night reports to bring Erik and me up to date on the printing. I look forward to them with anticipation and more than a little trepidation. I have never had weekly reports from a publisher.

On April 16, almost a month into the printing, I receive another Sunday night report. He sounds tired.

"I finished printing the first sixteen pages tonight.

This gave me the opportunity to fold all the pages into a signature. And it looks like a book. (<;)- For all intents and purposes, we have reached the twenty-five percent point. I must fess up and tell you that I took Sunday off, the first day off in the past month and a half. This signature was certainly a learning process that brought out some idiosyncratic flaws in the old press that I had not experienced until I started to use the full capacity of the bed and chase."

Hugh discovered damage in the far corner of the press bed, where a previous printer must have dropped a metal tool into the running press. Until now, his columns of text had miraculously missed the crumpled area, but *The Paradise Project* uses the full width of the chase, and some of the type is collapsing into the depression.

"I moved the quoins to raise the block of text another three-quarter inch and this corrected the problem," Hugh explains. "We are getting there, despite the Stupid Hughs, Stupid Eriks, and Stupid Merilyns."

If it's not one thing, it's another. For Hugh, these problems are the stuff of bliss; me, they keep in a state of constant dread.

One of my stories, he says, is too long. How can that be? I adjusted the typeface in my computer files to 14-point Garamond, with Hugh's chosen column width and length. By my tally, this story should fit easily within the designated pages, but apparently my computer's Garamond and Hugh's are different.

"I have been setting the final page of 'Fern' and, although I'm only at the second paragraph, the shingles are shaking on the roof. It looks as if the story will slip over onto a fourth page. That would normally be fine, but we didn't plan for a fourth page. We need a reduction of three lines total. I feel bad that I'm restricting you, but that's life in the big city. It is twelve thirty so I'm on my way to bed."

I don't mind cutting. I have worked as a magazine editor, so I understand the realities of having to make a story fit. No words are too good for the cutting-room floor, no idea so fine that it cannot be phrased more succinctly.

I send in the cuts by nine the next morning. At noon, he writes back.

"I have made a big mistake that has caused us both a bunch of headaches. I thought we only allowed three pages for 'Fern,' however I have discovered after several hours of confusion that we allowed four. I will go back to the original manuscript and bring the story to its proper length. You can even add some if you wish. Of course this buggers up my plan to make proofs and send them today. How can I say I'm sorry for the mix-up other than to say I'm sorry? Mark it against Stupid Hugh."

Our deadline is now set in stone. "Not that it changes the price of tea in China, but I have had a scientific paper on thinking outside the box accepted at a conference in Victoria on August 3. I have to be finished printing *The Paradise Project* on the 15th of July."

We are in good shape until early June, when he makes a mistake that can't be fixed.

"I confused two pages and printed one in the wrong

place. I can save half of the 300 run by cutting the page where the unopened section would normally be. That would save me reprinting one page, but I have to reprint the other, and this means I have to buy more paper. I have just spoken with Saint-Armand and they are not sure they have enough left to supply the 60 sheets we need. This will slow the process down but I still think I can make the deadline. I'm tempted to say 'shit' but I'll save that for a more devastating blow."

Hugh is not a horse, he's a bear. Determined. Intelligent. Curious. When I lived up north, the trailer down the road was broken into by a bear that sniffed at every window, then smashed one, and when he couldn't get through, he moved on to the next until he found a way into the trailer with its stash of food. I shouldn't be astonished by Hugh's energy and perseverance, but I am. He is clearly exhausted, but he's exhilarated, too, and never discouraged despite the endless irritations and obstacles in this process. The only time I ever see him down in the dumps is when he's between projects, with no trailer to figure out how to break into. What's his secret?

"I go by the Alice in Wonderland Plan. Start at the beginning and go to the end. We proceed line by line and make it all work. I had a good rest this afternoon and my tank is refuelled, so I will start again in the morning."

Hugh's print shop is weighed down under *Paradise*. In the front room—his former orthotics office—a table that spans the entire length is stacked at one end with folded paper ready for the press, and at the other with towers of freshly printed signatures. The print shop itself is awash in proofs and linoblocks, an island cleared at the work table where Hugh bends over the chase on his imposing glass.

"I wrote a poem," Hugh says. *When?* I think. He must have found the eighth day. "I'm performing it at the open mic tonight."

He is hedging, an entirely new look for Hugh.

"I'd love to hear it," I say. "That is, if you want a trial run."

"Sure. Sure. I call it 'The Mentality Poem.'"

Hugh starts waving his arms around even more wildly than usual. He is lurching in the sea of proofs, cursing I think, although the words are slurred. He points straight at me.

> So, ain't you seen nobody who's crazy
> > before?
> You there! Rich lady!
> You just want to pay someone to keep me
> > out of your face.
> You there! Doc, what are you doin' to help
> > me, pushing some new pill?
> You there, cop! You taser me and knock me
> > down!
> And you there, Rev, what are you doing in
> > your million-dollar church,
> Prayin' for the poor?

By the time he is done, I am shaking and so is he. If his bladder is too close to his eyes, then so is mine.

By mid-June, Hugh has forty pages printed. He is six days behind schedule. To help make up the time lost to Stupid Hugh's mistakes, he hires a neighbour to help with the typesetting, a young man named Richard who has just graduated from university. Between the two of them, he says, they can set and proof eight pages in fifteen hours.

I have to keep reminding myself that Hugh is seventy-seven. I don't know how he keeps this up. The printing occupies every waking hour and some of his sleeping ones, too.

"Just before waking this morning I could see page 37 in my mind's eye, and it had excessive negative word space. I had a look at it first thing and decided to make some changes, but I should have all the art work printed for the fourth signature in a few hours. Oh, and the sample endpapers just arrived from Emily. There are two that have some possibilities but even they don't do too much for me. I know you have nothing to do and it's raining. (<;)- If you are planning to come to Kingston, drop by."

For such a flexible man, Hugh is oddly rigid about the endpapers. We don't need them until near the end of the publishing process, so Emily has been producing samples while Hugh prints. From the beginning, he's wanted leaves and petals embedded in the handmade paper, and he is determined to have his way. If Emily can't do it, he'll find someone who can. He writes to Emily: "We have decided to cancel the endpaper project and seek out more conventional commercial options."

He uses the royal "we," but I'm not ready to cut Emily loose. She begs for another chance. Meanwhile, he is scattering emails like buckshot, trying to find a paper-maker with experience in embedded plants. Someone mentions surfactants and mordants, and Hugh careens down that blind alley.

"We could all work together to design experiments to determine which petal and leaf varieties are viable."

I am horrified. I remind him that we rejected commercial papers with floating flowers a year ago. I tell him that the garden is not a static thing to be harvested whenever it suits us. Nature has her own timeline, and at the moment she's not serving up the kind of plants he envisions.

"Keep Emily on the project," I urge. "We need to give her more direction."

I write to Emily and describe my vision for the book. "It's about human striving towards paradise and the various ways we attempt to make it." When I discover she hasn't read the stories, I send her a manuscript. I know the albinism affects her eyesight; I ask if she can find someone to read it to her. The boy with the ukulele?

"Hugh is reticent to be too prescriptive," I explain. Until now, I've taken a back seat in the production, but the horse is galloping towards the cliff; someone has to grab the reins. "The endpapers should be an artistic statement, in the same way that the illustrations are, and the typesetting, the printing. These artistic statements are all in response to the text, so you can see how important it is to read the book and bring your own vision to it."

She asks for pictures of my garden. I send her a stream of JPGs. She sends back image after image of new samples that look like gardens tossed in a summer breeze. Hugh and I both love what we see.

"Go for the gusto!" Hugh writes to Emily. It is June 30. He plans to put the press to bed in two weeks. How will she ever catch up? She says she can, and I believe her. Why not? This whole enterprise runs on a wild kind of faith.

It doesn't matter that July 1 is Canada Day, a national holiday. Hugh is in the print shop, pulling pages. At the typesetting station, Richard is joined by a burly young man named Dominic. "Call me Mico," he says when we are introduced. Hugh has finished the next-to-last signature, distributed the type, and is about to set the last eight pages. Emily has hired an assistant and promises the endpapers by July 10. The bindery is booked for July 16. I watch in awe.

I can almost hear the glee in the formal invitation that pings into my inbox late that night:

"Putting the press to bed will occur on Sunday, July 15, at eleven a.m. I am recommending that everyone wear their shirt inside out to show it takes crazy people to put these things together."

The first mechanically printed books were marvels in 1450, but they look pretty strange today. There are no page numbers: book buyers were expected to number the pages as they read, not a bad way, really, to remember where you left off. The titles of current bestsellers may be long—Mark Haddon's *The Curious Incident of the Dog in the Night-Time* or Dave Eggers' *A Heartbreaking Work of Staggering Genius*—but they're mere striplings compared to early titles, which weren't so much titles as page-long blurbs describing the entire book.

The books produced in those first fifty years were called "fifteeners" and eventually "incunabula," meaning "from the cradle." Gradually, the printed page evolved to what it is today, with a running head across the top to remind the reader what and who is being read, and numbers neatly inset at the top, bottom, or side. Paragraphs arrived to break up the solid columns of text, even though this increased the amount of costly paper required for a book.

On the last page, the scribe traditionally signed his name, and printers adopted the same practice. After 1500, the printer's name slowly moved from the back of the book to the front, along with the date and place of publication. When copyright laws were enacted, all the publication data was customarily gathered on the backside of the title page, on what is known as the imprint page.

Thee Hellbox Press has made it a policy to keep the

colophon in the back. Actually, it's more than a policy: Hugh is on a crusade.

"Perhaps you are not aware of the root of this word," Hugh writes more than a year before we actually start to work together on *The Paradise Project*. He wants to make sure I know who I am dealing with. I should have paid attention.

"Colophony was a city on the Silk Road that had an army whose strategy was to make a big charge at the end of every battle. The colophon is the printer's charge at the end of the battle of the book."

I like Hugh's version, but I check the etymological dictionaries just to be sure. The word "colophon" is Latin, derived from the Greek word *kolophon*, meaning "summit" or "finishing touch." And where did the Greek word come from? From the Greek city of Kolophon, now in Turkey. In early classical times, the city was famous for its strategy of deploying its crack cavalry late in a battle, as a kind of finishing touch.

Hugh is right: there's something back-asswards about putting a finishing touch at the beginning of a book.

In ancient Babylon and Assyria, the colophon was a clay tablet that came at the end of a series of tablets to indicate a piece of writing was done. From the sixth century on, the colophon was a personal inscription by the scribe, added at the end of a parchment scroll or codex. A colophon could be as minimalist as a printer's logo, but most early colophons were chatty, explaining to the reader where the book was printed and introducing all the people involved. Colophons have always been intensely personal, the one place where a scribe (and later a printer) could address the reader directly.

Curses, I am surprised to discover, were an important part of early colophons. Clay tablets were easily crumbled; illuminated manuscripts were beautiful and rare. The curses were intended to warn off thieves and thugs bent on damaging books that took so much time and skill to reproduce.

One of the earliest book curses, found in a colophon inscribed in a set of tablets in Nineveh, warned:

> He who breaks this tablet or puts it in water or rubs it until you cannot recognize it [and] cannot make it to be understood, may Ashur, Sin, Shamash, Adad and Ishtar, Bel, Nergal, Ishtar of Ninevah, Ishtar of Arbela, Ishtar of Bit Kidmurri, the gods of heaven and earth and the gods of Assyria, may all these curse him with a curse that cannot be relieved, terrible and merciless, as long as he lives, may they let his name, his seed, be carried off from the land, may they put his flesh in a dog's mouth.

Wow. I'm glad I didn't stumble upon book curses until after *The Paradise Project* was set and printed.

The earliest colophon found in a book printed on a Gutenberg press is in the back of the *Mainz Psalter*, published in 1457 by Johann Fust and Peter Schöffer, the financial backers who squeezed out Gutenberg before the psalter was completed. The colophon ignored the inventor and praises only his invention "fashioned by an ingenious method of printing and stamping without any driving of the pen."

At the time the *Mainz Psalter* was printed, its last words were not referred to as a colophon. The term wasn't coined until 1550, when Erasmus, a scholar whose books accounted for twenty percent of book sales in Europe in the sixteenth century, took to adding finishing remarks to his manuscripts, signing off with *Colophonem addidi*.

Once printing presses were mass-producing books, curses against the light-fingered were no longer needed. If someone stole a book, it could easily be replaced. The text itself, however, could be pilfered by an unscrupulous author. In the seventeenth century, copyright was invoked to protect such theft. Legal notice was moved up to the front of the book to warn readers right from the beginning of the consequences for stealing intellectual property. The practice of sharing details about the making of the book gradually disappeared except for some presses that, even today, include a note about the type in the last pages, a lingering vestige of the end-of-book colophon.

Erik and I agree on almost everything in the ebook design, but we come to blows over the colophon/copyright page.

"There's too much front matter," I say. "It takes too

long to get to the stories." In Erik's digital design, the first eight pages of *The Paradise Project* are devoted to titles, copyright, contents, and such. I point out that on many ebook sites, the first ten pages are free to read. I want people to get as big a sampling of story as possible. My digital friends tell me a praise page up front is essential, too.

Eventually Erik agrees. He moves the copyright information to the last page of the book. There is no need for a colophon, front or back. The user chooses the font, there is no paper, no endpapers, no Hugh, no Thee Hellbox Press. Erik's name is on the title page, together with mine. And I have become the publisher: Merilyn Simonds Publications.

With ebooks, colophons have all but disappeared, along with so many of the old trades involved in producing a book. Perhaps not disappeared, just evolved into something else. The rugged compositors are now pagemakers. There are still formatters and designers. There's still Erik. And colophons survive on websites, where a dedicated page lays out the details of how the website was created, the designer's name, and the technologies involved.

After the ebook is done and posted, I think, *I should have written more on that last page, told the world how this digital book came about.* I still can. That's the thing about ebooks: text is fluid and infinitely accessible. I can return to the EPUB file anytime and fix Stupid Merilyn's mistakes.

❦

Hugh has been thinking for months about what he will put in the colophon. It doesn't occur to him to curse the readers or warn them against making off with the book. But he does consider the colophon a prod, a way to get the reader to appreciate all that has gone into making this reading experience possible: the selection of paper, type, and ink, the plant material embedded in the hand-made endpapers.

"I think it would be a good idea to include a line in the colophon inviting the reader to consider how these materials and colours relate to the text," he writes to me as we close in on our mid-July deadline. "All this is just food for thought at the moment, just a couple of ideas that crossed my mind during the day. I'm always afraid that if I don't write them down or share them they will get lost or forgotten. Please don't worry about getting back to me on any of this. The good will stay on the table and the not-so-good will just fade away."

In 1976, Hugh was offered a job at Prince Edward Heights Hospital School for the Mentally Retarded, a facility in Picton, Ontario, for 1,500 developmentally challenged adults and children, many of them with foot problems. (The facility was closed in 1999.)

"I was paid the same daily rate as a physician, and I was obliged to dictate and sign the notes on my patients, the same as any doctor. I was taking liability, owner-ship for what I was doing. When I started the press, I thought, *Well Hugh you should do the same with the books you print. Take responsibility!*"

He started writing his colophons in the first person

and signing each one personally, in much the same way as an author signs a book at the front. He tried to convince his fellow book artists and letterpress addicts to do the same.

"When I read a traditional colophon written in the third person passive—'the type was set in 14-point Garamond'—I always want to ask, 'So who set the type, your mother?'

"When a writer publishes a book, their name appears on the title page. This is not ego; it is taking responsibility for the words. Similarly, in an effort to take responsibility for the design and printing, I write colophons in the first person and I sign them."

Hugh may blame Stupid Hugh in a moment of crisis, but in the colophon, like the scribes and printers of old, he owns up to his mistakes and writes paeans to the printing process he loves.

He also uses his colophons as a political platform. "In the last three or four books, I have included a critical statement about the Harper government, under the title 'Press for Responsible Government.' I am obliged to file a copy of every book I publish with Library and Archives Canada, and they are obliged to accept that book, at which point it becomes part of our national archive. It was my way of holding a finger vertical in hopes that Harper would see it."

Not a curse, exactly, but close enough.

The colophon at the end of *The Paradise Project* describes the Salad paper, the Garamond type, the chocolate ink, and Emily's endpapers. Like the earliest colophons in printed books, he acknowledges his proof-reader, Faye; his apprentice typesetters, Richard and Mico; as well as the bindery that will put the pages together. "It is always amazing the number of people it takes with differing skills to produce a book of this stature," he writes. "It has been a joy for me to take part in the process and you may find a few of my tears on page 31."

He goes on to enumerate the size of the run, which, due to the challenges of the past few months, is now 290 plus the number of copies that will be HC (*hors commerce*: not for sale but kept in the archives of the printer and the author). The colophon ends with "This is copy number _____" and Hugh's name. He will sign every copy as it is sold.

The colophon is on page 57. There are 58 pages reserved for text in the book. He sends me the colophon proof on June 28, with this note:

"Page 58 is blank. When you finish proofing this page, you can put your feet up and drink tea. And if you can manage a quick turnaround, there may be a bonus in your next paycheque. (<;)-"

PUTTING THE PRESS TO BED

The studio is so packed with people I can barely see the Chandler & Price. Hugh has invited everyone who worked on *The Paradise Project* to pull the last prints of the book.

Colophon

With the assistance of Richard Kohar and Mico Mazza, I have hand-set this book usiug 14 pt. Garamond Roman and Italic. The titles are set in 24 pt. Garamond Italic. The turtle press-marks are used to eliminate negative spacing when the ending word is too long and can't be hyphenated. The text paper is St. Armand's "salad" paper. Erik Mohr has created some outstanding lino-cuts that we elected to over-print in order to make them integral with the text. The covers are wrapped in Japanese Ajisai (hyacinth) Gold, and the spines are covered in Japanese Arashi (storm). The end-papers are designed and handmade by Emily Cook using abaca fiber mixed with lily fiber taken from Merilyn's garden. The book was case-bound by Smith Falls Book Binders. Faye Batchelor and the author lent their proof-reading eyes to each page during the printing of the book. It is always amazing the number of people it takes with dif-fering skills to produce a book of this stature. It has been a joy for me to take part in the process and you may find a few of my tears on page 31.

57

The edition comprises 321 copies: LD1 and LD2 are for legal deposit; 29 copies are marked Hors Commerce HC1-HC29 and are intended for those who took part in the making of the book. 290 copies are marked 1-290. This is copy number *103* .

Hugh Walter Barclay

Hugh Walter Barclay

We are putting the press to bed. It's an odd image, tucking this mechanical behemoth under the covers. It makes more sense in the garden, where putting the gardens to bed entails raking a blanket of leaves over the stubble of summer growth. Whatever I'm putting to bed—a garden, a press, a child—it provokes the same feelings. Sadness tinged with relief that a season, a project, a day is coming to an end. Joy that a memory has been made, something is complete.

"The first time I came here, the place was hanging with arms and legs," Antonino Mazza muses as we wait for the press to ink. Antonino is a Calabrian poet who has not entirely rerooted in Canada. He met Hugh when they both patronized the Italian Pastry Shop in downtown Kingston. At the time, Antonino was teaching English at Queen's, and Hugh was working full-time building innovative orthotics, the ink only just beginning to seep into his veins. Antonino was in the process of translating a poem by Pier Paolo Pasolini, the Italian poet, intellectual, and film director who was murdered in 1975 for being a communist or possibly for being gay. Hugh was immediately intrigued. He had found his next project: in 1985, he published *The First Paradise, Odetta*, the second book released by Thee Hellbox Press.

Antonino is here with his wife, Francline, and their son, Mico, the young man who spent last month typesetting with Hugh. Mico looks at the press the way he'll one day look at the person he loves.

"He let me run this thing when I was fourteen, and, ever since, I've wanted to come back. It was a big mistake," Mico says, shaking his head like a condemned man. "Now I never want to leave."

"The goal is addiction!" Hugh declares to no one in particular.

Hugh is in high spirits. He loves being a rebel and feels his cause most keenly when his print shop is full of acolytes. He consults the list in his hand. "Antonino, you're first. Don't worry, you'll all get a turn!"

We are not really printing the last page of *The Paradise Project*—it's number 48 of 64 printed pages— but in the complicated ballet that is the folding of the signatures, this page is the final one to roll off the press.

After Antonino, Francline steps up to the press. Then my son's wife, Tania, and their two girls, Astrid and Estelle. Then my husband, Wayne. Hugh has put us in order of the intensity of our contribution to the project. Next, Mico gets a turn, followed by Richard, the young neighbour who helped win back the six days that Stupid Hugh lost from the schedule. Emily couldn't make it, but Agnicia, who helped make the endpapers, steps up.

Now Erik comes up. The label on his shirt bobs as he bends to the press. We are all wearing our shirts inside out, as Hugh directed.

"Where does the tradition come from?" I ask, expecting another Gutenberg story. Hugh has so many of them. Sometimes he says he feels he is the reincarnation of the man who made today possible.

"Well. You need to know," Hugh begins, "you need to know that this tradition started a couple of weeks ago when I got out of bed and put my shirt on backwards. I thought, *We should do this when we put the press to bed.* And somehow I got all of you to do it!"

We feel a little foolish with our buttons rubbing against our bellies, our ruffles tickling our chests. We laugh.

"A thousand years from now," says Mico, "people will wear their shirts backwards when they put a press to bed, and they'll wonder how that tradition got started."

What an optimist, I think. Then again, fireworks and gunpowder were invented a thousand years ago, and they are still around. The fishing reel and stirrups were invented a millennium and a half ago, and *they* are still around. Maybe the hand-operated press will still be printing pages in the year 3000, too, 1,600 years after its invention.

In *The Social Life of Ink*, Ted Bishop travels the world looking at, making, and marvelling over every kind of ink imaginable, including printer's ink. He is making ink in Utah with a printing master and notices students wearing what look like folded paper baskets on their heads. His guru explains that the students each make a fresh hat every morning by folding one of the new sheets that has just come off the press. They're like hair nets in a chef's kitchen, he says. Printers have to keep their hair out of the press: a single strand on the type can ruin a page. After today I plan to tell Hugh. The lucky souls who work together on his next project will be wearing their shirts inside out and paper baskets on their heads.

Finally, it is my turn at the flywheel. I place the folded sheet of Salad paper upside down on the tympan as Hugh instructs. There is a small, pencilled number in one corner. 287. "Put the number on the left, at the top," Hugh says. "Centre the page between these two lines." He points to the pencil marks on the Mylar that by now are scarcely visible. I do my best to centre the page, then give the fly-wheel a whirl. I feel like a contestant on *Wheel of Fortune*.

287. 288. 289. 290.

I print my four pages. Hugh pulls the big lever on the side of the press. The Chandler & Price grinds to a halt.

The Paradise Project is printed. We're done.

I crack open the bottle of single malt scotch, although it is not yet noon. Hugh christens all his projects this way. When we are each holding a snifter or tumbler, we raise our glasses, and Wayne recites a poem he's written for the occasion:

> It started with stories like plump morning
>   glories
> that sprouted from Merilyn's head
> Not enough pages
> And too many haitches
> Now we're putting the press to bed.

He goes on, verse and after, finally coming to the end.

> *The Paradise Project* is printed at last
> And soon it will be read
> Now after that riot
> Thee Hellbox is quiet
> We're putting the press to bed.

We raise a huzzah and toss back the scotch. We toast Hugh and the press and Erik's images and my words and the typesetting skill of Richard and Mico and the keen proofreading eye of Faye and the gentleness of the golden retriever that wags around our knees.

As the bottle is passed around, I lift the last page off the press. It looks the same as all the others, nothing to declare its special place in these four and a half months of printing, this year-and-a-half marathon of production. Ironically, page 48 is the beginning of the story "Twig," the last one I wrote for this collection. In it, Peter complains to a woman he meets in a park that his children and his children's children have "no sense of history. No sense at all."

I'm reading the story again, thinking how fine words sound when they are beautiful on the page, when I notice, in one corner, a faint smudge. I peer more closely. The smudge is clearly a fingerprint. The print of Hugh's long, angled Peter Pointer.

"Oh dear," I say, showing the page to Hugh. "Should we print another?"

"We should charge extra!" Hugh exclaims, dismissing my question with a wave of his hand. "We're not striving for perfection here. That fingerprint—that's what makes this copy distinct. Human. It says, 'Somebody printed this.' Imagine what it would be worth, a book with Gutenberg's fingerprint!"

BOOK
BOOK
BOOK
BOOK

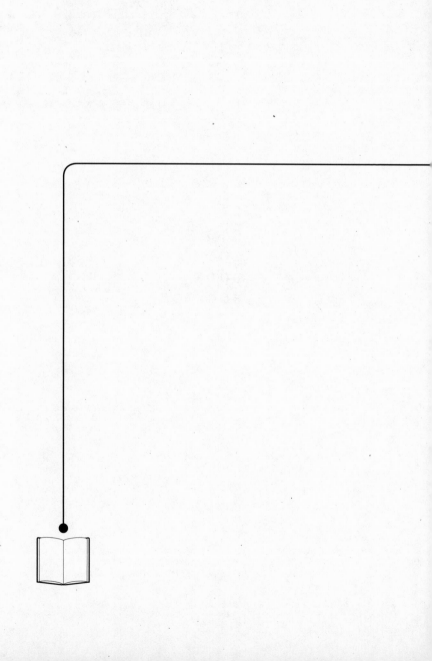

FIRST IMPRESSIONS

Wayne has recited his poem and the scotch has been sampled. I assume the party's about to adjourn to Hugh's back garden for lunch.

"Just one more thing!" Hugh calls out.

For a little guy, he has a very big voice. Our chattering stops abruptly, a needle lifted from vinyl. We turn as one to the centre of the room, where Hugh is standing in front of his imposing glass. When he has our attention, he dips out of sight then bobs up again, a long, thick white envelope in his hand.

"This is for you!" he shouts, handing it to me. In case I had any doubt, three-inch cherry-red letters scream from the front: *FOR M*. I recognize the wooden type he keeps in his corner cabinet, lovely old shapes that seem carved from some ancient unknown species, worn smooth by ten thousand pressings.

"What is it?" I ask, thinking, *Dammit, I should have brought him a gift.*

"Open it if you want to find out," he tosses over his shoulder. He is busy handing out similar white envelopes to Erik and Richard and Mico and Faye.

After a year of working with Hugh, I recognize the tooth of the paper in the handmade envelope. I stroke it appreciatively before dipping my fingers into one end and sliding out a book.

My book. Oh, and it is a beautiful thing, the cover an explosion of pale golden petals, the spine a tempest in a forest canopy. My name and the title of the book, *The Paradise Project*, are deeply embossed in a wonderfully footed font. I run my finger in the grooves left by the bite of the type, over the gloss of chocolate ink. The others are doing the same with their presentation copies, which Hugh has had bound in advance.

"This isn't just another book," he announces, and I'm thrown back to something I read last night in *Life Notes*, personal writings by contemporary black women. I was reading an excerpt from "The House That Jill Built" by Rita Dove, a woman of about my age, who won the Pulitzer Prize for Poetry and was poet laureate of Virginia. In the memoir, she recounts her experience working with a printer who produced a handprinted book of her poems.

On first seeing her printed book, Rita Dove feels

The Paradise Project

Merilyn Simonds

Block prints by
Erik Mohr

Thee Hellbox
Press 2012

"abashed." Embarrassment and puzzlement and a kind of wide-eyed, gaping astonishment mashed together with a sense of toppled composure, unseated confidence.

I know exactly what she means. The accumulation of Garamond words pressed into this thick, leafy Salad paper, pages upon pages of them, is overwhelming.

Did I really write this? Did I really have a hand in making it?

I have held a lot of books in my life. Thousands. Maybe hundreds of thousands. But never a book like this. The DNA of my garden is embedded in the endpapers. My own DNA is in the words. Hugh's DNA and Erik's are on the pages. I know every hand that has touched these words as they moved from the scribbled leaves of my notebook to this crisply printed page: the hand that chose the paper, cut and folded it, set the type, carved the image, stirred the ink, ran the press.

I look up at Hugh.

"This book is worth more than any price we can put on it," he says simply.

We both have tears in our eyes.

CREDIT TO THE CODEX

Gutenberg may have invented the printing press and the movable metal type and oil-based ink that made printing possible, but he didn't invent what we know as the book. In fact, it was the book—the codex—that made Gutenberg's invention possible.

Imagine what would have happened if scribes were still copying their texts onto parchment scrolls when Gutenberg wandered into Strasbourg. Would he have made the leap from writing on a long roll of sheepskin to printing on a flat, discreet page? Not likely. It was because the shape of the book already existed—flat sheets stacked between covers—that Gutenberg could envision the transition from handwriting to mechanical printing.

Scrolls were the repositories for stories and essays and laws for at least 2,000 years of human history, a definite improvement over a stick in the sand or crumbling clay tablets. Fragments from Roman and Greek pottery show people reading scrolls, leisurely unrolling one side as they roll up the other, like the music roll in a player piano. Scrolls were used for everything from counting sheep to recording prayers, and they ranged in size from thumbnail small to thirty-foot-long scrolls that make our doorstop novels look puny.

When I was very young, I came down with an extended bout of measles just as my baby sister was born. I was sent to my grandmother's house. In an upstairs closet, she kept toys for such occasions: a wooden cart and horse with tiny wooden bottles of milk that fit into miniature crates, sweet porcelain-faced dolls, and an educational toy that I think of as a very early version of a computer. About the size of a square suitcase, the top lifted like a laptop, its hinged arms connected to a base that was a chalkboard. The "screen" was a thick scroll moved by wooden knobs. I'd turn the knobs, and the scroll would move to reveal architectural drawings, a train in perfect perspective, songbirds and their eggs, flags of the world, the complete Morse Code, a lady with a hat that if you squinted became a Bengal tiger. Really, everything a girl needed to know. As I fix my cursor to scroll down my computer screen, I often think of that other scroll and of the Romans, especially the marble sculpture of a young girl, discovered in Pompeii, a small scroll held loosely in her hand.

From tablets and scrolls to scrolling tablets and, in between, the codex we call book.

The Romans designed podiums with top and bottom rollers to lighten the load of reading heavy scrolls. They stored the texts in what looks like a wine rack. They also developed wooden tablets smoothed with wax—an early version of Etch A Sketch—small enough to carry with them to scratch a few notes. The convenience of reading from a discreet "page" on a wax tablet led to the creation of personal notebooks made of parchment pages that could be washed or scraped and reused, the parchment pages known as palimpsests (from the Latin *palimpsestus*, to scrape again). Some historians suggest that Julius Caesar, in the first century BCE, was among the first to reduce scrolls to bound pages in the form of a notebook. His contemporary, Cicero, mentions recording his letters on a palimpsest.

The first codex book appears a hundred years later, in the first century CE. The word "codex" comes from the Latin *caudex*, which means the trunk of a tree, or a block of wood, perhaps because that's what the stack of pages looked like. At the time, the pages of a codex would have been made from plants (papyrus) or the skins of sheep or goats (parchment) or lambs, calves, and kids (vellum). Instead of writing on an extended roll of papyrus or vellum, a codex allowed a person to record the world on individual pages that were piled up, one on top of the other. Sometimes the pages were held together with loose stitching down one side—usually on the left but not always.

The first reference to a codex is by the Roman poet Martial, who praised its virtues over the scroll. The codex was sturdier, more compact, and much easier to read. Because pages were written on on both sides, the codex held more words and therefore consumed fewer skins. And because pages were distinct, the codex paved the way for numbering that would allow a person to dive into a text at any point and reference bits to share with others.

Martial was an early adopter. Like most new forms, though, the codex was not generally enthusiastically embraced. Because it was descended from erasable palimpsests, it was dismissed as informal and transient, appropriate only for passing thoughts. Scrolls were held in much higher regard, the proper way to present important ideas.

The codex and the scroll co-existed for several hundred years, the codex slowly gaining popularity until, by 300 CE, the two were equally in use. After that, the scroll gradually fell from favour. By 1000 CE, scrolls were used only by governments and institutions for recording legislation and making decrees. By Gutenberg's time at the end of the Middle Ages, scrolls were a niche market, in use only for religious purposes, a practice that continues today. The Torah, for instance, is still copied scroll to scroll by highly trained, learned, and pious scribes, and small scrolls inscribed with particular Bible verses are produced for the mezuzah that marks the door frames of many Jewish homes.

The codex evolved independently in the Americas, where its trajectory was more tragic. When the conquistadores arrived in Mexico in 1519, they found a civilization that was reading books written on paper made from the inner bark of the wild fig tree, a much more durable substrate than papyrus. Mayans coated their fig-tree paper with lime plaster, creating a smooth white surface that was perfect for their intricate, highly coloured glyphs. Some codices were also made from deer hide. The pages weren't loose, as in European codices: they were folded accordion-style into "screen-fold" books. A reader opening the book could read several pages at once, like a scroll, but the pages were distinct and folded up to a flat stack, like a European codex. The *Codex Borbonicus*, an Aztec calendar, was made from a single folded sheet of fig-tree paper forty-seven feet long. Intent on stamping out Aztec and Mayan cultures, the Spanish burned almost all the Mexican codices. Among the few that were spared is the *Dresden Codex*, folded into thirty-nine leaves, written on both sides. It dates from the eleventh or twelfth century and is the oldest surviving book in the Americas.

Book-burning is a favourite tactic of conquering heroes and political megalomaniacs. In the early 1990s,

I co-wrote a book called *The Valour and the Horror* that drew the wrath of Second World War veterans. A 500-million-dollar lawsuit was launched against us, the biggest class-action suit in Canadian history at the time. A senate hearing was also called, and within the solemn stone walls of Canada's parliament, senators rose to recommend that the book be destroyed. The lawsuit went to the Supreme Court of Ontario, where the judge declared there were no grounds for legal action, quite the opposite, but the image of my own book being burned has never left me.

Paper books are too ubiquitous to be wiped off the face of the earth by burning. More likely, they will follow the survival curve of the scroll. Just as radio continued after the advent of television, and CDs are still produced even though most of us download our music directly onto our devices, printed books will likely be with us for a long time yet. The pace of change is accelerated but, even so, a hundred years from now printed books and some form of electronic reader may happily co-exist, text scrolling on a screen the usual way of reading, printed books reserved for special purposes, still held in the highest esteem.

RIDING THE ROCKET

Hugh and I set the book launch for August 26, six weeks after we pulled the last page of *The Paradise Project* from the press. Surely this will give Hugh plenty of time to get the pages bound. He has decided not to bind all 290 books at once. The binding alone costs $15 a copy, and he has pre-sold only fifty books. I'll bind a hundred, he says, maybe 125.

Binding is the process of physically assembling printed pages into a book. The parchment notebooks of the Romans contained folded pages and sometimes they stitched a few wax tablets together along one side. These two concepts—folding and sewing—are the basis of all book binding.

Bookbinding hasn't changed much in 500 years. A medieval bookbinder, a hand bookbinder today, and a contemporary commercial bindery all face the same three basic questions: how to hold the pages together, how to protect the pages and cover them securely, how to label and decorate the cover.

Early codices were sometimes stored with pieces of wood laid on top to keep the loose pages square and protected, but it wasn't until the fifth century that pages were bound together and fitted between hard covers made from thin wooden boards covered with leather. Because vellum was notorious for swelling during hot, humid weather, the wooden covers of these first bound books were often secured by leather or metal straps and clasps known collectively as furniture. (The word "furniture" comes from "furnish," to equip, so that clasps on a book and pieces of wood in a printer's chase are all furniture—necessary equipment. When I do a substantive edit of my books, I often refer to the process as "moving the furniture.")

Even after the fifth century, books didn't always have covers. As late as the nineteenth century, books were often sold in plain paper wrappers, the pages temporarily sewn together by the printer. Books without covers were cheaper to transport, and publishers weren't willing to go to the expense of binding a book if it wasn't going to sell. Often as not, especially for expensive books, the buyer was expected to take the book to his own binder to have it bound to match his personal library. The 1854 edition of *Walden* by Henry David Thoreau is an early example of a book bound by its publisher. It is a half-bound leather book, which means it has a leather spine but cloth sides, which made it relatively cheap to produce.

Hugh has produced some interesting covers. When he published *The Last Paradise, Odetta*, Antonino Mazza lent him a bronze medal that had been cast in honour of Pasolini after his murder. Hugh made a polypropylene mould of each side of the medal and created 115 paper facsimiles using raw fibre from Saint-Armand. The binder inset the paper disks into the front and back covers, the medal split by the pages of the book to reflect the violence of the poet's death.

For the Christmas keepsake he made in honour of Verla the year she died, Hugh built a number of hand looms and invited her friends to weave strips of cloth that he glued to the spines, a unique handwoven spine for each book.

The Paradise Project will be a more traditional hardcover, casebound book, which means the pages will be bound into a "textblock" attached to a "case" made of matte board covered with paper. (It could also be covered in leather or cloth, hence the term "cloth binding.") With casebound books, pages are typically glued or sewn.

Open a book. If the pages lie flat, the pages are sewn. *The Paradise Project* will be Smyth-sewn, a hallmark of library quality or archival books because pages are physically stitched into the book using binder's thread, then further reinforced with fabric backing and adhesive at the spine. Case bindings are both secure and tamperproof. Individual pages won't come loose, and a page can't be removed without compromising the entire binding.

David Smyth patented his book-sewing machine in 1879. "Perfect" binding—gluing instead of stitching—was invented twenty years later, but it was rarely used until 1931, when Germany's Albatross Books introduced the first paperback. These inexpensive books were greeted with enthusiasm by impoverished readers craving escape from the reality of the Depression. Four years later, Penguin Books adopted the format, and in 1939, Pocket Books in America started producing its most popular titles in paperback versions.

Early paperbacks were bound with cold glues that grew brittle over time. We've all tossed out dozens of those books, spines cracked, pages fluttering to the floor. (I admit I have a few favourites still held together with rubber bands.) In the 1940s, the DuPont company developed a hot-melt adhesive that made for longer-lasting paperbacks with more integrity, but no glue can ever solve the inherent problem with perfect binding: open the book flat, and the pages are likely to pop out.

The Paradise Project will be bound at Smiths Falls Book Binding, which operates in a small town an hour's drive north of Kingston. In 1739, Leipzig, Germany—a town with a population of only about 35,000—boasted twenty-two book binderies, but such enterprises are rare birds now. The one in Smiths Falls survives by servicing libraries in need of archival binding, individuals looking to conserve and restore their old books, and self-published writers wanting print-on-demand and bind-on-demand books.

When Hugh started his press, he was adamant that his books be handmade down to the last detail. He commissioned a local book artist to hand-bind the pages and covers of the first two Hellbox editions.

"The books cost $50 each to bind—and that was twenty years ago!" Hugh exclaims. "I had to find a less expensive way. I decided I would do it myself. How hard could it be?"

For the next decade, he sewed pages himself, using linen thread and one of Verla's needles. Being Hugh, he didn't just use a simple knot to tie off the thread that bound the pages together.

"If the book was a bit brash and earthy, I tied the knot on the outside. It was my way of saying, 'This author has balls.' Otherwise, I tied it on the inside." Phil Hall's poetry collection *X* has the double knot on the outside, as does *The Truth About Rabbits*, a debut collection by spoken-word artist Winona Lynn. The knots on several others are discreetly hidden inside.

Most of the time his stitching held, but when I open

my copy of *Where Do I Start*, that collection of emails from Hugh's daughter about her work on Vancouver's downtown east side, I find the endpapers wrinkled, the pages separating from the covers.

"I wasn't very good at it," he admits. "I should have gone to a commercial bindery from the beginning. But eventually I got smart."

Binding is a three-step process. The pages have to be sewn to create the text block, the covers have to be constructed, and the text block has to be attached to the covers. With *The Paradise Project*, the first and second steps take place together.

Hugh delivers the printed signatures to Smiths Falls Book Binding and, at the same time, hands over the Japanese Ajisai (Hyacinth) Gold paper to wrap the covers and the Japanese Arashi (Storm) paper to wrap the spine. Once the covers are made, they'll be shipped back to Hugh to be printed while the text blocks are sewn.

The spine is made from a narrow strip of thin matte board; the covers are from a heavier stock. The spine and two covers are laid out on the work table like a spine sandwich. A long strip of tape, or "hinge," is glued to one side of the spine, then to the cover on one side. When both hinges are set, the full cover is turned over. Storm paper is glued to the outside of the spine, extending an inch or so onto the front and back covers. Next, Hyacinth paper is glued over the outside of the front and back covers. The full cover is turned over again, and the spine and cover papers are brought to the inside, trimmed, and neatly glued.

Hugh fits the front cover sideways onto the platen and prints *The Paradise Project* and my name across the lovely Hyacinth paper.

There is no title on the spine. "Why?" I ask.

He looks embarrassed. "I guess because I never thought about printing on the spine!"

In this, he is more faithful to Gutenberg than he knows. The first bound books were stored flat on a shelf, spines facing the back. The owner would write the title in ink along the fore-edges of the pages, the way we used to print *MATH* and *GEOGRAPHY* on the fore-edges of our high school textbooks so we'd know what we were grabbing from the jumble inside our lockers. Around the sixteenth century, readers began to stand their books up on the shelf, a practice that was standard by the 1700s. To identify the standing book, printers added the title, author, and publisher to the spine, first as a printed or penned strip of paper, and later by printing on the spine itself.

While Hugh is printing the covers, the bindery is busy creating the textblocks. Before taking the pages to the bindery, he gathered them into signatures, carefully choosing impressions with similar ink coverage so that each book will appear uniform. At the bindery, each signature is stitched individually through the fold with threads that go through the paper several times. Then all four signatures are stacked in order and stitched, chained together with a single linen thread.

If I peer down into the spine of my presentation copy of *The Paradise Project*—indeed, into any well-bound book—I can count the individual folded signatures, proof that it is either a handsewn or a Smyth-sewn book.

Two weeks before the launch, I get an email from Hugh: "This book is blowing people out of the water. If you have heard a rumour that I'm excited about the launch I'm sure it's not true. I don't know about you but I'm going to have withdrawal symptoms when this book is done."

He spoke too soon. Before the day is over, the bindery calls. Stupid Hugh has been at it again: some of the pages are gathered upside down. Hugh spends a day putting more signatures together and drives them up to Smiths Falls. The following Monday, he delivers the printed covers. The bindery confirms he can pick up the finished books at the end of the week.

"Good news!" he writes. "We will have 125 books bound in time for the launch and I'm well on my way to finishing the sleeves for the page-openers. Now I'm leaving it in your hands to arrange for good weather."

The launch is Sunday. All through the week, the bindery staff works long hours to meet our deadline. It looks like they'll make it. Then, first thing Thursday morning, Hugh gets another email: some of the endpapers are too short. Can Hugh get more?

The endpapers do more than look pretty: they bind the textblock to the cover. Emily produced her endpapers in matching pairs, one for the front and one for the back. Each endpaper is folded in half. One half is glued to the inside cover, and the other is glued narrowly at the inside edge of the first or last page of the book, so the endpaper is attached but also free-moving like a separate page. Because the endpapers are handmade, they vary in size. Too big is okay: it can be trimmed to fit. Too small is a disaster.

Hugh emails Emily. She has another 150 pairs of endpapers ready, but by the time she can get them to the bus and the bus gets to Kingston and Hugh drives them up to Smiths Falls, another day will be lost. Hugh emails the bindery and tells them he'll get them there Friday morning. If need be, he'll stay to help until all 125 books are bound.

The to-ing and fro-ing is playing havoc with Hugh's timeline. He still has to finish making the sleeves for the books, another ripple caused by my offhand suggestion to leave some of the pages unopened. Hugh decided we had to supply a paper knife. How, then, to attach the knife to the book? A book sleeve, of course. And how would a book buyer know what to do with it? Include instructions, what else?

"I can see it all quite clearly," Hugh wrote the night before he made the first sleeve. The knife would tuck into slits in the front of the sleeve, like a darning needle through a sock. A folded paper printed with instructions would be tucked under the knife. I wrote a brief treatise on the proper use of a paper knife; Hugh printed it and set to work constructing and sewing 125 sleeves. Between the two of us, we cornered the Kingston market on a certain slim metal letter opener, and I ordered fifty more online, dropping them into Hugh's mailbox the morning they arrived.

"Mother never said that this publishing business would be easy, but the important thing is that we will be ready. I have the sleeves made and the paper knife instructions printed, I just need to mount the knives and notes, which I will do on Sunday morning. Don't you just love these mad dashes to the wire?"

I can almost hear him chuckling.

"Keep your fingers crossed, Author. We're riding the rocket in the eleventh hour!"

THE READIES

This book that I am writing, *Gutenberg's Fingerprint*, is called a manuscript even though I am not writing it by hand. I'm typing it on my MacBook Pro in a program called Scrivener. I'll send the finished "manuscript" to my editor by email. She'll make suggestions with Track Changes, a feature of word processing programs. The designer will format the book digitally. And I'll receive the final edit not as galleys—the old, long, curling sheets of typesetting—but as a PDF file. Much of the printing of the paper book will be accomplished on digital presses. This book will assume a physical form only in its very final stage: a print butterfly emerging from a pixelated chrysalis.

The ebook version of *Gutenberg's Fingerprint* has a final physical form, too—on an ereader, the most recent stop on the moving frontier of the digitization of publishing. Long before ereaders were invented, physical books were being converted to pixels through Project Gutenberg, founded in 1971 when Michael S. Hart, a graduate student at the University of Illinois, decided to type up the Declaration of Independence and make it available for free public download. The Declaration became the first ebook; the United States Bill of Rights and the Bible were second and third. Hart went on to found the first digital library, offering public-domain books for free download as ebooks to be read on personal computers.

Over a thousand titles were on the virtual shelves of Project Gutenberg's free library by the time ereaders came on the market. The first prototype—a floppy-disk-driven, six-inch reader called Incipit—was developed at the University of Milan in 1993, but it wasn't until 1998 that two ereaders—SoftBook and Gemstar's Rocket eBook Reader—were introduced to consumers, along with websites where ebooks could be downloaded for a fee. The Millennium and the EveryBook came out in '99; the Cybook launched in 2001. Those first ereaders weren't very different in principle from the next generation of Kindles, Kobos, and their ilk, except for storage capacity, which was limited to 1,500 pages (about five books) and Internet connectivity, which was dicey enough to provoke significant download frustration.

Ereaders may not have been invented until the 1990s, but the idea was articulated sixty years earlier in an essay called "The Readies" by Bob Brown, which appeared in the journal *transition*. In 1930, after watching a "talkie" movie, he got the idea that books, too, needed a shot in the arm, "a machine that will allow us to keep up with the vast volume of print available today and be optically pleasing." Brown wasn't an inventor, so nothing came of his idea, but he did predict that such a machine would allow users to adjust the type size, avoid paper cuts, and save trees. He also predicted that eventually words would be "recorded directly on the palpitating ether."

I saw ereaders long before I could buy one. I was a Trekkie. Through the late 1980s and early 1990s, *Star Trek: The Next Generation* was my eye candy of choice, a television series that showcased fantasized, twenty-fourth-century technology while basing its plots on the works of Raymond Chandler, Herman Melville, Sir Arthur Conan Doyle, Charles Dickens, William Shakespeare, and even Gilgamesh. At quiet moments, Captain Jean-Luc Picard would retire to his cabin with a cup of "Tea—Earl Grey—hot!" and a book, some-times an antique twentieth-century paper book, but often a small rectangle that he held before him like a mirror, reading pages that scrolled before his eyes.

Despite the futuristic prep of *Star Trek*, the first ereaders provoked the virulent love-hate reaction that so often greets new technologies. Some writers jumped on the bandwagon: Stephen King's novel *Ride the Bullet*, released in 2000, appeared first as an ebook. Within five years, however, the limited memory and download irri-tations cancelled out the desirable novelty of the device. By 2003, manufacturers were going out of business and Barnes & Noble was closing down its ebook sales division.

Ha! print-lovers gloated. A flash in the pan.

Their triumph was short-lived. Just one year later, Sony released LIBRIé, the first ereader to use electronic ink technology. Finally, words on the screen had almost the same clarity as words printed on paper.

In 2007, Amazon introduced the Kindle, the first truly reader-friendly ereader. It was pretty basic—it didn't pretend to be anything but a hand-held plastic page—but it connected to Whispernet, Amazon's private data storage and retrieval system that held millions of books, an avid reader's wet dream.

Other online book retailers followed suit. Barnes & Noble brought out the Nook, Chapters/Indigo the Kobo, Sony its Sony Reader, all of them digital devices designed solely for reading. They don't run email or Twitter or Facebook or any other distracting applications. They are just books—super-thin, spineless, coverless books, not so different from a codex, with pages that appear one at a time to be read singly, not in spreads that open like, well, a book.

Dedicated ereaders are exactly that: dedicated. They are like printed books in the way that they are content to sit patiently on a bedside table or in a purse or a glove compartment, waiting to be picked up, flipped open, and read. They exist only to be read. People like them precisely because they seem so familiar.

But this very appealing strength is also a great weakness. The tethered distribution systems of a Kindle or a Kobo forces a reader to shop at only one store—a gigantic store, but even so, the ereader comes with built-in boundaries. With my Kindle, I can read only what Amazon offers.

This fenced-in ereader world was about to blast open. In 2008, BooksOnBoard.com started selling ebooks that could be read on Apple's brand new iPhone, introduced just the year before. In 2009, Sony hooked up with a digital wholesaler, OverDrive, offering their ereader customers access to the ebook holdings of any participating library. That same year, a Sony Reader loaded with textbooks was given to every student at Blyth Academy, a private school in Toronto, Ontario—the first high school in the world to distribute digital texts to its classes.

When Apple introduced the first iPad tablet in 2010, I was at the sales counter. It was bigger than a cellphone or any dedicated ereader and had a better screen. The iPad came with a built-in app called iBooks, but I could also download Kindle and OverDrive and Kobo. Since then, tablets have proliferated and no wonder. They unchain us from a single mega-retailer monopoly. We can buy stories from iTunes, novels from Amazon, download a nineteenth-century novel from Project Gutenberg, share EPUB files of our self-published ebooks. My Kindle languishes on the shelf. I can't give it away. I've tried.

In the first quarter of 2012, according to the Association of American Publishers, ebook sales surpassed hardcover sales for the first time. By 2014, fully half of all American adults had an ebook reading device, either an ereader or a tablet. (Forty-five percent had tablets, nineteen percent owned ereaders, some owned both.)

But here's the thing: although half of American adults owned an ereader in 2014, that same year only twenty-eight percent claimed to have read an ebook. This makes me wonder if the tide has really turned. Maybe this is just another case of techno-lust: in a few years, people may be tossing their ereaders into the same box in the basement that holds their Game Boy, their Discman, and their eight-track tapes.

Only about four percent of the people who read books are digital-only. The rest are like me and my friends, people with both ereaders and shelves of printed books. A very unscientific poll reveals that my friends prefer ereaders for travel, for genre fiction—fantasy, mystery, romance—and for research, because digital is so searchable and text can be highlighted and bookmarked onscreen as you read. With literary fiction, people like me tend to buy the ebook first and, if we really like it, we'll buy the print edition, too. Knowing this, many publishers now bundle an ebook in with the print book. A website called BitLit started up in 2014 to put readers together with these publishers. BitLit now offers an app, Shelfie, that will take pictures of a book-shelf so a reader can download free ebook or audiobook editions of paper books.

The advantages of ereaders are legion. They are lighter than printed books, less likely to cause bruising for those of us who like to fall asleep with stories. Ereaders now have vast memories, capable of holding not five, but 15,000 books. In the early 1990s, when I travelled to Mexico for the winter, I took one small suitcase of clothes and one very large suitcase crammed with books. Now I take my iPad and a print book or two not yet released in digital format. I am exactly in the demographic that is the most active consumer of ebooks: seventy-five percent are women and seventy-seven percent are over forty-five. Most are between fifty-five and sixty-four. Not kids, then, and not techno-geeks. Women of a certain age.

I read a lot of ebooks, but even so, I score the experience fairly low on the literary aesthetic scale, compared to holding, smelling, feeling, and turning the pages of a printed book. The thingness of a printed book is still important to me. A paper book presents ideas and stories in a way that is increasingly unlike any other way I receive such information. There are no links to lure me down one rabbit-hole after another. No electrical cords to tether me. No Big Brother to decide what I can buy and whether I can keep it. A printed book is a world I can hold in my hands, a world I can step into and out of as I choose. It is limited and self-contained, which changes how I interact with it. The experience isn't necessarily better, but it is qualitatively different. Print books encourage depth; digital encourages breadth.

Naomi Baron, in her book, *Words Onscreen: The Fate of Books in the Digital World*, reports on her studies with university students in the United States, Japan, Slovakia, Germany, and India. Ninety-two percent of them said they concentrate better when they read in print. And it's not just concentration that's affected. "The problem with reading digitally is that it encourages us to keep going," she writes. "Print gives us the leeway to pause and think."

Ereaders, dedicated or not, are almost certainly a transitional technology. We'll look back on the so-called state-of-the-art digital technology we're using today and see these ereaders as Model Ts compared to the ways we'll be reading in twenty, ten, even two years from now. Ereaders may end up like television: astonishing when it came into my living room in 1956, essential through the moon landings, assassinations, famines, wars, and *Downton Abbey*s of the '60s, '70s, '80s, '90s, and the first two decades of the new millennium, then suddenly and swiftly made obsolete by Internet streaming. Who knew we would abandon television so completely, with hardly a backward glance? It is equally impossible to predict the future of ereader technology, but I suspect ereaders will eventually leave our lives, too. Before they do, they will drift even further from the discrete thingness of printed books, further from the traditional publishing model that today informs ereaders as much as it does paper books.

At the moment, ereaders are a lot like printed books partly because of copyright laws. But suppose notions of ownership around written text change. Suppose readers could control not only what they read and how they read, but how they engage with the text. Suppose the boundaries that make reading a print book a discreet, isolated experience come tumbling down. Suppose ereaders fully embrace all that digital can do.

Hugh McGuire, co-founder of Rebus, founder of PressBooks and LibriVox, and co-editor of *Book: A Futurist's Manifesto*, listed his own future-book-reading wish list during a talk at the WWW2016 Conference:

I would like to connect the books I read to a service of my choosing that helps me view and track the books I have read, and organize that experience in different ways.

I would like to be able to make links between the books I am reading, to arrange, say, my annotations from multiple books from a particular topic into a single place.

I would like to be able to easily bring my annotations—along with rich metadata about where they come from—into other tools, perhaps Word to write an article, or WordPress to write a blog post.

I would like to track when I am reading books, and what the impacts are on my sleep habits.

I would like to be able to plug into a service that will map out all the locations mentioned in the books I have read and show them to me.

I would like to plug into a service that will automatically build for me

a reading list based on all the books
mentioned in the books I've read.

I would like to plug into a service
that will let me ask an AI chatbot
to search for references to the book
I am reading in other books.

At the moment, he can't do any of these things.

Ereaders have come a long way in the decade and a
half since they were first introduced. They have surpassed
anything the creators of *Star Trek* imagined. Phone
screens are getting bigger to accommodate books as
well as browsing. Tablets are sending dedicated ereaders
into obsolescence. Publishers have figured out that the
experience of reading onscreen is different from that of
reading on the page, and they now hire skilled designers
like Erik to create ebooks that are visually distinct from
the printed version. Higher design standards are having
an impact on self-published ebooks, which at first were
the electronic equivalent of mimeographed handouts.

Bob Brown's prediction of almost a century ago is
well on its way to coming true. The Readies are not
only increasingly inexpensive, accessible, and function-
ally sophisticated, they are set to become delightfully,
satisfyingly "optically pleasing."

Hugh arrives early, struggling across the lawn with his hitching gait, barely visible behind the tower of cardboard boxes in his arms. He lowers them to the grass under the spreading apple tree where I've set tables for the book display and signing. The day promises to be killingly hot: the food and drink are cooling inside.

"Your wand has worked very well on the weather," Hugh says. "Good job!"

"And good job on the books," I toss back.

Hugh is laying the books on my grandmother's white linen tablecloth in numerical order. For months I have been looking at lines of type, random pages, disconnected images. Seeing these parts brought together, not just in one book but in the hundred lined up along the tables, moves me more than I thought possible. Each book rests in its own lovely sage-green sleeve, a metal paper-knife glinting in a slit along one side, the instructions trapped gently beneath the blade. A book plate on the front of the sleeve lists the title, the author, and the number of the book. At one end of the table, a printed sheet lists all the advance buyers and the book Hugh has assigned to them.

We are expecting about eighty people: friends, family, colleagues, country neighbours, and many of those who bought books in advance, including my dentist, who bought four. Next week Hugh will ship copies to out-of-town buyers, including the rare book libraries, but he has brought these books to the launch, too. He sets a stack in front of me.

The Paradise Project

Merilyn Simonds

Thee Hellbox Press

Copy number *103*.

The Paper K...

We have included the pa...
to cut the uncut pages of...
Lay the book on its side...
between the pages at the...
at a 45 degree angle, the...
with a slight sawing mot...
these pages, you are takin...
of the book, releasing M...
world.

"These want your Jane Henrietta."

I remove the first book from its sleeve, pick up my pen, pop off the lid, then freeze, Montblanc in mid-air.

"With this? Can I write on this paper with a fountain pen? Is the ink archival?" I turn to the last page and, sure enough, Hugh has signed and numbered the colophon page in pale lead. "Pencil is archival, right? I'll go get a pencil."

My mind is racing through HB, 2B, my father's 1960s mechanical pencil, the collection of late-nineteenth-century ladies' mechanical pencils I've accumulated over the years.

Hugh puts a hand on my arm. "Relax. Sign it in fountain pen—because it is you, because it is period friendly, and because it ain't an f'n ballpoint."

I pick up my pen, and Hugh picks up his needle and thread.

"Still finishing up?" I say, as I lay my signature in the first book. It feels like a desecration.

"Just a few left. You can help, Apprentice. When you've finished there, slide some of these knives into their sleeves."

Still riding the rocket, right up to the minute the first cars pull into the lane.

❧

The gardens are a bit past their prime but still beautiful, the pinks and blues of early summer long since retired in favour of the earthy yellows, burnt oranges, and reds of late summer. The Datura Belle Blanche shrubs are intoxicating; the August Lilies in full, fragrant bloom. The canna lilies and castor bean plants rise to exotic peaks; daylilies lay their long spears at their feet, offspring of the leaves that Emily immortalized in the *Paradise* endpapers.

Each set of endpapers is different, each one a garden. People stand around, staring in wonder at their books, holding the endpapers up to the light, comparing their Emily Cook gardens. Others sit on lawn chairs and benches, hunched over their books, slicing the pages open with the paper knife.

The crowd seems evenly split between those who can't wait to open the pages and those who intend to release the stories one by one as they are read. "I don't think I can cut these pages at all," one friend confesses. I tell her about the rare book library that has purchased two copies: one to open and one to leave uncut. "If only I could afford that!" she moans.

Halfway through the afternoon, Hugh hushes the crowd to say a few words to officially launch the book.

"What have we really accomplished by producing this book?" he asks, waiting for the question to sink in before he answers it himself. "I speak more for those of us who have been intimately involved in the writing and production. I'm sure that when Merilyn created these stories such a collaboration never entered her mind. However, she had the courage to take a chance on me, an unknown person. We hooked up with Erik, certainly unknown to me, but then I always look for the good and build on that.

We then met with Emily, who we were able to fool into thinking we were intelligent. What we had accomplished at that point was the assembly of four creative people. I'm sure that we all bit our tongues from time to time, but we managed not to shoot one another. As a matter of fact, we each started to appreciate the skills of the others. I think it must be outside the ordinary for four creative and, yes, headstrong individuals to get along so well in a collaboration. Thank you for this opportunity. It has been one of great joy for me."

At Hugh's urging, I say a few words, too, then read from the book. I start with "Tree," raising my eyes from the page now and then to look past the assembled crowd to the Norway maple and the mountain ash that inspired the story of a man who planted a tree for each of his children. I read "Stone," my back to the field from which the boulders were lifted to build the wall where people sit. I feel giddy, light-headed, as if the stories have come alive and are walking around in the landscape, whispering in my ears, the words no longer inert pebbles in my mouth or ephemeral shapes on a computer screen. The book in my hand pulses with stories, the ones I am reading and the ones I was part of with Emily and Erik and Hugh. The place where I'm standing inspired this book, its harvest is embedded in the pages, and the people who made every word visible, who made them permanent on the page and protected them with such grace and beauty between covers— these people are all standing with me on the grass.

The feeling is oddly familiar, and with lightning-bolt

shock I realize that here, today, my book and the wider world are linked in a way that I assumed was solely digital, connections zapping off in all directions, limitless.

What can I do but laugh and weep with joy.

※

The Paradise Project is my sixteenth book. My other launches have run the gamut from, "Look, honey, my book arrived in the mail!" to a wall-to-wall party that took over an art gallery where Erik's paintings hung on the wall and Karl provided ambient music with his group, Lion.

Launches have always been celebrations, a birth announcement to those who have asked patiently for years, "When is the book coming out?" In recent years, as newspapers shrink, reviews dwindle, and radio and television interest in books has all but disappeared, launches have evolved from personal parties to a vital piece of a book's marketing campaign. A book isn't launched just once, it is launched in city after city in the hopes that the launch, if not the book, will stir media interest. Launches have become so entrenched as a marketing tool that there are endless blogs offering advice: "How to Organize a Book Launch" and "Twelve Tips for Successful Book Launch Parties," including How to Build Your Crowd, Prizes and Giveaways, and How to Sign. (I should have read that one, but I have a feeling archival paper isn't discussed.) Guests are expected to buy books in droves. As marketing guru Tim Grahl shamelessly said of a client's forthcoming event, "Our goals for the launch are to hit both the *New York Times* and *Wall Street Journal* bestseller lists."

When Erik finished the design for the ebook of *The Paradise Project*, I posted the book on Amazon, Kobo, and iBooks. While I was on those retail sites, I created an author profile. My web mistress and I worked to freshen my website to showcase the new ebook I was launching together with two other backlist ebooks and three estories. I hired Karl, now a sound designer, to record me reading excerpts of the stories and posted the

Paradise Project

ROOT

He loved everything about the plant: its vigorous growth, its prolific bloom, and especially the dark purple fruits that glistened like sweet jellies among the leaves, though they were bitter, unpalatable even to the birds.

He found it growing on a hard piece of earth behind an outbuilding near the first place he lived, a downstairs apartment with access to a small yard that he was encouraged to improve. He dug up the plant, a spindly thing, and moved it into the sun, top-dressing it with sheep manure. It thrived.

After two years, he left. The pattern of his working life was set early, for he was a diplomat of minor account. He didn't mind. He got quite used to moving on, finding small houses to rent, rarely apartments, for he felt the need to step out his door onto earth, into audio files, introduced by his rich baritone, on the site, too. I finished a few days before my birthday, so I waited and, as a present to myself, I sent out an email on that day to all my friends and associates announcing the new *Paradise Project* ebook. I tweeted and posted Facebook comments. I had a postcard made with the gorgeous Erik-designed covers of all six new digital and audio books to leave at bookstores and hand out at workshops and literary gatherings.

I was pretty pleased with myself until, months later, I Googled "How to Launch an Ebook." I got dozens of hits: ebook launch plans, launch tips, launch strategies. Step-by-step action plans. Keys to successful ebook launches. A 30-Day-Ebook-Launch-Formula workshop that I could attend for only $75. The most astonishing site recommended setting the launch date *before* writing the ebook, as a personal incentive. The blog went on to recount how one young woman sat down in March, set a launch date for June, then wrote her book, finished it on schedule, and sold 359 copies of the ebook in the first week!

One of the launch tips suggested releasing sample chapters in advance, to whip up public appetite for the ebook, an oddly anachronistic strategy. That's pretty much how books were promoted 400 years ago. In the early years of mechanical printing, books were expensive, bought by what publishers today would call a niche or a premium market. In order to increase sales, publishers in the seventeenth century produced books in instalments called fascicles. By the nineteenth century, the fascicles were being serialized in magazines.

Charles Dickens' *The Pickwick Papers*, first serialized in 1836, is the book that established serialization as a profitable and appealing marketing strategy. In France, *The Count of Monte Cristo*, by Alexandre Dumas, was meted out in 139 instalments. The economic benefits worked both ways. The circulation of the magazines that carried book serials soared. And when the full novel appeared—just before the final instalment—it was snapped up by readers who couldn't wait even one more day to find out how the story ended.

Serialization was one of the reasons nineteenth-century novels were so long: it was in everyone's best interests—especially the author's, who was paid by the line and the episode—to keep the public panting for more. *Uncle Tom's Cabin*, written by Harriet Beecher Stowe and published in 1852, was one of the biggest hits in early American literature, selling 10,000 copies in the first two weeks. Her publisher threw up his hands to the clamouring public: "Three paper mills are constantly at work, manufacturing the paper, and three power presses are working twenty-four hours per day, in printing it, and more than one hundred book-binders are incessantly plying their trade to bind them, and still it has been impossible, as yet, to supply the demand."

If Gutenberg had printed my book, it would likely have been launched by hiring a young lad to hand out flyers that said something along the lines of "We are pleased to announce that *The Paradise Project* is now for sale direct from the printer, Hugh Barclay, at Thee Hellbox Press." In fact, that's pretty much what we did. We sent out announcement emails, we sent a press release to the local newspaper, and we posted news of the print release on various literary websites. For a few months prior to the launch, I posted bits about the making of the book in what I very loosely called a blog.

Discoverability has always been the issue when launching a new work. Typically a print book is listed in the publisher's catalogue, from which a store orders copies for its shelves. Readers see it on the store's shelves or read reviews of it in a newspaper, and they buy it. Sometimes, a reader discovers the book at a public reading and buys a copy from the person selling stock at the back of the room—a bookstore, the publisher, or the author herself.

In the heyday of CanLit, Jack McClelland, the master impresario of Canadian book promotion, pulled all sorts of pranks to make readers aware of the books he'd just published. In 1980, to launch Sylvia Fraser's *The Emperor's Virgin*, he hired a chariot to drive down Toronto's Yonge Street—in a blizzard—carrying himself, Fraser, and the charioteers, dressed in togas and sandals.

Jack's world was relatively small: just the million or so people in Toronto. The world a book drops into today is as big as planet Earth.

BRICOLAGE

The common wisdom is that publishing is a business that aspires to make money by producing books. Seen from that perspective, it is no different from any business that makes money by producing widgets.

But Hugh doesn't care if he makes money, so long as he's relatively certain of his next meal. Money is involved, but he is pretty clear that it's more likely to go out than come in. For him, a publisher is someone who makes *good* books. Like many small presses, especially literary presses, he practises publishing as art.

Almost as soon as mechanical printing was invented, so too was the art of publishing. In much the same way that Gutenberg brought together the essential physical elements of paper, ink, mechanical type, and press, a Venetian by the name of Aldus Manutius raised the careful selection of each of these elements to an art form: exactly the right paper, the perfect colour of ink, a particular shape of the letters and their design upon the page, the arrangement of the covers, the skilful and artistic binding of all these elements into a physical object that would present a carefully selected text. Manutius wrote *epistulae*, or short letters, in the front of the book to introduce his favoured texts—the precursor of today's forewords and jacket copy.

Not much has changed in traditional publishing since Manutius created Aldine Press and founded a dynasty of great printer-publishers. A good publisher still chooses with care the manuscripts that will be published and oversees every step of production to release the most perfect book possible into the world of readers.

"If you think this is an unworkable enterprise," writes Roberto Calasso in *The Art of the Publisher*, "you may remember that literature loses all of its magic unless there's an element of impossibility concealed deep within it. I believe that something similar can be said about publishing, or at least this particular way of being a publisher."

Calasso and Hugh have a lot in common: a yearning for the impossible.

Calasso himself is the publisher of Adelphi Edizioni in Milan, a house known for its exquisite books and high-quality literary authors. "Part merchant, part circus impresario, the publisher has always been considered with a certain mistrust, like a clever huckster," Calasso continues. At the same time, he says, "publisher" can also be among the most prestigious titles in the working world, if the job is done right.

Calasso describes the first book published by Manutius—*Hypnerotomachia Poliphili*, or *The Strife of Love in a Dream*—which Calasso refers to as a novel in the same vein as James Joyce's *Finnegans Wake*, written in a mash-up of Italian, Latin, and Greek. "The vast majority of bibliophiles regard it as the *most* beautiful book ever printed."

Manutius not only had the aesthetic sensibility to create a beautiful book, he was also innovative. In 1501, he introduced inexpensive editions of Greek and Latin classics, small enough to fit in the hand. He called them *para forma*—we would call them pocket books today—and they revolutionized not only how people read but also the number of people who took up books.

Calasso cites another example of a remarkable publisher: Kurt Wolff, a wealthy young German who, during the First World War, released a series of slim black books containing a single story by writers who would become the brightest lights of German literature. Like Manutius, Wolff selected the texts he published with the greatest care, then passionately and obsessively controlled every element of the bookmaking process to ensure that the physical form reflected the quality and character of the content.

Calasso makes the case for calling this kind of publishing "*bricolage*," an odd French word that is sometimes translated as "do-it-yourself," although DIY doesn't come close to the true meaning of the word. Bricolage is a process of making something in a way that is opposite to the practical, rational process of moving from a goal through various means to an end. In the 1960s, Claude Lévi-Strauss used the word "bricolage" to describe how a society creates something new by using what already exists, as in the creation of a mythology.

Fine publishing, Calasso says, is bricolage. Gutenberg was a bricoleur. Hugh is a bricoleur. This is also how Sherry Turkle, in her book *Life on the Screen*, recommends Internet programmers should work.

Publishing is always casting about for new ways to make books, but never before with the creative zeal driven by digital innovation. In 2006, Wattpad started up: a free site where writers share their works-in-progress. With more than forty-five million subscribers in 2016, Wattpad is used to serialize finished books, too. Since then, many serialization sites that offer books in bits to readers have emerged, most recently Tapas

Media, an app-based platform for mobile devices. Team publishing is a hybrid model between self-publishing and the traditional approach. At Booktrope, authors whose manuscripts were selected for publication were admitted onto a platform where they chose their own team of editor, designer, and marketer of the print-on-demand book. Everyone shared in the profits. In May 2016, after six years and four million copies of one thousand titles, Booktrope closed its doors.

Self-publishers, serializers, team publishers, and traditional print publishers all start with the text, choosing a manuscript for publication because they feel a connection with the writing and because they think others will, too. The publishing guru Brian O'Leary calls this "focusing on the container." He believes that publishing is set to shift gears, to focus instead on "context": who wants the book and how it will be sold, rather than what it is about.

At the fringes of publishing today are nimble new digital start-ups that are reversing the publishing paradigm. They start with what readers want—convenience, specificity, discoverability, easy access, and connection—and produce books that offer all this and more. O'Leary asks us to imagine a world where storage is plentiful, where writing and editing tools are cheap or free, and where content can be sent out in multiple formats to multiple platforms at the push of a button. In many ways, that digital world already exists. In it, instead of giving priority to *what* will be published, publishers will focus on *how* to make what is published discoverable.

The container—the book—has to be rich, layered, linked, and relevant. Readers born in the digital age won't accept anything less. My sons, my granddaughters, and I, in increasing intensity, live in an open and accessible world in which we expect to be able to find what we want easily and quickly, where we expect to be able to mix and match and create something of our own from what already exists. Bricolage.

Does this means that the branders have taken over the artist's studio? I don't think so. In a way, beautiful books, electronic or print, are now a given. The challenge for a publisher is to create and embed into their ebooks sophisticated ways for readers to find a book and engage with its ideas.

Digital thinking is sideways, experimental, the opposite of hierarchical. It is how creative leaps have always been made. In fact, it is how the manuscript for *Gutenberg's Fingerprint* is being written, not by having a vision of where I am going and planning every step in advance, but by wandering around inside an idea, figuring out how this, then that works, standing back and assessing where I am and where I want to go next. Despite what our teachers told us in grade eleven history class, progress is rarely straightforward, *A* to *B* to *C*. More often, the movement from idea to articulation is lateral, circular, spiral, expanding like waves in a pool when a hook is dropped in, like the swirling, limitless links in a digital universe.

The declines I've received from publishers are what my husband likes to call "rave rejections": *We love your work, but it isn't right for us.* I used to think this was just a polite way of telling me my writing was crap, but now I wonder if Calasso isn't right when he says, "Why does a publisher reject a particular book? Because he realizes that publishing it would be like putting the wrong character into a novel." Calasso sees a publisher's entire list as the equivalent of one book, each individual work like a chapter in the longer oeuvre that reveals the publisher's principles and tastes.

"Let's get together," I write to Hugh after the launch of *The Paradise Project*. Our visits are more relaxed now, and often involve lunch at the Star Diner, which hasn't changed its turquoise stools, its boomerang Arborite, or its menu since the 1950s. After our hamburgers and fries, I propose going back to his house for tea. "I want to see all your books."

"What's a book?" he responds.

It is a serious question. Hugh has produced posters and monographs, keepsakes and broadsides, thousands of pages collected in various ways. Some are so slim the word "book" does not immediately spring to mind.

"Anything over forty-eight pages," I toss back, following the definition adopted by the Canada Council for the Arts.

When I arrive, he has all the books he's produced in his thirty-five years as a printer-publisher stacked in a wobbly tower on the kitchen table. They are in chronological order, starting at the top with *A Letter to Teresa*, published in 1983. At the bottom is *The Sky These Days*, a poetry collection by Susan Gillis, hot off the press.

Every book is different in size and shape and colour. A range of genres is represented: poetry, memoir, essays, fiction. It's hard to grasp a binding thread through all these Hellbox books, in either form or content.

Hugh seems a little shy, faced with his oeuvre. Or maybe he's tired. In recent months, he's been having some trouble with his heart. I peer across the table at the tower of books, but really I'm looking at him. His colour is good. The prickle of anxiety at the back of my neck wanes a little.

I pick the top book off the pile, turn to the first page, and read aloud: "The old chief who made us welcome in English and then offered prayer in the soft poetic tongue of the Ojibwa radiated a concern for the future and the past of the North American Indian."

Hugh leans across and flips forward to an illustration of a warrior that seems to dance across the page. "I wanted to show the dynamics of the powwow, a bit of the dance," he says. "So I carved three images and over-printed them in progressively fading colours."

He digs into the pile of books and pulls out *The First Paradise, Odetta*, published with Pasolini's original Italian on the left of each spread, Antonino Mazza's English translation on the right.

"Pasolini was a communist, he was spurned for that," Hugh says, his voice trembling with emotion. "That's why I put his original words on the left. And you see how, when I typeset the lines, I biased them to the left.

There is less white space on the left of every line than on the right."

He closes the book and holds it up to the light. The cover paper is herringbone. "Look from this angle. The title seems to float on the high points. Pasolini was bipolar, so I did this to show that he wrote in the high points of his cycle." He grins at me. "Of course, everyone sees that right off!"

Then, for a moment, he is uncharacteristically introspective. "I'm not sure why I do this. It is a neat thing to do, of course. I hope there is some person out there who will pick it up."

The early books are few and far between. Hugh was occupied with getting his tilt wheelchair into the marketplace. Then Verla died, and he sold the wheelchair business. It was the press that kept him going. In 2009, he published *Piecing It Together*, a collection of poems by Queen's University student Tanya Neumeyer. He had been in Cuba with her a few years before, taking a course on Che Guevara led by his friend Susan Babbitt, who teaches in the department of philosophy at Queen's.

"Tanya was a spoken word artist. In one of the poems, she was coming out. That was the main reason I did the book. It took great courage, it seemed to me, the same kind of courage Che had, so I illustrated that poem with a soft-block portrait of the revolutionary."

I am starting to glimpse the thread: it's the personal connection that Hugh has to feel with a work before he can choose it as a Hellbox book; it's the uncanny attention to detail that makes even the most minuscule aspect of a Hugh Barclay book significant to what the words are saying.

Hugh hands me *Out of the Mouth* by Shane Neilson. The rough burgundy cover is cleaved by a silver shard headed for the word "Mouth."

"The poems deal with his son Zack, who started having seizures at age two," Hugh explains. "That shard shows there is a break in his brain." Deeper into the book, I come upon a collage of shards in silver and gold. "The silver is the seizure, and the meds are in gold. You see? The meds never completely cover the seizure." Pasted into every one of the 104 copies of the book is a bookmark made from the same green fabric that surgeons wear in the operating room. On the final page, a soft block made from a painting by Zack. "I wanted to give him the last word in the book. He deserves it!"

Who else would publish these books? Who else would publish them in this way?

And who, at almost eighty, would see every book as a fresh opportunity to stretch himself, stretch the reader? When he published *The Truth About Rabbits*, by a young poet who divides her time between Paris, France, and Kingston, Ontario, he developed a collaboration with Larry Thompson, a fellow letterpress printer in Merrickville, Ontario. Hugh printed the text, then drove the pages up to Larry, who reprinted the pages with the wood engravings he'd carved.

"I even got him to write his own colophon in the first person, beside mine," Hugh chuckles. He reads it aloud to me: "I am Larry Thompson . . . whose happy task it was to cut the wood engravings that adorn this book, here under the Sign of the Gothic Tree, in the picturesque village of Merrickville while the promise of spring could just be felt in the sunshine."

Paging through the book, we come upon a signature of upside-down pages. "Oh dear," Hugh says, "I'll have to take that one apart." There is no moan and groan in his voice. He makes the correction sound like a treat he can't wait to get at.

And that's part of what makes Thee Hellbox Press unique: these books are flawed. They don't pretend to be made with machine precision. They are made by human hands, a human mind, an exquisitely human heart.

The tower has tumbled into a sprawl of books between us. A lovely jumble. A bricolage.

LASTING IMPRESSIONS
LASTING IMPRESSIONS
LASTING IMPRESSIONS
LASTING IMPRESSIONS

People often say that writing a book is like having a baby, to which I usually reply, "I wish it only took nine months." Writing may not be like childbirth, but *producing* a book is. The minute that longed-for creature is in your hands, the hard parts are forgotten. Hugh is not irritating at all; he is a genius. I look back on the grubby print shop, where we lurched from one near-disaster to another, with a fondness I recognize in Rita Dove's memoir of the making of her letterpress book of poetry.

"I love the world of the print shop," she writes in "The House That Jill Built." "There is a calm and order, an *adagio* sense of time that permits the appreciation, the *heft*, of each detail—the positioning of a comma, the measured appraisal of every letter and space, the sheer physical investment of setting a page of type. Isn't this how every writer imagines writing, setting down each letter with deliberate care, setting it to last, tamping it in?"

The nostalgia I feel for the Hellbox production of *The Paradise Project* is part of how I feel about all books. I *love* books. An irrational, deep, joyous, fierce, sometimes enraged love. I cannot imagine my world stripped of printed books. And I'm not alone. Something about printed books elicits strong emotion. People refer to them as friends, as companions, as the scripted playlist to their lives. In part, this may be because language provokes the emotion that attaches to the sensory cues so important to the memory-storage process. But that doesn't explain why printed books, in particular, become such heartfelt icons for so many people.

Clearly, books are more than plot, more than characters, more than ideas.

"Books sell a house," our real estate agent told us when we listed our country place for sale. By the time we put the grand old stone farmhouse on the market, we had moved the heart of our library of 10,000 books to our city house. "I wish you'd left them here," she said. "Buyers love books!"

From the 3,000 or so we left behind, she made stacks of oversized books to serve as lamp stands and side tables. She laid out books with covers that matched the walls, the floor, the furniture of each bedroom, the living room, the kitchen. When we were ready to deliver the books we didn't want to the Symphony Sale, she asked if she could take some. "Sure!" we said, naively delighted to have a reader for a realtor. For an hour she sat on the floor, pulling out all the books with red spines, white spines, deep blue spines, to decorate other houses she was staging to sell.

Books are a brand. Restaurateurs buy them by the yard to paper the walls of their bars and bistros. Books have been glued together to make bed frames, couches, chairs, benches, even an outdoor bench in Berlin, where the books are renewed each season. In Sweden, a floor-to-ceiling partition was made of books laid flat, end to end, like thin bricks. An Australian bookseller made a waist-high counter for his shop entirely from books. A British company makes chandeliers from the fanned pages of unwanted books. A gift shop in downtown Kingston has two mannequins in its window, one wearing a very swish suit and the other an evening dress, both made from pages of books by Ovid and Noël Coward.

The sight of those orphaned pages makes me queasy. Printed pages are meant to be read. What does it mean when they're used as decoration, as decor, as art?

In novels, books are a kind of short-hand that indicates a character is educated, sensitive, enlightened, worldly. The books that line the rooms in Alan Paton's *Cry, the Beloved Country* spell emancipation. In *Fahrenheit 451* they symbolize freedom of thought and free will, everything the fascist society is not. In *The Book Thief*, by Markus Zusak, books are identity, immortality, an emblem of hope. But what is the meaning of a book on a restaurant wall?

My local used-book dealer told me about a fellow who came into his store looking for a book. Not a certain title or a certain author; he just wanted a book about yay big by yay thick. He spent hours roaming the aisles and finally came to the counter triumphant. He was carrying his Kindle on top. His plan was to cut out the pages of the paper book to make a carrying case for his ereader.

He should have waited. Amazon now sells a Kindle cover that looks exactly like a leather-bound book. You can even order a hand-bound book to hold your reader "that perfectly imitates the look and feel of a classic hard back book." The titles on offer: Jane Austen's *Pride and Prejudice*, Harper Lee's *To Kill a Mockingbird*, Jules Verne's *A Journey to the Centre of the Earth*. Book covers for iPads include *Alice's Adventures in Wonderland*, *Dracula*, *The Great Gatsby*, and *The Theory of Relativity*, depending on whom you admire and whom you want to impress. You can also order a "book case" for your smartphone.

I've seen old books reamed out to hold flasks, secret documents, and house keys. I can wear actual pages from *Pride and Prejudice* pasted over a big wooden bead to hang around my neck. Or a pendant made of a glass bottle containing a page of *Wuthering Heights*. Or a brooch in the shape of a bird covered with a varnished "original page from damaged copies of Harper Lee's classic" *To Kill a Mockingbird*. At the Grimsby Wayzgoose this year, an artisan printer was selling teensy books to wear as necklaces.

Copying quotations and likenesses of authors is one thing. But repurposing actual pages of actual printed books strikes me as sacrilege until I look over at the frame on the wall by my bed. It contains a page from a nineteenth-century book, *The Language of Flowers*, showing an early lithograph of roses, violets, and tulips. Brought together in a bouquet, the flowers say, "Your beauty and modesty have forced from me a declaration of love." A razor-bladed book page has been staring me in the face every morning for twenty years, and I've only just noticed.

It gets worse. Amazon sells a candle called New Book that promises a scent reminiscent of the beautiful smell of a newly opened book, what they call "an unabridged blend of lignin paper, ambered glue, and fresh India ink, narrated charmingly with white ginger and sweet pine resin."

Such bookish paraphernalia would not be sold unless people were buying it. I suppose there are those who would wear "old book" perfume if it were offered. If nothing else, these earrings, candles, and page-dressed mannequins tell me one thing: people may not be reading printed books, but they still want the smell, the touch, the sight of them close at hand.

And what does all this say about what a book means in our culture? I think it says the brand is still fresh. A book is intelligent and thoughtful. Not old and fusty. Books still matter.

What is a book?, Hugh asked me.

It is not an idle question. When scientists with the Human Genome Project finally sequenced all the genes in human DNA in 2003, they called it a book—the book of life. When I worked in magazines, every issue was called a "book." A book can be a whole packet of knowledge, as in "Who wrote the book of love?" In fact, it can be any gathering of like things: a book of matches, or the number of tricks I need to win in a game of bridge before I can start scoring. For half a millennium, humans regarded a "book" as a stack of pages between covers, but I wonder how many pages have to be in the stack before it earns the title. And what about ebooks, which have neither physical pages nor covers?

The *Oxford English Dictionary* cites the original meaning of book as "a writing tablet," a definition that expanded to include any sort of written narrative, record, list, etc. Eventually, a book was defined generally as a collection of sheets of paper, written or printed on, and "fastened together so as to form a material whole." Contemporary online dictionaries such as the *Cambridge English Dictionary* pry the definition open a little wider: "a written text that can be published in printed or electronic form." The notion of stacked pages and fastening on one side has disappeared. Instead, the word is often modified: print book or ebook; paper book or digital book. Rarely just book.

I spend some time pondering a definition of my own. It starts out long and convoluted, but in the end, the only inclusive, conclusive meaning I can come up with is this: "A book is a longish written work published in some form." I recall the wording in a film contract I was once offered and feel tempted to add, "in some form now existing or yet to be invented anywhere in the universe."

A few years ago, Hugh McGuire took a stab at what he calls "a format-agnostic" definition of a book that would articulate what the various kinds of books have in common: "A book is a discrete collection of text (and other media), that is designed by an author(s) as an internally complete representation of an idea, or set of ideas—emotion or set of emotions—and transmitted to readers in various formats."

Both the writer and the reader have a place in his definition. I wish I'd thought of that.

In the beginning, ebooks were little more than printed books in digital form. Copycats. But think about what software can do and apply that to books. When we open a book, whether paper or pixel, we expect it to be the same as when we last opened it. But an ebook could be automatically upgraded, the way our Adobe Readers and operating systems are. Applications now tell us when an upgrade is available, but future upgrades may well be seamless and invisible, version-less. Or maybe with books, versions will still be part of the picture. Academics revel in different versions of a text, and so do readers. We love the glimpse into process that multiple versions afford. My editor was recently in Rome where she stumbled across a library in an old palazzo museum that had a display of fifty or sixty of the earliest versions of *Orlando Furioso* (*Roland's Rage*), the sixteenth-century Italian epic poem that was a major influence on Spenser's *The Faerie Queene* and

Shakespeare's *Much Ado About Nothing*. Each version in the exhibit was different, and beautiful in its own way.

So-called "enhanced ebooks" have been evolving for two decades. At first, the approach was essentially info-loading, embedding links to anything remotely related to the text. This has evolved until now, the embedded "assets" feel like natural extensions, deeply relevant to the narrative. They don't take you out of the story, they drive you in deeper.

Early on, digital storytellers spun their narratives around the "choose your adventure" model of alternate story paths and endings that put creation into the hands of readers. The latest digital stories, however, preserve the role of the author who constructs the original narrative, start to finish, but readers are encouraged to explore and engage with the text. The reader's role is no longer passive, it is active, even though he or she can't actually affect the outcome.

The latest catchphrase—which may well be obsolete before this book is printed—is "augmented reality," or AR: virtual images laid over real ones to create an "augmented" display. AR integrates graphics, sounds, touch (haptics), and smell into a real-world environment, blurring the line between the actual and the computer-generated. Caitlin Fisher is the Canada Research Chair in Digital Culture and co-founder of York University's Future Cinema Lab. Digital technology, she says, has already transformed narrative and storytelling. I listened to her speak on the subject for over an hour, and she never mentioned the word "book," instead referring to "story worlds," "story frames," "narrative spines," and "interactive narratives" with the unrestrained enthusiasm with which people must have talked about the first printed books 600 years ago.

Serialization and platforms such as Wattpad have given new urgency to reading, a sense of "I have to read this now, I have to be part of this conversation." (Some books on Wattpad get over a billion reads.) There's a spirit of community to this kind of reading, of reciprocity when readers can engage directly with the story. "What does a novel look like," asks Caitlin Fisher, "when it is spacialized and hundreds of thousands of readers own a piece of it?"

We get a glimpse of this narrative future in *Inanimate Alice*, a digital novel I've been reading since it was first released in 2005. Developed by Canadian novelist Kate Pullinger and British graphic designer Chris Joseph, *Inanimate Alice* uses images, text, and sound to tell the story of a young girl who travels the world. The reader/viewer determines the pace of the story and has to perform certain actions for it to continue; there are embedded puzzles, games, and other "digital assets." The storyline is riveting, told in six episodes, the most recent released in 2016, free to read on a computer browser or purchase to download with purchase.

Book apps have been around for a while. The first one I downloaded was for my granddaughter, who was seven at the time. Now Google's Editions at Play hosts "books" that are essentially websites built to be experienced on a mobile device. With music and visuals, reading has the quality of world-building games. One of the 2016 titles, *Strata*, was developed in partnership with Lex Records and Penguin Random House U.K.: clearly, traditional publishers are banking on this becoming a trend.

Read—or more accurately, participate—in a digital story, and a printed book will seem as old-fashioned as a player piano. My generation may still prefer a static text, but children growing up today expect media to be participatory. They add comments to everything they look at, whether it's a simple "like" on Facebook, a retweet, or a full blog discussion. A multidimensional digital book will seem as normal to them as a paperback did to us.

As a writer, this excites me. I've always maintained that a book isn't finished until it's read, that writing is a collaboration with readers who ultimately read a different book than the one I wrote, finding themes that I wasn't consciously aware of developing. But traditionally, a writer rarely communicates with readers: a life with words is a solitary one. When *The Convict Lover* was adapted for the stage, I went to all the rehearsals and came home deeply envious of playwrights who have actors to help them work out their dialogue. Since then, I have dabbled in collaboration, from reading with jazz bands to producing the foundational script for an experimental-music symphony that included huge projected photographs, narration, an opera singer, and multimedia effects.

The letterpress and digital versions of *The Paradise Project* were also collaborations of a sort. I can feel myself edging along the book continuum: it's only a matter of time until I move past print and digital to dive headfirst and full-body into whatever lies beyond.

THE PRICE OF TEA IN CHINA

At the launch of *The Paradise Project*, friends mill about, picking up their books. They each paid $150 for this slim volume of stories. When we set the price, I felt embarrassed. Would I pay that much for a book, even one that is made by hand? I'm not sure.

Rita Dove had the same reaction when it came time to price her letterpress book of poems.

"Rita, how much time did you put into each word, each line?" her printer asks. "They've been set by hand and handprinted on fine paper and the bindings glued by hand and sewn by hand. How long have you worked on this book? How long have we worked on its conception, and now, the book?" Then, very gently, "This book is worth more than you can ever ask for it."

Hugh says almost exactly the same thing to me after I send an email to friends and colleagues announcing the book.

"I notice that you apologize for the price of the book," he writes. "May I suggest that you point out the unique characteristics and suggest that, in view of the fact that such books occur only once every twenty years or so, this book is very well priced. If you bought a folio of Erik's linocuts alone, you would expect to pay at least this much. Seen from almost every perspective, your book is a bargain."

He's right. This isn't a book, it's art. And you can't put a price on art.

Even so, I'm not used to thinking about the price sticker on my books. That's one of the arguments for going with a traditional publisher: they take care of all financial matters. Not with Hugh. As I've discovered, he expects the author to put her finger on every pulse point of the process.

In the early days of printing, books were sold *before* they went on the press. Printers would advertise that a subscription was available. Sometimes writers went door to door, as American ornithologist and painter John James Audubon did. In 1820, he decided to paint every bird in North America. While he painted, he knocked on doors to solicit financial backers for the project. Finding none in the United States, he travelled to England, where he garnered little monetary support but did come across an excellent engraver and printer. Audubon travelled for three years, giving talks and meeting people whom he signed up to receive 435 prints of his life-sized watercolours of birds, five at a time, in a pay-as-you-go subscription. A dozen years of painting and knocking on doors, and still he was able to print only 200 sets of the treasured *Birds of America*.

It was during the nineteenth century, as the mechanization of bookmaking progressed, that the various trades involved in the process became specialized. The writer wrote, the designer designed, the printer printed, the publisher (as a role distinct from the printer) arrived on the scene to oversee production and distribute the book. By the late–nineteenth century, bookstores became the go-to place to purchase a book. Even then, the local general store would usually stock a few psalters and almanacs; street kiosks would sell popular fiction and political treatises; and itinerant hawkers would have some engravings and calendars among their wares. Increasingly, though, bookstores sprang up in cities, towns, and villages as reading and literacy spread.

In its early days, no doubt because of the threat of sedition, bookselling was strictly controlled. In France, Napoleon created a system whereby a bookseller who wanted to set up shop had to supply four references and a certificate from the mayor attesting to his morality, as well as four further references that confirmed his professional abilities as a bookseller. If successful in his application, the bookseller then had to swear an oath of loyalty to the regime.

Restrictions relaxed towards the end of the nineteenth century, and the number of bookstores proliferated. In England, W. H. Smith set up bookstalls in every railway station in the country; in France, Hachette followed with Bibliothèques des chemins de fer. In Berlin, just before the First World War, there was a bookstore for every 3,700 citizens; in Leipzig, one for every 1,700. Kingston, Ontario, the city where I live, has a population of more than 100,000, and until five years ago, it had six bookstores. Now there are only four: two used and two new, including a chain and an independent.

That's one for every 25,000 citizens. Online megastores that deliver books electronically or by mail order (and soon by drone) have changed everything.

Hugh's profit margins are so slim, and often non-existent, that there is no room for a middleman. He sells his books himself, on his website and at the book fairs where he sets up his stall. He relies on the author to pass business his way. When we were selling *The Paradise Project*, he left it to me to stir up interest. Since then, he has taken a card from Audubon's hand and offers a discount for pre-purchased books, with solicitations sent by email—the portal-to-portal equivalent of door-to-door.

Hugh may be more forward-thinking than he knows. In *Book: A Futurist's Manifesto*, media consultant Brian O'Leary argues that in the content-flooded near-future world of books, sales may change from fee-per-purchase to a subscription model, where for a monthly payment readers can have access to books of a certain type, or by a certain author, or unlimited choice, models that already exist in some form with Kindle Unlimited and Scribd. He counters the complaint that the Web, already filled with lolcats and ego noise, is no place for selling books. "The question isn't what stupid things people have put on the Web in the past but what great things we could do if books were connected on the Web in the future. That's what sets people who love books, and the Web, to dreaming."

Paper is a plastic screen; type is a million shifting, floating balls; ink is seen as pixels; Gutenberg's press has disappeared; local bookstores are vanishing, too. But all of this is just window dressing to the truly fundamental change that ebooks have wrought.

Stephen King called books "portable magic." Now the magic is truly ephemeral.

Ebooks have set words loose in the ether. Words no longer have substance, shape, heft. I can't feel them as a series of marks on a page. I can't hold them in my hand, knowing they will be there tomorrow and the day after and a hundred years from now, barring floods and fires and the negligence of my species.

Three thousand years of creating an alphabet, learning to write, experimenting with damp clay and rolls of donkey hide, stirring lampblack into egg white and grinding cinnabar into oil, carving letters from wood and lead and antimony, rubbing and pressing and stamping, sewing and gluing and fixing one surface to another have brought us full circle. Once again, words are ephemeral, disappearing as easily, as completely, as if spoken into the wind.

I have approximately 1,200 books on the shelves at my back as I write. Imagine if I turned around one day and *poof!* they were gone. That's what happened to Allene, who tells her sad tale on the Amazon forum "Books Disappeared from my Kindle." True, she only had 340 books on her Kindle, and SReads only had 71, and someone named Castro doesn't say how many were on his Samsung tablet when it froze.

A quick call to customer service can usually restore accidental deletions, but it is chilling to know that digital retailers can—and do—delete ebooks that a reader has bought and stored in her digital library. On Friday, June 12, 2009, anyone who had purchased an ebook of George Orwell's *1984* from Amazon woke up to find it gone from their Kindle. This was not a prank, although it was highly ironic given that in the Orwell novel, Big Brother gets rid of embarrassing stories by sending them down an incineration chute called "the memory hole." In real life, it was Amazon.com that remotely deleted both *1984* and *Animal Farm* from the Kindles of their paying customers. The company later explained that it was a legal issue—Amazon had bought the ebooks from a company that didn't hold the rights—and they refunded the cost of the books. But nothing could take back the sudden, absolute realization that ebooks are not ours to keep, not even when we pay for them.

Like most people, I rarely read the fine print of user agreements before clicking, "I agree." A close inspection of the Amazon agreement, however, reveals this clause:

"Unless otherwise specified, Digital Content is licensed, not sold, to you by the Content Provider."

In other words, an ebook is not purchased in the way that we buy a physical book, which we own once we pay for it. What we buy from Amazon and Kobo and their ilk is a perpetual license to *read* an ebook.

Our transactions in a physical bookstore are

completely different. They are anonymous. They can't be traced. If a bookseller discovered the books he was selling were illegal merchandise, he wouldn't be able to find you to take back your copy. And even if he found you, he certainly couldn't break into your house and take it off your shelf. Because Amazon is selling you a license, however, they can revoke it at any time, and because the transaction is tracked, they know exactly where to find your book. Perfectly legal, but unsettling nonetheless.

The terms of ebook ownership are constantly being tweaked in response to what readers want, what is economical, and what is possible. At the moment, Amazon allows a Kindle owner to share five ebooks with other owners and so does Apple through its Family Sharing program, although with Apple, only entire libraries can be shared, not individual titles. Bloggers like to paint eretailers as power-crazed Big Brothers, but the truth is that it is still too technically complicated to tether unconnected devices without compromising individual privacy.

Outside the mega-retailers, self-published authors are thinking up new ways to sell their digital-born books. Pay-what-you-want pricing, for instance, is a sales strategy so common now that, like BYOB, it has its own acronym: PWYW. Basically a book is offered for sale with a suggested price that buyers can pay or not, as they choose. Most people tend to pay the suggested price or more, but they go away feeling like they got a deal because *they* chose the price tag.

My own financial arrangement with Hugh was loose. Very loose. We had no contract. This is uncharacteristic:

I've taught financial workshops for artists. I would never recommend such a thing. But the book project evolved erratically: there was never a good time to bring it up, and, besides, my relationship with Hugh seemed to have so little to do with money. When the book was finally published, he sent me an accounting. He would earn back his costs as soon as the first hundred copies were sold. After that, he suggested, we should split the proceeds. That sounded fair to me.

The truth is, I won't likely make any money from *The Paradise Project*. Not from Hugh's letterpress edition, and not from the ebook version either. I will have to sell a lot of $10 ebooks to earn back the $2,000 I spent to have the text professionally designed, edited, formatted.

For a few years in the 1990s, it seemed reasonable to expect to make a living as a writer of books. That no longer seems realistic, except for the very few.

Writers are still trying to grasp the financial fallout of the transition from physical to digital, which has occurred, for some of us, within the span of time it takes to conceive and produce a book. In certain genres, such as paranormal, romance, and "new adult," ebooks now account for up to ninety percent of sales. Even for literary fiction, a third of my royalties are from ebooks.

The shock waves from this transition continue to push at what we've known. Author and editor tools are so easy and accessible that everyone, it seems, is now writing a book. Professional writers' incomes are dropping as copyright laws are being dismantled and publishers are starting to release DRM-free ebooks.

DRM stands for digital rights management, which is basically a lock put on digital books to prevent a reader from sharing or creating course packs and mash-ups. Increasingly, independent publishers are releasing books without DRM or any other form of copy restriction.

The debate around DRM is both moral and financial: should a creator have rights to what they create? Should someone who uses a creator's work for another purpose pay for that privilege? Maybe some new way will be developed to prevent unauthorized use, but my guess is that all text will soon be available to anyone who wants to share or reassemble it.

Soon indie writers will far outnumber those who are traditionally published. In fact, they probably already do. There will be way more "books," but it will be harder to find books you want to read. Writers will become permanently disabused of the notion that writing is a profession that will earn them enough to pay the rent and the electricity bill to run the computer. Looked at from another perspective, we may not get rich, but we may have way more readers.

Only the future knows whether the digital disruption will be a good or a bad thing for books, for writers, for readers, for literature. But Pakistani author Kamila Shamsie asks a provocative question: "Are we hearing all the complex, nuanced human voices we need to help us understand our own times, our fellow citizens, the world in which we live? No. But we could. And we must. And that should be publishing's bottom line."

Hugh doesn't own an ereader or a tablet, and he pecks

at his computer keyboard with one crooked finger. I'm pretty sure he has never laid eyes on the digital version of *The Paradise Project*. But I can see him nodding, bright-eyed, at Kamila Shamsie's words. More voices, yes!—and who gives a tinker's damn how they come to us.

IMPLANTING FORGETFULNESS IN OUR SOULS

Each of the paradigm shifts that pushed human communication forward has met with stiff resistance. Even the invention of writing. From the perspective of the twenty-first century, such resistance seems incomprehensible, almost ridiculous. What kind of knob would say no to the written word?

Socrates, for one. In his dialogue *Phaedrus*, Plato has Socrates tell the story of the ancient Egyptian god Theuth, who invented geometry and astronomy, games of chance, and—his greatest invention of all—writing. Thamus, king of the Egyptians, admired all of these gifts except writing, which he refused to teach to his subjects, claiming that "if men learn this, it will implant forgetfulness in their souls; they will cease to exercise memory because they rely on that which is written, calling things to remembrance no longer from within themselves, but by means of external marks. What you have discovered is a recipe not for memory, but for reminder."

Socrates tells the story to explain why he refuses to "write" his thoughts "in water" with pen and ink, "sowing words which can neither speak for themselves nor teach the truth adequately to others."

According to Plato, Socrates called writing "inhuman." In striving to establish outside the mind that which can truly live only *inside* the mind, writing transforms thought into object, no longer of flesh and blood. Reading, in his view, was just as despicable. Because readers would be able to "receive a quantity of information without proper instruction," they would "be thought very knowledgeable when they are for the most part quite ignorant."

Almost 2,000 years later, the advent of the printed book provoked the same response. The humanist Italian editor Hieronimo Squarciafico was at first enthusiastic about books. But in 1477, less than a decade after Gutenberg died, Squarciafico wrote an imagined discourse between the spirits of great authors passing their time in the Elysian Fields. Some authors lauded the new printing press, but others complained that "printing had fallen into the hands of unlettered men who corrupted almost everything." Yet even the naysayers felt they had to accept Gutenberg's invention: "Their works would perish if they were not printed, since this art compels all writers to give way to it."

This sounds a lot like what writers today say about digital books, and self-publishing, too. They are the modern incarnations of that Florentine bookseller, Vespasiano da Bisticci, who said that a mechanically printed book should be "ashamed" to be set beside a hand-copied manuscript.

Squarciafico has become famous for his aphorism, "Abundance of books makes men less studious; it destroys memory and enfeebles the mind by relieving it of too much work." It is well to remember that he wrote this at a time when books were still enormous, chained to lecterns, long before Manutius released them to everyone's hands with his *para forma*.

The rotting impact of reading on the mind wasn't the only criticism levelled against books. Inexpensive and easily available, books would devalue the work of scholars and undermine religious authority, spreading sedition and debauchery. And perhaps these critics were right. Luther's Ninety-Five Theses would not have spread so far and wide without a printing press to publish his posters, and it's unlikely the Enlightenment would have had the impact it did without the rise in literacy that the printing press made possible.

But is it true that writing and reading books have stolen our memories, made us stupid?

That argument was levelled against calculators (a small handheld device that could add, subtract, multiply, and divide at the press of a button). Keep them out of schools! our parents said. Children will lose the ability to add up long columns of numbers in their heads! Which they probably did, since that skill quickly became redundant in the face of a machine with the ability to calculate complicated equations in seconds.

With the Internet fully upon us, the same old criticisms are being voiced once again. "Is Google Making Us Stupid?" Nicholas Carr asked in the *Atlantic*. "Over the past few years I've had an uncomfortable sense that someone, or something, has been tinkering with my brain, remapping the neural circuitry, reprogramming the memory. My mind isn't going—so far as I can tell— but it's changing. I'm not thinking the way I used to think. I can feel it most strongly when I'm reading."

I know exactly what he means. I feel it, too. Even writing these short vignettes, I interrupt myself a dozen times to check facts, scan incoming email, confirm my bank balance. My brain functions seem less linear, more scattered. More nimble, too, if I'm honest. Less able to focus, perhaps, but better able to make connections. In his seminal folklore text, *The Singer of Tales*, Albert Lord suggests that the act of writing drives us to a linear way of thinking, that oral memory is patterned differently than written memory. Perhaps computers are taking us back to a different—not necessarily inferior—spatial form of memory.

For at least five years, bloggers have been monitoring the phenomenon. "I used to be a voracious reader. What happened?" one moans. "I can't read *War and Peace* anymore," another admits. "I've lost the ability to do that. Even a blog post of more than three or four paragraphs is too much to absorb. I skim it." "What if I do all my reading on the Web not so much because the way I read has changed, but because the way I THINK has changed?"

It's a terrifying thought. Clearly, as a species, we aren't crazy about change. We resist it at the very moment we embrace it. And we are right. There are monsters as well as ghosts in the machine. We know this from experience (even if we don't remember it). Nicholas Carr cites the example of the mechanical clock, which came into common use about a hundred years before the printing press. In his book *Technics and Civilization*, the historian and cultural critic Lewis Mumford describes how the clock "disassociated time from human events" and "helped create the belief in an independent world of mathematically measurable sequences." The scientific mind with its measurable truths evolved in part because of the mechanical clock. A significant benefit, to be sure, but we lost something, too. We stopped paying close attention to our bodies and to the physical world around us. We eat at noon even when we aren't hungry. We go to sleep at ten p.m. whether the summer sun is still shining in our northern sky or we are pulling up the blankets under a dark winter moon.

Reading onscreen may indeed be turning us into informational magpies, and writing probably did weaken the part of our minds in which long poems and speeches were stored and shared orally with friends and family. My nostalgic self yearns for what I can only imagine: a huddle of loved ones, all eyes fixed on the storyteller, knowing as I listen that the story this time won't be the same as when I last heard it, or the next time, either, every moment fresh, unique, pure in itself.

Socrates and Squarciafico knew something in their bones that we no longer believe. Or at least, it is a truth that we fight against: life is ephemeral, it is different one millisecond to the next. No amount of pressing words onto paper or digitizing them on a screen will ever stop that flow.

LEARNING TO READ

I don't remember a time before books. My mother used to say I was born knowing how to read, but of course that can't be true. Still, I don't remember learning. I can't remember a time when *A-B-C* struck me the way Arabic or Greek letters appear to me now. Utterly foreign. Impenetrable. Without meaning.

I do remember the day my firstborn son learned to read. More precisely, the day I learned that he could read. It was winter. I was pregnant again, huge with a post-Christmas child. Karl was sitting on the floor at my feet with *The Little Engine That Could.*

"I think I can! I think I can!" he said in his sweet child's voice.

I had read the book to him often. I assumed he was remembering my words.

"What are you doing?" I said.

"Reading."

"Really?" I sat up and closed my own book. "Are you reading every word?"

He read the next sentence perfectly. I wasn't convinced. He was only three, after all.

"I can read!" he said.

"Can you read the newspaper?"

"Sure I can!"

He heaved himself up and toddled over to the basket beside my chair. He opened the newspaper to its full size and spread it on the floor. He sat on top of it, laid his finger on a line, and read every word.

In her memoir, *Ex Libris*, Anne Fadiman recounts a story about the Irish novelist John McGahern. When he was a small child, his sisters unlaced his shoes and removed them, while he was reading. He didn't seem to notice. They put a straw hat on his head. Still nothing. Only when they pulled his chair out from under him did he "wake out of the book."

I understand this phrase. Emerging out of a story is like rising unwilling from Atlantis. I've wandered semi-conscious through the house for hours after I left the pages of a Colm Tóibín novel or an Alice Munro story. I've seen my granddaughters emerge from their rooms with the same glazed eyes, Kobos limp in their hands.

Parchment, paper, electronic particles: does it matter what the portal is made of that leads us into story?

Maybe.

Julian Barnes, in his acceptance speech after winning the 2011 Man Booker Prize, made a plea for the survival of printed books. Umberto Eco in his published conversation with Jean-Philippe de Tonnac, *This Is Not the End of the Book*, voiced the belief that printed books *must* always be with us.

Spend time with someone reared reading digital books and the printed page will seem as old-fashioned as a horse and carriage. Charming, but impractical. What, it's not searchable? You can't change the font? I have to squint at that tiny type? If I forget it at home, that's it, nothing to read? Are you kidding me?

But Julian Barnes and Umberto Eco and Mark Helprin aren't talking about practicalities. It is the way we relate to a book that these defenders of reading the printed page are determined not to lose.

Clearly, the interface of reader and printed page is different from the interface of reader and screen. Defenders of print talk about the feel of the paper, the sound of a page turn, the heft of pages in the hand. The invitation of broad margins to receive a personal comment, a squiggle, a tick. The way the mind remembers how far into the thickness of a book a specific passage was. I can still remember exactly where I first met the word "ubiquitous," in the pages of *The Rise and Fall of the Third Reich*. I was fourteen years old, and I'm pretty sure I could lay my finger on that word in that book today.

Digital text discourages that kind of personal, visceral engagement. In his heretical book, *Where I'm Reading From*, novelist and translator Tim Parks asks, "But are these old habits essential? Mightn't they actually be distracting us from the written word itself?"

It's an interesting question. Over the past 4,000 years, all of the paradigm shifts in communication have worked to make the experience more impersonal, more pared down, more generic. Writing took ideas out of the head and turned them into objects built of words. As the poet-typographer Robert Bringhurst puts it, "Writing domesticated language." The alphabet reduced images—pictures of everyday things we recognized—to lines and shapes that had meaning only because we ascribed it to them. Mechanical type substituted mass-produced letters for individually recognizable handwriting. And digitization has made words ephemeral, without any physical substance at all.

Each stage has been loudly lamented, but Parks invites us to consider what reading is really all about. Unlike sculpture or painting, there is no essential artifact, and readers aren't required to respect the artist's timing, the length of time the experience should take, as they are with music. Joyce is Joyce is Joyce whether set in Baskerville or Times New Roman, whether shouted or read silently. The only requirement is that the words be read in the order in which they were written. Everything else is up for grabs. So what is the literary experience, at its core? To Tim Parks, it is "the movement of the mind through a sequence of words from beginning to end."

Even Socrates might agree with Parks that writing is "pure mental material, as close as one can get to thought itself." Not thought itself, but close.

Still, the books in my house are more than repositories of near-thought. They are also mnemonic devices, reminders that I have read those words, enjoyed them, taken them in. Scanning my shelves, my eyes light on the book my Aunt Marion gave me the day I was born, the *Fun with Dick and Jane* book that taught me to read, the Bible I read cover to cover when I was eleven, the Hardys and Salingers and Capotes that fed my adolescence, the *Gone with the Wind* I read straight through the night my older son was born, the myriad volumes, slim and fat, ragged and pristine, that make my life flash before me. The same thing happens when I look at the covers displayed on my iPad: the list is shorter because I only have a decade of digital reading stored there, but those covers do the same for me as the spines on my library shelves. They are my Proustian *madeleines*, opening stories in my memory without ever clicking on the book or pulling it from the shelves.

When our library was bulging, we had nothing on our walls but books. No paintings. No photographs. Anyone coming into that house might have thought we had a book fetish or a deep need to show off our familiarity with famous works.

I wonder if Tim Parks is right when he says that digital text, by eliminating all distractions except the naked words themselves, actually brings a reader closer to the essence of the literary experience. He compares the transition from paper to screen to the moment when we passed from reading illustrated children's books to reading adult books in which the pictures were gone, leaving only words.

"This is a medium for grown-ups," he concludes.

His theory is appealing. Yet the more I think of it, the more Parks' argument strikes me as narrowly intellectual. We are more than brains: we have ears, noses, fingertips, all of which engage with a physical book. Even so if I let go of the nostalgia and think about the last book I read on my iPad—*The Mercy Journals* by Claudia Casper— I can't imagine how my enjoyment of that post-apocalyptic novel could possibly be heightened.

When I moved from picture books to my mother's books, fat novels by Thomas B. Costain and John Buchan, nothing else in my world could lift me so fully out of my life and set me down in Scotland or England or Italy. There were movies, but that was a different experience entirely, one packaged for me, one that manipulated my emotions like a mad puppeteer. A book was a book and nothing else. Opening the covers was like tapping on the stone in front of Aladdin's cave and saying, "Open sesame." Only a book held the treasures that consumed me.

Such immersion, I think, is not solely the purview of paper.

Recently, I was sitting in my car in a parking lot, waiting for my husband. I was reading a book when two young women walked past, all legs and bare midriffs. They were clearly heading for the mall bookstore.

"I, like, read so many books! Most weeks, ten at least."

"Me, too," said her friend. "I read fifteen last week."

I practically jumped out of the car and hugged them. Anyone worried about the state of reading should hang out in the parking lots of bookstores. But that wouldn't tell the whole story. My granddaughters, who are now fifteen and thirteen, love paper books and collect certain series. Their bookshelves, at their house in the city and at the farm, are bulging. We talk about the books on their shelves, but I have no idea what they are reading onscreen. Those titles are hidden within their digital devices.

Lucky kids. I had to sneak forbidden books into the house. They can read them right under their parents' noses.

In *The German Ideology*, which lays the foundation for Karl Marx's theory of history, Marx writes: "Is it not inevitable that with the emergence of the press, the singing and the telling and the muse cease; that is, the conditions necessary for epic poetry disappear?" He was referring to the notion in epic poetry that the metre served as an *aide-mémoire* to an oral poet reciting a long narrative work. Take away the necessity for remembering and the raison d'être of the metre is removed, opening epic poetry to mutations in its form.

The invention of the printing press might have robbed us of a certain kind of literary memory, but it also collapsed the information monopolies of the church and the universities. Literacy increased by leaps and bounds. When sixteenth-century philosopher Michel de Montaigne wrote his famous *Les Essais* in 1580, just 140 years after the invention of the printing press, he had a library of 1,500 works in his tower in the Dordogne. His short ruminations, printed in a book that could travel the world, went on to influence René Descartes, Ralph Waldo Emerson, Friedrich Nietzsche, and Isaac Asimov—an impact unthinkable just a century before. Imagine the implications if those books had not been written, those thoughts not fixed for future generations to read.

In his book *The End of Absence*, Michael Harris quotes *The Justification of Johann Gutenberg*, a novel by Blake Morrison in which the inventor argues with an abbot not about the content the printing press is spewing forth, but about the *way* that text can now be read. "The word of God needs to be interpreted by priests," the abbot exclaims, "not spread about like dung."

⚡

According to Alison Gopnik, a Berkeley psychologist, the act of reading reshaped our brains long before the Internet came along. Parts of the brain once devoted to vision and speech have been "hijacked by print." Instead of learning through doing, through apprenticeship—the way Hugh learns—I'm dependent on books.

As evidence, Gopnik points to dyslexia and attention disorders and learning disabilities. All signs, she says, that our brains were not designed to deal with such a profoundly unnatural technology as reading.

Marshall McLuhan, who spent his life studying the relationship between the medium and the message, seems to blame reading and writing for drawing us away from our natural thinking selves. "The eye speeded up and the voice quieted down." He attributes our "shrill and expansive individualism" to Gutenberg's invention.

The printing press let loose an explosion of books. Digitization has turned that grenade into an atomic bomb. I wonder how much of that disruption is obvious at the time it is going on. A shift in jobs is one immediate indicator: 500 years ago scribes were thrown out of work almost overnight; the herders who produced the vellum were made redundant. At the same time, the printing press created a burning need for typesetters and inkmakers and papermakers and bookbinders, trades no one had imagined a decade before. Similarly, as print shops close down, computer programmers, ebook designers, electronic marketers, and software developers are filling the gap with entirely new kinds of work.

There was a time when we thought computers would usher in a paperless world, when we believed those who said the book would soon be dead. We may not be able to anticipate the fallout from these dramatic paradigm shifts, but one thing is inevitable: there will always be someone on the podium, shaking their fist, warning of dire consequences and an impoverished future. Yet no one predicted that the social media revolution would create a culture in which everyone reads, and that includes books.

According to the twelfth annual Publishers Forum, 2016 marked "the end of the digital beginning." Perhaps we have enough experience now to make some viable predictions. For instance, Ingenta, a publishing software provider, predicts that the print book will have staying power and so will the ebook: the two will diverge as each finds its own readers. (Agent/publisher/author/critic Andrew Lownie is less optimistic: he predicts traditional publishing's share will drop to ten percent.) New on the horizon are digital audio book formats and audio podcasts: both are expected to grow exponentially. Andrew Rhomberg at Jellybooks is using data collected on digital reading devices to tell us how books are being read. (Ninety percent of readers give up after five chapters; readership declines sharply during the first hundred pages; those who make it past a hundred pages will likely keep going to the end.) David Crotty of *The Scholarly Kitchen*, a blog published by the Society for Scholarly Publishing, predicts that in our age of ever-expanding media abundance "the value of curation will continue to be increasingly vital." Readers will be looking for networks, bloggers, reviewers, publishers they trust to filter the flood of books, to point them to what they want to read.

More readers, more writers, more books. Who can complain about that?

MOVING INTO OVERDRIVE

I went searching for the collective noun for books, hoping it would be something fanciful, like a shimmer of hummingbirds or a quiz of teachers, a cloudier of cats. I imagined a puzzling of books, a provocation of novels, a delight of poetry. But no, a gathering of printed pages bound on one side is exactly what one would expect: a library of books.

The word "library" was coined in the late fourteenth century, after the wholesale copying of books in scriptoriums made collections possible but before Gutenberg invented his mechanical press. The word comes from the Old French *librairie*, meaning a collection of books, which comes from the Latin *librarium*, meaning a chest containing books—at the time, as many volumes as a person was likely to own. The root of *librarium* is *Liber*, Latin for "book," which derives from *leub*, meaning to strip or peel bark, which is ironic, given that books today are made from trees. The word "library" now stretches to cover the collection of text bytes in our digital devices, and Amazon continues to use the word "library" to refer to my personal collection of ebooks. (I also have an app called Delicious Library that digitally tracks and manages my collection of physical books by scanning their bar codes.)

At the beginning of the shift to computers, I was wary of digital libraries—what if the power goes out?—but surely the libraries of the future couldn't be any more fragile than those of the past. The most famous ancient book hoard, the library at Alexandria, accidentally burned to the ground during the Siege of Alexandria in 48 BCE, when a fire set by Julius Caesar's troops spread from the docks into the city.

By some estimates, ninety-nine percent of ancient Greek literature has been lost through fire, war, and the whims of history. Of the nine volumes of verse written by the Greek poet Sappho, only one complete poem survives. Of Livy's 142 books on the history of Rome, only 35 can still be read today. Ovid's version of *Medea*, Gorgias' philosophical *On Non-Existence*, seventy-four plays by Euripides, some ninety plays each by Aeschylus and Sophocles, the entire works of the Greek philosopher Epicurus—all gone. And these are just the books that we know are missing because we've found some reference to them. There must be tens of thousands of works by authors we don't even know existed.

The books themselves may be missing, but we have

a good idea what an ancient Roman library looked like. When the eruptions of Vesuvius buried Pompeii in 79 CE, the lava also flowed over Herculaneum, burying the town and a mountainside villa purportedly owned by Julius Caesar's father-in-law. In 1752, the villa was excavated from under its burial shroud of ninety feet of stone and ash. Among its splendidly intact loggias and galleries was the only private library that survives from antiquity: a small room housing hundreds of papyrus scrolls stacked horizontally on shelves and some packed in travelling scroll boxes called *capsae*. Eight hundred books in all, with only a precious few culled for an aborted escape from what has come to be called the Villa die Papyri, the Villa of the Papyrus Scrolls. Some believe that this library was only an antechamber, that the main library has yet to be excavated.

In the 265 years since the magnificent library at Herculaneum was found, not one scroll has been read. Ironically, the ash that charred the papyrus also preserved it. The minute these buried treasures are exposed to air they start to deteriorate and disappear, this time permanently. And as soon as anyone tries to unfurl the scrolls, the paper crumbles to dust. So there the books sit in their ashy tomb, tantalizing repositories of some of the world's great stories, a verbal exposition on the way of life of an entire civilization. Words from the past that could speak to us, but can't.

Over the centuries, various means have been used to try to soften the scrolls enough to unfurl them: rose water, mercury, "vegetable gas," sulfuric compounds, papyrus juice, and, most recently, a cocktail of glycerin, ethanol, and warm water. Every attempt did nothing to ease open the tightly wound papyrus and in fact caused significant harm. Archeologists came to accept that the scrolls might never be physically unfurled, but in the mid-1990s, they began to consider digital technology as a way of penetrating the scrolled pages, reading the words without laying a finger on the artifact. They tried multispectral imaging, or MSI—developed by NASA for use in mapping mineral deposits during planetary flyovers—to make the scribed letters stand out from the charred background, but they weren't readable. Then Brent Seales, a software engineer, proposed putting one of the unopened scrolls inside a CT (computed tomography) scanner, a kind of X-ray used to make 3-D images of human bones and organs. First, he experimented with homemade papyrus scrolls and other old documents and, finally, in 2009, got permission to scan an unopened Herculaneum scroll. Nothing. A physicist at Stanford came across an article about the attempt and thought his synchrotron—a kind of particle accelerator that can be "tuned" to look for certain particles—might make the iron in the iron gall ink legible. Like magic, the writing on the ancient papyrus became visible. In ten years, reading the scrolls had gone, as Seales put it, "from impossible to plausible, even probable." An article in the January 2015 issue of *Nature Communications* announced that the "virtual" unwrapping of a Herculaneum scroll had worked: without physically touching the charred remains, a French team had found writing scattered across the papyrus and had managed to make out one chilling phrase—"would fall."

Digital technology, accused of killing the paper book, may yet succeed in saving whole libraries.

Perhaps it is the ephemeral nature of every sort of communication that makes our species so intent on finding a way to hang onto our written words. Project Gutenberg, for instance, takes as its mission the archiving of all the great cultural works of every continent. When Project Gutenberg was first announced, many writers—myself included—were concerned that it would digitize *all* books, past and present, and post them online for free download, breaking copyright and compromising the ability of authors to make even a paltry living from their work. But that got sorted early on, and today most of the 50,000 books in the Project Gutenberg collection are digitized only after the rights have reverted to the public domain. The rest are digitized with permission. In the forty-five years that Project Gutenberg has been in existence, there have been massive changes in technology, yet from the beginning, the team was committed to creating downloads in long-lasting open formats that could be read on almost any computer.

The first books were entered manually into computer files by volunteers at Illinois Benedictine University. After optical character recognition scanners were invented, the process became streamlined, and today the site is hosted by ibiblio at the University of North Carolina at Chapel Hill. Books are available in plain text and, wherever possible, in formats such as HTML, PDF, EPUB, MOBI, and Plucker. New books are added at a rate of about fifty a week. Most are in English, but works in other languages are increasingly available as Project Gutenberg spreads around the world. When I download from Gutenberg.ca, it is on the understanding that these books conform to Canadian copyright laws.

When Michael Hart invented the digital library, his mission was a noble one: "To provide as many ebooks in as many formats as possible for the entire world to read in as many languages as possible" and to "break down the bars of ignorance and illiteracy." It's true that Project Gutenberg books aren't very pretty and often lack colophons to establish which version of a book was scanned. The books selected for scanning may not be the ones I would choose: this is a crowd-sourced project, after all, run mainly by volunteers. And occasionally, Project Gutenberg–scanned books have made their way into the commercial marketplace, especially into the Amazon digital bookshop, where they are sold for a profit.

But it is hard to argue with the extended life this huge, accessible library has given to books that might otherwise be lost to us.

Libraries full of books provide an interesting meeting ground for technology: old printed books need digitization to give them immortality; the online world still needs paper books to feed its insatiable appetite for content. People want to read, not only new books but old books, too. It was inevitable that commerce would come into the mix, as it has with the ambitious Google Books Library Project, which set out to digitize the contents of *all* the world's libraries. Started in 2002, it had scanned some thirty million books by 2015, when it was stalled by an ongoing lawsuit in which authors and publishers contend that Google was infringing on their copyright, scanning books without permission. Google didn't declare its project as non-profit and so left itself open to the accusation that it intends to profit from the work of others. Authors and publishers continue to struggle to retain control of their copyrights, but despite the challenges, Google carries on. If the moral and legal issues get resolved, by the end of this millennium, Google Books Library Project will have scanned all the world's titles, which in 2010 they estimated at 130 million.

So many books. So little time.

❧

At the moment, my husband is writer-in-residence at the Haig-Brown House in Campbell River, British Columbia, far up the eastern coast of Vancouver Island. When he first arrived, he was given strict instructions about using the Haig-Brown library. He was told not to touch a book without first slipping on a pair of the white cotton gloves mounded in a basket on the large square coffee table at the centre of the room.

The books are arranged not alphabetically by author or by title. They are arranged by the birth date of the author. This boggles my mind, especially given that the system was developed in pre-digital days when it wasn't so easy to discover when anyone was born. The oddness of the system is not unique. I've seen home libraries shelved according to the height of the books or colour of the spines. The main character in Nick Hornby's novel *High Fidelity* organizes his record collection autobiographically, in the order they were acquired. Public libraries use the Dewey Decimal System to shelve books alphabetically by author within numbered subject categories that often makes for strange bedfellows. That system divides knowledge into ten main classes with decimal subclasses. Library of Congress has twenty classes represented by capital letters. B is Philosophy, F is History, P is Literature. Only G for Geography makes any kind of sense.

In our country house, we organized our books in rough categories by room. The dining room was Canadian fiction, my study was international fiction, the hallway was sociology and history, the kitchen was culinary, and the third floor was science and nature. Within each category, books were shelved alphabetically by author. A few years ago, when we suffered our renovation disaster, we decamped to a hotel for six weeks while cleaners in hazmat suits took down every book, cleaned it of silica dust, and packed it into a box; when the air in the house was clean again, the boxes were returned and unpacked. We took pains to describe our shelving system and how important it was for two writers to be able to find their books. Unfortunately, the alphabet was *terra incognita* for the workers reshelving the books.

As we moved those thousands of books to the house in the city where we now live, I couldn't help envying friends who have converted to a digital library. Public lending libraries are trending in the same direction. OverDrive's partnership with local libraries makes digital books available to library members. This is a free service. In 2011, Amazon monetized Carnegie's philanthropic notion of allowing everyone access to books through public lending libraries by introducing the Kindle Owners' Lending Library (KOLL), available only to Amazon Prime members. For an annual fee, Prime members have access to nearly 5,000 books that they can read at a rate of one a month, with no due date.

In 2014, Amazon launched a new subscription service that lets users read Kindle ebooks (on Kindles or through apps) for a fixed fee instead of buying individual titles or becoming an Amazon Prime member. Subscribers to Kindle Unlimited have the choice of over a million books and can read as many of them as they want for $9.99 a month, although they can only have ten on their Kindle at a time. (In 2016, readers buying books from online retailers could choose from 4 million titles on Amazon and 4.7 million on Kobo.) Some of the money earned through Kindle Unlimited is set aside in a monthly pool that is paid out to self-published authors whose books are borrowed, originally on a per-borrowed-book basis, now on a pages-read basis. In February 2016 some three billion pages were read; the pool was $14 million. The amount paid to authors was less than half a cent per page.

Other ebook subscription systems sprang up—Scribd, Entitle, Oyster—but they were short-lived. In

2015, Oyster was bought out by Google and closed its edoors, as did Entitle. Scribd ended its all-you-can-read-for-$8.99 subscription plan and now allows only three ebook reads a month for that price. By early 2016, Kindle Unlimited was the only subscription service still offering all-you-can-read for a monthly fee, although the Big Five publishers (Penguin Random House, Simon & Schuster, HarperCollins, Macmillan, and Hachette) don't participate, leaving readers with a reduced pool of self-published books and those from participating small and mid-sized publishers.

The number of books now accessible to an individual reader is astounding. To the thousands of print volumes in my local lending library, I can add millions through ebook subscription services, Kindle Lending Library, Google Books, and Project Gutenberg. Why have a bookshelf in the house at all?

It's not the weight or bulk of printed books that keeps me from clearing all our shelves in favour of an electronic library, my own or one I subscribe to. I would miss browsing. Not the scattered hunt and peck of a Firefox search, the kind that strains the eyes and exhausts the brain. I would miss the browsing I do when I stand in front of my wall of books, a browsing that is something like daydreaming, an unleashing of the brain to wander where it will, making connections unguided by the rational mind, scanning past Homes, Høeg, Ishiguro, Kingsolver, and in the muddling of those works coming up with an idea for an altogether new kind of literary cocktail.

My books are my brain and my heart made visible.

When my house in the woods was in danger of being engulfed by a forest fire, it was books I carried out in my arms. The diaries I began to write when I was seven have accompanied me through twenty-six apartments and houses. As cumbersome as they are to haul with me through my life, I'm not sure I could write without the works of Elena Poniatowska, Doris Lessing, and Eduardo Galeano at my back.

INTO THE WOODS

Years ago I read a calculation of the true cost of heating with wood. Considering the hours felling, bucking, splitting, and hauling wood, the cost of chainsaw, tractor, and splitter, the wear and tear on back muscles and knees, it was in the tens of thousands of dollars. The article was tongue-in-cheek, but it makes me wonder about the true cost of paper books, when reforestation, pulp-mill pollution, fossil-fuel extraction for manufacturing presses and inks, and transporting books are factored in. Ebooks aren't much better. An individual title may be cheap and have a tiny environmental footprint, but we pay the equivalent of a new bookshelf for a device to read it on, a non-biodegradable plastic device that will be obsolete in a couple of years. It's as if we're back in Gutenberg's day, paying for the pages and paying again for the covers to keep them safe.

But cost isn't the point. The real concern is the

longevity of our literature, the worry that we are risking our written culture on something doomed to disappear.

Hugh claims his books will survive 500 years or more, or he'll give a reader their money back. He says it as a joke, but he means it, too. He likes to think his books will be around long after he has turned to dust, and they likely will be.

In the summer of 2015, a scroll discovered fifty years before among the ruins of Ein Gedi, a Jewish village levelled by fire in 500 CE, was digitally scanned, read, and translated. The charred remains were from a Torah scroll, part of the Book of Leviticus, and were the most ancient of the five books of Moses to be found since the Dead Sea Scrolls. The year before, parchment scrolls the size of a garden snail were discovered inside three phylacteries, small leather boxes with Biblical verses written on them worn during Jewish prayers. No one had thought to look inside the thumb-size leather cases until an archaeologist took them to a hospital and put them through a CT scan.

Literary survival depends on two things: the ability of a book to last through time, and the ability of readers in the future to recognize what they see.

Buried beneath the foundations of Kingston Penitentiary, Canada's first and most formidable prison, is a copy of *St. Ursula's Convent, or, The Nun of Canada*, Canada's first novel, written by Julia Catherine Beckwith and published in Kingston in 1824. Books have long been part of time capsules buried under buildings and in back-yards—bottled optimism, as Glenn Fleishman refers to them in his 2016 article in the *Atlantic*. He describes how, in 1999, the *New York Times* set out to create a new kind of time capsule. The editors met with techies who quickly dissed the notion that digitally encoded information would survive more than a couple of decades. Better to preserve the thing itself, they said, so that whoever finds it in the future can interpret it directly. But the editors persisted until they found a process that could store 10,000 standard letter-sized sheets of text on a 2.2-inch-diameter nickel plate. Several such plates were embedded in the *Times* Capsule, a two-ton stainless-steel above-ground sculpture. The same plates will be used to store the two million words and 14,000 photographs from the Hi.co website when it ended its service in September 2016. The plates have a lifespan of 10,000 years and can be viewed with a 1,000-power optical microscope.

By comparison, from our vantage point in the early part of the twenty-first century, digital books seem a dangerously fragile technology, dependent on electricity and specific software and hardware that could and probably will be outdated within a matter of years, maybe months. Applications and operating systems are upgraded at an alarming rate. Already, my AppleWorks files from a few years ago are unreadable by my new laptop. My floppy disks from a decade or two ago are good only to level my desk. My hard disks should be in a museum. I still own Apple's first portable computer, which I jokingly refer to as a "luggable" because it is the size of an airplane carry-on and about as heavy. Given my experience with technological change, it seems unlikely to me that 1500, 500, or even 50 years from now the digital version of *The Paradise Project* will still exist, let alone be readable on any devices then in use.

But those tiny scrolls and that charred fragment of Leviticus suggest otherwise. A cave preserved the physical objects until an entirely new technology—one that the scribes who wrote those scrolls could never have envisioned—made it possible to read their ancient words. We can't even imagine what technologies will exist a century or a millennium from now that will keep our digital books alive and readable.

In Norway, a Scottish installation artist named Katie Paterson has begun a project that demonstrates extraordinary—some might say foolhardy—faith in the survival of the book. Every year for the next hundred years, a writer will be invited to prepare a manuscript that will be sealed, as both printed text and on a thumb drive, in a special room in the new Deichman Library in Oslo until the year 2115. Margaret Atwood was the first. She called her text "Scribbler Moon." It is unlikely that anyone alive today will live long enough to read it. As part of the inauguration of the Future Library project, a forest of one thousand trees was planted; a century from now, the trees will be pulped to supply the paper to print an anthology of the one hundred sealed texts.

The assumptions embedded in this project are staggering: that someone four generations in the future will know how to make paper from trees; that printing on paper will exist; that the language in which these texts were written will be understood; that a story written today will have resonance with a reader a hundred years from now. The last seems most likely: the human heart doesn't bullet forward with the same relentless speed as technology.

"We are growing a book over a hundred years," Katie Paterson says. The point of the exercise is to show how important today's decisions are for the generations that follow.

I can't decide if this is an act of faith in the future, or an astonishing example of hanging on to the past.

"It's very optimistic to do a project that believes there will be people in a hundred years, that those people will still be reading, that they will be interested in opening all of these boxes and seeing what's inside them, and that we will be able to communicate across time, which is what any book is in any case, it is always a communication across space and time," Atwood mused for a video camera as she leaned against a tree near the newly planted forest.

What will technology be like a hundred years from now: that's the million-dollar question. Perhaps printed books will have gone the way of the scroll. Just in case, Katie Paterson has arranged for a printing press to be stored in the library so that future generations can figure out the process for printing a paper book.

"Future Library is hopeful in its essence because it believes there's going to be a reader in the future," says Katie.

Atwood smiles her characteristic wry smile. "Nature doesn't really care whether there are human beings or not."

Or books, for that matter.

The paradigm shift that Gutenberg's invention provoked took hundreds of years to unfold. No one person's lifetime spanned the entire transition. Technological innovation moves faster now but, even so, digitization is not a moment, it's an era. We are in a privileged and horrifying position: we see the before and we catch a glimpse of the after, but we will never see it all.

In the course of these many months of thinking about books, I have come to view them as very odd things. Thoughts and stories locked into a form. Inflexible. Inert. I suppose that's their charm. But it is also their great failing.

In 2015, book lovers pointed to a momentary decline in ebook sales with relief. "See?" they cheered. "The sky is not falling!" Maybe ebooks would be the eight-track tapes of literature, after all.

That same year, for the first time since 2007, sales of printed books showed an upturn. News headlines were jubilant. But a closer look showed the increase was only 0.3 percent. Moreover, the uptick was due in large part to the popularity of adult colouring books. There was a slight bump in backlist sales, but sales of newly published print books continued to decline. When the stats were broken down by genre, classics and horror sales jumped thirty-three percent while photography, art, and design book sales rose sixty percent. Adult fiction sales were up marginally at two percent.

It's true that 2015 ebook sales were down eleven

percent. Overall, the big decline was in YA, mostly due to a lack of a big Harry Potter–style mega hit. Adult ebook sales were relatively stable. But that is the story only for ebooks sold by print publishers. Amazon doesn't share its detailed sales figures, and in 2015, that eretailer listed four million titles, up from 600,000 six years ago. A third of their best-selling ebooks are self-published.

It is safe to say that the horse is out of the barn. The worm has turned, and so has the milk, and there is no turning either one back. Digital and print may well co-exist comfortably for hundreds of years—the resilience of print has surprised almost everyone in the industry—but ebooks are not going away. Chances are good that ebooks or some further refinement of the electronic principle will eventually push printed books to the margins, just as the codex eventually made scrolls obsolete. As publishing critic Jane Friedman notes, we crossed the digital divide in 2008 and are well on the other side. It's not a question of making peace between print and digital. The digital world is here. Now.

It is curious that we are still so resistant to a cycle that plays out again and again, throughout history and our own lives. In a hundred different ways, ebooks are more convenient and reading them is every bit as pleasurable as reading in print. In just as many ways, paper books are pure delight. Why not embrace both? Maybe scrolls have a place, too. I look at those elegant sculptures rescued from Pompeii, the woman with a scroll draped lightly from one hand to the other, and I think, *Yes! Imagine the silky feel of vellum under the finger.*

Imagine how easy it would be to lay down a scroll and never lose one's place. Diversity, whether in a forest or in publishing, is essential for survival. Perhaps, if books are to survive, we *must* have it all.

The book is not dead. Let me be more specific: the print book is not dead. Its demise has been prematurely proclaimed. Paper and ink bound on one side has a lot of life left in it yet, although my bet is that it won't last forever.

And with apologies to my geeky friends, digital is not forever, either. Something better will come along, and we'll ditch pixels as gaily as we tossed aside our quill pens. Just wait and see.

What we are experiencing is an interregnum, or perhaps a purgatory. As Paul La Farge puts it in "The Deep Space of Digital Reading," we're in the crouch before the leap. The reading brain will adapt to what it reads: the more we skim, the more we will skip lightly across sentences; the more we dive deep, the more we'll be inclined to explore.

Technologies come and go. What is eternal, it seems, is the human craving for story. In 2012, there were 300,000 new publisher-produced books and 391,000 self-published books in the United States alone, as well as ten million reissues and reprints. Clay tablets, parchment scrolls, vellum codices, paper books, bytes on screens—it hardly matters how we get our fix so long as there is a way to read what we want to know of the world.

The awful, wonderful truth is, we humans are deeply flawed. We are all Stupid Merilyns and Stupid Hughs.

This is why we so desperately need stories: to escape our fate, to cope, to learn, to remember. And it is why every technology we invent to share our stories is bound to fail eventually, to prove inadequate to the task, each defect paving the way for the next best thing.

Any blemish, any glitch or slip-up, any smudgy fingerprint on pristine paper may become tomorrow's treasure, the answer to some unimagined, unimaginable question. The thrill that keeps us going is we never know which weakness will save us, or which strength. We have to be discerning, vigilant, savvy. We have to remember to have fun. To play. If the making of *The Paradise Project* has taught me anything, it's that our humanity doesn't dwell in one in technology or another. It rests in our ability to create, to see the world from more points of view than just our own. We need stories. How we read them doesn't matter one single whit.

At ten o'clock on the night before the launch, I receive an email from Hugh. He's finished. One hundred and twenty-five books are printed, bound inside their covers, and each slipped into its handmade sleeve fitted with a paper knife and instructions for cutting open the pages and releasing my stories. I read on, expecting to bask with him in what we have accomplished. But no.

"I have an exciting new project," he writes. "Mother never said it's going to be easy, but don't you worry, I'll figure it out."

SELECTED BIBLIOGRAPHY

PAPER

Basbanes, Nicholas A. *On Paper: The* Everything *of Its Two-Thousand-Year History by a Self-Confessed Bibliophiliac.* New York: Alfred A. Knopf, 2013.

Hunter, Dard. *Papermaking: The History and Technique of an Ancient Craft.* London: Dover Publications, 2011. Originally published in 1943.

TYPE

Baron, Naomi S. *Alphabet to Email: How Written English Evolved and Where It's Heading.* New York: Routledge, 2000.

Bringhurst, Robert. *The Elements of Typographic Style.* Vancouver: Hartley & Marks, 1992.

Dair, Carl. *Design with Type.* Toronto: University of Toronto Press, 1967.

Goudy, Frederick. *The Alphabet, and Elements of Lettering.* New York: Dorset, 1989. Originally published in 1918.

Lawson, Alexander. *Anatomy of a Typeface.* Boston: David R. Godine Publishers, 1990.

Sacks, David. *Language Visible: Unravelling the Mystery of the Alphabet from A to Z.* Toronto: Alfred A. Knopf Canada, 2003.

INK

Bishop, Ted. *The Social Life of Ink: Culture, Wonder, and Our Relationship with the Written Word*. Toronto: Penguin Viking, 2014.

Book printed with the author's blood: underware.nl/publications/the_book_of_war_mortification_and_love/general.

Nietzsche, Friedrich. *Thus Spoke Zarathustra: A Book for All and None*. Translated by Thomas Common. Originally published between 1883 and 1891. Available on Kindle or for free download at holybooks.com/thus-spoke-zarathustra-friedrich-nietzsche.

PRESS

Man, John. *The Gutenberg Revolution: The Story of a Genius and an Invention That Changed the World*. London: Review, 2002.

BOOK

Battles, Matthew. *Library: An Unquiet History*. New York: W.W. Norton, 2015.

Calasso, Roberto. *The Art of the Publisher*. Translated by Richard Dixon. New York: Farrar, Straus and Giroux, 2015.

Carrière, Jean-Claude, and Umberto Eco. *This Is Not the End of the Book: Two Great Men Discuss Our Digital Future*. A conversation curated by Jean-Philippe de Tonnac. Translated by Polly McLean. London: Harvill Secker, 2009.

Carr, Nicholas. *The Shallows: What the Internet Is Doing to Our Brains*. New York: W.W. Norton, 2011.

Coady, Lynn. *Who Needs Books? Reading in the Digital Age*. CLC Kreisel Lecture Series. Edmonton: University of Alberta Press, 2016.

Fadiman, Anne. *Ex Libris: Confessions of a Common Reader.* New York: Farrar, Straus and Giroux, 1998.

Ferris, Jabr. "The Reading Brain in the Digital Age: The Science of Paper versus Screens," *Scientific American*, April 11, 2013.

Harris, Michael. *The End of Absence: Reclaiming What We've Lost in a World of Constant Connection.* Toronto: HarperCollins Publishers, 2014.

Helprin, Mark. *Digital Barbarism: A Writer's Manifesto.* New York: Harper, 2009.

Lyons, Martyn. *Books: A Living History.* London: Thames & Hudson, 2011.

Manguel, Alberto. *A History of Reading.* Toronto: Alfred A. Knopf Canada, 1996.

Manguel, Alberto. *City of Words.* CBC Massey Lectures Series. Toronto: House of Anansi Press, 2007.

Parks, Tim. *Where I'm Reading From: The Changing World of Books.* New York: New York Review Books, 2015.

Socken, Paul, ed. *The Edge of the Precipice: Why Read Literature in the Digital Age?* Montreal: McGill-Queen's University Press, 2013.

Suarez, Michael F., S. J. Woudhoysen, and H. R. Woudhoysen, eds. *The Book: A Global History.* London: Oxford University Press, 2013.

Wolf, Maryanne. *Proust and the Squid: The Story and Science of the Reading Brain.* New York: Harper Perennial, 2008.

The Future Library: KatiePaterson.org.

The History of Bookbinding: lib.msu.edu/exhibits/historyofbinding/index.

ACKNOWLEDGEMENTS

Without Hugh Barclay, this book would still be a rattling of random thoughts in my brain. He not only published *The Paradise Project* as an exquisite handmade letterpress book, he welcomed me into his personal paradise, where an honest, inquiring mind and an unfettered spirit are valued above anything, where joy is the objective. Hugh has changed my life, and I thank him for that.

My sons have changed my life, too, in more ways than I can count. What a pleasure it has been to work with Erik to produce the digital version of *The Paradise Project* and with Karl to produce the audio versions of my stories. And what a delight to follow the paper/ink/book trail back through our lives together. My two sons mean more to me than anything in this world.

Thank you to all the creative folks involved in the making of *The Paradise Project*, both print and digital, especially Emily Cook, Mico Mazza, Richard Kohar, Faye Batchelor, and Laura Elston.

I am grateful to all the writers from the distant past to the immediate present who have thought deeply about words and stories and books and set those thoughts to clay, parchment, paper, and pixel for magpies like me to feast upon.

I especially appreciate my ongoing conversations with Carla Douglas and Kate Pullinger about the future of books. They have been prods throughout my process, forcing me deeper into that word, "book," and all it did and can and might mean.

Thank you to my agent, Martha Webb, for her steadfast faith, her hard work on my behalf, and her many kindnesses. Thank you to Sandra and Richard Gulland for encouraging me to pursue what seemed like a passing idea. Thank you to Alison Pick for introducing to me to Scrivener, which speeded the writing. And thank you to the Canada Council of the Arts for providing the material support that made it possible.

How lucky I have been to work with Susan Renouf, an editor with a deep love of books and a rare appreciation for the arcane. She deserves more thanks than words can convey. The entire team at ECW Press is a writer's dream. I want to thank, especially, Jen Knoch and Rachel Ironstone for their copy-editing acumen and enthusiasm, Sarah Dunn for her innovative and indefatigable promotional zeal, Crissy Calhoun for her patience and fine visual sensibility, and Jack David and David Caron for keeping this publishing house vibrant and growing to become one of the best of Canada's indie presses.

As always, my deepest gratitude to Wayne Grady, my loving partner in all things literary and in life.

A NOTE ON THE TYPE

The body text of *Gutenberg's Fingerprint* is set in Adobe Caslon. Considered the first original English typeface, it shares many characteristics of the Dutch Baroque type fonts of the era, and may be a variation on the Dutch Fell type fonts cut by Voskens or Van Dyck at that time. From 1725 through to 1730, three books printed by William Bower used roman and italic fonts cut by Caslon. The fonts were popular throughout the British Empire including the American Colonies, where they acquired their distinctive appearance from the exposure to salt air during the voyage from Britain.

Gutenberg's Fingerprint also features Akzidenz Grotesk, first published in 1891. Originally named "Accidenz-Grotesk," the design originates from Royal Grotesk light by royal type-cutter Ferdinand Theinhardt. The Theinhardt foundry later merged with Berthold and also supplied the regular, medium, and bold weights. The great German corporate designer Anton Stankowski (1906–1998) announced in an advertisement in 1989, "I only accept functional typefaces. The one you are reading right now is the one I preferred for 60 years now. It is Akzidenz-Grotesk."

Published by ECW Press
665 Gerrard Street East
Toronto, Ontario, Canada M4M 1Y2
416-694-3348 / info@ecwpress.com

LIBRARY AND ARCHIVES CANADA
CATALOGUING IN PUBLICATION

Simonds, Merilyn, 1949–, author
Gutenberg's Fingerprint : Paper, Pixels
and the Lasting Impression of Books /
Merilyn Simonds.

ISSUED IN PRINT AND ELECTRONIC FORMATS.
ISBN 978-1-77041-352-8 (hardback)
also issued as: 978-1-77305-003-4 (PDF)
978-1-77305-002-7 (EPUB)

1. Books and reading. 2. Handprinted books. 3. Electronic books.
4. Communication and technology. I. Title.

Z1003.S56 2017   302.23'2
C2016-906358-5   C2016-906359-3

Editor for the press: Susan Renouf
Cover photo: Wayne Grady
Author photo: Wayne Grady

The publication of *Gutenberg's Fingerprint* has been generously supported by the Canada
Council for the Arts which last year invested $153 million to bring the arts to Canadians
throughout the country, and by the Government of Canada through the Canada Book Fund.
*Nous remercions le Conseil des arts du Canada de son soutien. L'an dernier, le Conseil a investi 153
millions de dollars pour mettre de l'art dans la vie des Canadiennes et des Canadiens de tout le pays.
Ce livre est financé en partie par le gouvernement du Canada.* We also acknowledge the Ontario
Arts Council (OAC), an agency of the Government of Ontario, which last year funded 1,709
individual artists and 1,078 organizations in 204 communities across Ontario, for a total of
$52.1 million, and the contribution of the Government of Ontario through the Ontario Book
Publishing Tax Credit and the Ontario Media Development Corporation.

PRINTED AND BOUND IN CANADA   PRINTING: FRIESENS   5   4   3   2   1